REACHING FOR THE STARS..
AND GRABBING ONE

PETE RAMIREZ

Dedication

To Julie, my wife, best friend, and pillar; as well as my son Erik, and my daughter Rita. They fill my heart with love and joy each and every day.

PROLOGUE

2

"La educacion nadie se los quita." [Literal translation: An education no one can take away from you.] My father, Pedro G. Ramirez, instilled in me and my two brothers the importance of getting a good education to help us avoid, as much as possible, the shallow waters and reefs one encounters in life. His mantra became the cornerstone of my personal and professional life. My parents were born and raised at their parents and grandparent's ranches located in the relatively isolated ranching community of Encino, South Texas; they knew full well the hardships and disadvantages of education limited to the primary grades as my grandparents could not afford to send them on to high school. Attending high school in the 1930s, located in the county seat of Falfurrias located 25 to 30 miles to the north of Encino, entailed living in a boarding house or with relatives that lived there or commuting 25 to 30 miles by horse or a mule-driven wagon, both unfeasible options. My parents' families did not have automobiles and could not afford to send them to high school. My father remained at the Las Cuatas Ranch to help his father with

ranch work until he was drafted into the U.S. Army at the age of 18. My mother stayed at home to help her mother with housework, cultivating and harvesting crops in their fields. They both experienced hard labor at a young age and stressed to my two brothers and me the importance of obtaining a good education and grades and trying our best. They did not want their sons to face the same hardships they did. Their love of family and compassion transcended all aspects of their lives. One of my professors, Dr. Maurice G. Hornocker, at the University of Idaho graduate school, added substantial reinforcement to the foundation of my professional career with the U.S. Fish and Wildlife Service (FWS). He emphasized the importance of reaching out to the public and not limiting wildlife research to gathering dust in a scientific journal in a university library accessible only to academics. Dr. Hornocker also had one of his graduate students, Gary M. Koehler, assist me with field work during my first summer conducting my study on small mammals. Gary's backcountry skills and sense of humor left an indelible mark; he took his responsibilities seriously and somehow managed to laugh in the face of adversity. The two years I worked with Gary led to a lifelong friendship. Maurice also introduced me to Esther Louie and her husband, Wayne Beymer. During my first five years with the FWS in Corpus Christi, Texas, my coworker Gerry A. Jackson repeatedly stressed that "data is power" in our efforts to conserve fish and wildlife habitat. His influence and guidance served as a guidepost to my 41-year professional path as an environmental contaminants specialist with the FWS.

Contents

Chapter 1: Environmental Enlightenment

Armed with my dad's .22 rifle, I walked quietly through the live oak mottes (groves) and mesquite trees, scanning the gnarly tree branches for fox squirrels, but spied a hawk instead. I raised the rifle, aimed at the bird's chest, and fired; the raptor quickly fell to the base of the mesquite tree. I walked up to the bird, which was still alive, looked at its piercing eyes, and watched as they dimmed, not realizing that extinguishing the raptor's free spirit would imprison it in my soul. I carried the dead bird home and showed it to my Dad. Back then, people considered predators a threat to domestic animals. Expecting praise from my father, I held the bird up by its legs to display my deed. "Why did you kill it? *Pobre* animal (ah-nee-mahl)." My Dad, Pedro Sr., responded gently, shaking his head in disapproval. His mournful reaction draped me with a shroud of shame at what I had done. To this day, I don't know what compelled me to shoot the hawk; it was probably my foolishness and immaturity as a teenager. Years later, while in graduate school at the University of

Idaho at Moscow, I read conservationist Aldo Leopold's book *"Sand County Almanac,"* which includes his essay *"Thinking Like a Mountain."* In his essay, Leopold describes killing a wolf. "We reached the old wolf in time to watch a fierce green fire dying in her eyes. I realized then, and have known ever since, that there was something new to me in those eyes — something known only to her and to the mountain." His essay struck a chord with me as I thought of the day I shot and killed that hawk and my dad's reaction when I showed him the lifeless raptor.

Growing up in the wildlife-rich ranch country of Brooks County, Texas, I spent many days hiking at my dad's ranch, coursing my way through mesquite and prickly pear as well as the oak mottes. I learned much later in life how the paths on which we walk during our formative years chisel into the trails that we follow in our life's journey. The legacy of my Dad's 300-acre ranch, where my love for wildlife and the outdoors developed, extended back to 1872, the year my great-great-grandfather, Gregorio Villarreal, purchased the 22,142-acre La Encantada grant conveyed by Mexico in 1834 to Jose Manuel de Chapa. Early ranchers in what is now Brooks County lived along the Rio

Grande, the only perennial source of water between the Rio Grande and the Nueces River 120 miles to the north. Historical maps labeled this stretch of land the Wild Horse Desert. It was branded as such due to an estimated one million wild horses that inhabited the area. Historians believe these mustangs descended from horses left behind from 16th century Spanish expeditions and other horses that crossed the Rio Grande from Mexico into what is now Texas. The Spanish explorers described the area between the Rio Grande and the Rio Nueces as *'las mestenas'* or the "wild horse desert." Spanish explorer José de Escandón, from Soto de la Marina, four miles west of Santander, Spain, explored the area that is now South Texas in 1747 and named the area extending from the Pánuco River in Mexico to the Guadalupe River in Texas as Nuevo Santander. He founded over 20 towns or villas and a number of missions, including Camargo, Reynosa, Mier, and Revilla, south of the Rio Grande and Laredo, and the mission Nuestra Señora de los Dolores Hacienda, north of the Rio Grande. Following the settlement of Nuevo Santander, residents were assigned the land grants promised by Escandón.

My second cousin, Raul Longoria, Jr., traced the Longoria family, including my mother, to Captain Lorenzo Suarez de Longoria, who was born in the city of Oviedo, Spain, in 1592. Captain Suarez de Longoria left Spain in 1603 for Veracruz, New Spain, and traveled north-northwest to Monterrey, a distance of slightly over 1,200 miles. Monterrey was established in 1582 by Spanish and Portuguese settlers, who were encouraged to settle there by Philip II, King of Spain. In 1775, only a few hundred residents lived there. Settlers located Monterrey adjacent to the foothills of the Sierra Madre Occidental mountain range, with the settlement serving as a waypoint for Spanish explorers venturing northward to what is now South Texas. The Spanish explorers described the area between the Rio Grande and the Rio Nueces as *'las mestenas'* or the "wild horse desert."

The Wild Horse Desert is a savannah with mesquite, prickly pear, and other woody vegetation, including grasses such as little bluestem and switchgrass. Areas with aeolian sands probably supported scattered live oak mottes. The Wild Horse Desert was much less brushy 400 years ago than the area is today. Much of the area between the Nueces

River and the Rio Grande is dominated by honey mesquite, which scholars believe was introduced from Mexico into South Texas by cattle and horses roaming the area. The Aztecs called it *mizquitl*, which the Spaniards pronounced it as mesquite (mess-key-teh). Early Anglo-Texans spelled the word in a variety of ways: mesquit, mezquit, muskeet and musquit. Mesquite trees grew mainly along rivers, creeks, and draws in South Texas, although this thorny tree/shrub also grew on the open prairie. What has increased since then is not the mesquite's range but its density. Livestock ranching, rather than a quest for gold and silver, played a major influence in the eventual settlement of the Wild Horse Desert by the Spaniards. The Wild Horse Desert remained sparsely populated through at least the mid-1800s. William A McClintock kept a journal of his trip to Corpus Christi from 1846 to 1847 and described the area from San Patricio to Camargo as follows:

"Crossing the Mustang, or wild horse desert, either from the Nueces or the bay, the country is almost level as the ocean, which it strikingly resembles when clothed with the tall grass that is ever fanned by the bland southern breeze. Excepting a motte or small chaparral of them bushes at long intervals, it is destitute of timber. No running water is found in this region unless it may be for a few days during the rainy season. A miserable substitute for this inestimable element is found in holes and ponds. But these are few and far between. A found these water holes thousands of wild horses, deer, antelope, wolves, leopards, cats, cougars, rattlesnakes, and horned frogs, with other numberless reptiles and fowls, congregate." McClintock describes steamboats navigating up the Rio Grande "between Brazos, and Santiago or Matamoras (Matamoros) and Carmigo (Camargo)."

Diversion of river water for irrigation lowered the depth of the river downstream of present-day Rio Grande City and Brownsville and put an end to steamboat navigation on the lower Rio Grande sometime between 1900 and 1910.

Raul Longoria was able to trace my father's family to Dionicio Ramirez, born in 1734, presumably in Spain, who immigrated to Camargo, New Spain, in the late 1700s. Descendants of the Longoria family in Monterrey eventually made their way to Cerralvo, Nuevo Leon, 58 miles to the northeast, and ultimately to Camargo, Nuevo Leon, located on the south side of the Rio Grande. Camargo was founded on March 6, 1749, on the eastern bank of the San Juan River, about six miles from where it empties into the Rio Grande River. The initial settlers were primarily from Nuevo Leon and consisted of 40 families and a few soldiers. Capt. Blas Maria de la Garza Falcon was placed in charge of Camargo. Native Indian tribes living in the area included the Tareguanos, Pajaritos, Venados, Tejones, and Cuero Quemados. Spain assigned land grants on the north side of the Rio Grande in long, narrow half-mile to one-mile-wide tracts from 5,000 to 12,000 acres in size called *'Porciones'* (Portions) extending 14 to 15 miles away from the river to provide access to water since the nearest perennial source of fresh water was the Nueces River 132 miles to the northeast. Three of Juan Diego's sons and one daughter received Porciones from the King of Spain, with *Porcion* 94 (4,650 acres) granted to Pedro Longoria Chapa. La Grulla is located on the opposite bank of the Rio Grande from Camargo and a few miles downstream. It is situated in Porcion 94, initially granted to Pedro Longoria in 1767. Juan Longoria was probably the first Longoria actually to reside in La Grulla. In *"Memories from La Grulla on the Rio Grande,"* Josefina Vera writes, "In the year 1836, Juan

Longoria Flores, his wife Yrinea Villarreal, and their small children moved across the Rio Grande to settle in that part of their Porcion 94, and called the settlement "*Los Mesquititos*" (The Little Mesquites). The *portales* and *jacales* were hidden by dense mesquite and retama. Thick log fences were built around the yards. Armed men guarded the place day and night. Through a small peephole in the fence, they could see anyone approaching." This was the beginning of the settlement known today as La Grulla (the official post office designation is "Grulla"). The timing of Juan Longoria's move across the river coincided with Mexican general Santa Anna and his troops crossing the Rio Grande to quell the revolution at the Alamo 215 miles to the north in present-day San Antonio. On March 2, 1836, Texas declared its independence from Mexico. The Alamo fell on March 6, 1836, and Santa Anna was defeated in the Battle of San Jacinto on April 21, 1836. Texas became a republic resulting in a land rush as Anglos ("*gringos*") from East Texas and neighboring areas such as Louisiana, Alabama, Mississippi, and the territory of Arkansas, started forcing non-Anglo landowners off their lands and confiscating them as their own. To maintain possession of their lands, the non-Anglo citizens had to live on them and fight to keep them. This is probably what compelled Juan Longoria to relocate his family from Camargo to the north side of the Rio Grande in 1836 in what is now the town of La Grulla, thus succeeding in maintaining possession of his lands. Many of the land grants were converted to Texas grants in 1852. To this date, some of Juan Longoria's descendants still live in La Grulla.

Dionicio Ramirez was born in 1734, presumably in Spain, and later immigrated to New Spain, where he was assigned Porción 78 [1] in Reynosa.

However, he did not take possession of that tract; instead, he was granted possession of Tract 77 as requested since his mother, the widow of an original settler, already had livestock grazing there. Permission was granted, and Dionicio Ramirez officially took possession of Porcion 77 on May 20, 1768. Porcion 77 was 5,536 acres in size and is located in present-day Hidalgo County, Texas. Mexico gained independence in 1821 after an 11-year war with Spain to relinquish their rule. A year-and-a-half after La Encantada was granted to Chapa, the first shots in the Texas revolution were fired in Gonzales in 1835. Four months

---

[1] http://www.raullongoria.net/Genealogy/FamilyTree/index.html).

later, Mexican general Santa Anna marched his troops across the Rio Grande to quell the revolution at the Alamo. According to family history, the Longorias moved their ranch headquarters and residences to the north side of the river to protect their lands from the Anglo Americans moving into Texas from Arkansas, Louisiana, Kentucky, and Tennessee. In Andres Tijerina's book, *"Tejano Empire - Life on the South Texas Ranchos,"* the author describes 1835 South Texas as follows:

"The Tejanos, the native Mexicans who had originally established Texas, found themselves in an unusual situation with the Anglo settlers after 1836. During the Texas Revolution, most Tejanos had joined the opposition to the centralist Mexican government of General Santa Anna. But many Anglos in the Republic of Texas quickly forgot that Tejanos had also fought for Texas' independence. Most Anglo Texans distrusted Tejanos, particularly after Santa Anna massacred the Anglo rebels in the Alamo and at Goliad. The Mexicans north of the Rio Grande were attacked by Anglos as well as by the Mexican armies. The Mexican armies abused them as traitors, and Anglos never accepted them as fellow Texans. One of the ironies of Texas history is

that the original Tejano families, who by this time had been in Texas for almost one hundred years, were still considered 'Mexicans' by the Anglos, implying that they were foreigners in the Texas Republic. On the other hand, Anglos who had been in Texas for no more than a few weeks called themselves 'Texans.'"

After Texas gained independence from Mexico, the newly formed Republic of Texas defined the Rio Grande as the border. Mexico, on the other hand, considered the Nueces River, 160 miles to the north, as the boundary between the two nations. The area became a lawless frontier fraught with Comanche raiders, horse and cattle rustlers, and land robbers. Anglos established ranches and towns such as Gonzales, Goliad, Refugio, and San Patricio near or adjacent to rivers and perennial streams that provided freshwater for their homes and livestock. La Encantada grant changed hands three times before my great-great-grandfather Gregorio Villarreal purchased it in 1872. Historical accounts of ranching in South Texas paint a picture of cyclical and prolonged droughts, which caused landowners to either sell their livestock or their land. In the book *Falfurrias - Ed C. Lasater and the Development of*

South Texas, Texas A&M University Press, College Station, TX, 1985, author Dale Lasater writes that "a sharp decline in livestock prices forced ranchers to sell or have their lands sold by the county sheriff to cover delinquent taxes. The feast-or-famine nature of the South Texas climate combined with the ups and downs of livestock markets paved the way for the transfer of Mexican American-owned ranches to well-educated Anglos, giving rise to the large ranches within or adjacent to the La Encantada grant: the King Ranch – Encino Division, Skipper Ranch, El Coyote Ranch, and the Tepeguaje Ranch.

Family historical lore has my great-grandfather Ponciano Longoria moving up to the San Juanito Ranch located within the 39,855-acre La Encantada land grant to protect his family's livestock and ranch from rustlers and unscrupulous land grabbers in the late 1800s. He moved his wife, Maria Rita Villarreal de Longoria, and their six children to the Santa Rita Ranch in 1908 after constructing a board-and-batten house on the ranch. A 2007 study of historical ranching in South Texas prepared for the Texas Department of Transportation states that the Santa Rita Ranch was established during the early 1900s by my great-grandfather in what was then Hidalgo County. My maternal grandmother, Maria, her mother and her siblings fled Monterrey, Nuevo Leon, Mexico, for South Texas during the Mexican Revolution in 1915 or 1916. Maria and her sister Elvira worked as housekeepers at the Santa Rita Ranch. My grandmother married Juan Longoria, one of my great-grandfather's sons, in 1916. In *Tejano Empire – Life on the South Texas Ranchos,* author Andres Tijerina writes that "A typical Tejano ranch family of the time included great-grandparents, their married sons and daughters, grandchildren, and great-grandchildren, all in the same household, though not all in a single house. The Tejano family might occupy several small homes around the casa mayor of the grandparents, but the various units of the family depended on each other for their daily necessities." Tijerina adds that these small ranch communities "gave strength to the colony and to conduct daily life on the ranch." They only had each other to depend on for security as the nearest law enforcement officers were located 20 to 40 miles away in Falfurrias, the county seat of Brooks County, and 35 to 40 miles to the southeast in Edinburg, the county seat of Hidalgo County, a full-days ride on horseback. Texas Historical Commission records describe the road through Encino as "A soft sand thoroughfare constructed in 1918 extending from Falfurrias and terminating at Encino. One year after establishing the Texas Highway Department, plans were drawn for the Brooks County segment of what would become U.S. 281. A caliche, a hardened natural cement of calcium carbonate, was applied onto the road surface in 1920. The communal living in the ranches facilitated the growing and sharing of food. The families grew, harvested, and preserved their fruits and vegetables by canning and storing them in a root cellar located near the houses. Livestock was slaughtered for meat during the cooler months of winter, and what was not consumed was preserved by drying it into jerky.

Ponciano Longoria and his heirs were fortunate to hold on to their homes and ranches during the 1920s, surviving droughts and depressed livestock prices prior to and during the Great Depression. Families living in the La Encantada grant raised crops and cattle, augmenting their meager incomes as ranch hands at the King Ranch and other large ranches in the Encino area. The succeeding heirs of the Santa Rita Ranch divided the ranch, which made the tracts of land smaller and smaller with each passing generation. My parents grew up on their family's ranches during the Great Depression of the 1930s. My mother, Ester, and her two sisters spent their childhoods doing household chores and helping their four brothers weeding and harvesting crops that included corn, cotton, and an assortment of vegetables. The oldest son, Lisandro, ran the ranch for my grandmother Maria after my grandfather Juan passed away at the age of 48 when my mother was 12 years old. My grandmother passed away in 1963 at the age of 68.

My dad grew up in the Las Cuatas Ranch, one of two children born to my paternal grandparents, Brijido and Maria. His brother, Ernesto, died at 15 in March 1944. My Dad grew up in Las Cuatas (the Twins) Ranch, about 1 mile southwest of where my brothers and I grew up. Las Cuatas Ranch was named for two playa lakes at the ranch. I assume that when families moved from the ranches along the Rio Grande north to the La Encantada land grant, they established their homes near Playa Lakes, which provided them with a source of water. They must have moved north during a wet spell. Later, they had the tools to dig wells, which provided them with water. The ranch compounds consisted of several houses and a separate 'house' or one-room building for the kitchen. The main house was occupied by the owner of the ranch and his wife. At the Las Cuatas Ranch, Macario Ramirez and Estefanita Diaz established the ranch. Macario inherited the land from his father, Juan Ramirez. When Macario and Estefanita (Stephanie) Diaz's children became adults and married, they built separate houses consisting mainly of two, maybe three, bedrooms. Two months after his brother died, my father was inducted into the US Army at Fort Sam Houston in San Antonio, where he spent six months training for what would eventually be a decisive battle leading to the defeat of Nazi Germany's occupation of western Europe.

As an adult, I felt comfortable asking my dad if he was anxious when he received his draft notice when he was 18 years old. He responded that he had no idea nor concept of war as news was limited to word-of-mouth and local events happening in their small ranching community. He left for Basic Training at Fort Sam Houston in San Antonio, Texas, in May 1944 and joined other recruits six months later in New York City to board the RMS Queen Mary bound for Scotland. From Scotland, he and other soldiers set foot on LA Havre, France. My father spoke very little of his experience during the war. What little he did say was that war was hell, adding that when his unit, K Company in the 9th Infantry Regiment, 2nd Infantry Division, marched through France *en route* to the Rhineland, the corpses of dead soldiers on the roadside brought the horrific reality of war front and center to him. Growing up in an isolated ranching community with no electricity, hence no radio, and probably no newspapers as well, my father had no idea what he would be facing as a soldier. K Company headed towards the front lines in the Ardennes in Belgium, where my father experienced the coldest winter ever to grip Belgium in 60 years. My father had never experienced snow and below-zero temperatures in South Texas. Huddled in a foxhole in temperatures of 20 degrees below zero or lower left my dad with a lifelong disdain for cold weather. A U.S. Army report characterizing the weather in the Ardennes during the Battle of the Bulge states: "The weather that occurs in the Ardennes and Eifel terrain during the winter generally is severe, and it was in 1944. This is a mountainous country with much rainfall, deep snows in winter, and raw, harsh winds sweeping across the plateaus. The heaviest rains occur in November and December. The mists are frequent and heavy, lasting well into late morning before they break. The structure of the soil will permit tank movement when the ground is frozen but turns into a clayey mire in time of rain. A single snowstorm often deposits a depth of 10 to 12 inches in 24 hours. On 28 December, the weather had favored the Americans, in the air and on the ground." In early December, the experienced 2nd Infantry Division was tasked with capturing the crossroads. The 2nd and 99th Divisions retreated to the Elsenborn Ridgeline and their subsequent stubborn defense blocked the German tanks' access to key roads in northern Belgium, which led to Antwerp, a major seaport and key objective for the Germans.

Historian John S.D. Eisenhower noted, "...the action of the 2nd and 99th divisions on the northern shoulder could be considered the most decisive of the Ardennes campaign. The German forces were plagued with "overcrowding, flanking attacks, blown bridges, and lack of fuel." The only details my father offered of what he saw and experienced in the Battle of the Bulge were of German Panzer tanks rolling over foxholes and physically crushing the soldiers within them. In 2001, I found an online blog on World War II history that led me to postings on the 9th

Infantry Regiment. I made several inquiries for information on K Company and received the following replies.

Letter – no date "Dear Mr. Ramirez,

I am sorry, but I do not have a roster of Co. K, 9th Inf. Reg 2nd Division. I was with Co. K from August 13th, 1944, to Dec 18th 1944. Co. K was captured on Dec 18th, 1944, in the Battle of the Bulge. We were in that battle 22 hrs. before capture. I did not know your dad. He must have joined Co. K when they reorganized after we were captured. I was in the battles for Brest, France, in late August 1944, Sept. 18th, 1944. Our Co. left Brest and moved to the German Belgium Border on the Siegfried Line in early October. We stayed there until Dec 10th, 1944. We were relieved by 106 Div. Our company was engaged in battle on Dec 15th & 16th at Wehlerscheid. Co. K entered the Battle of Bulge on Dec 17th and was captured on Dec 18th. I was held prisoner until the war ended on May 8th, 1945. I was in Czechoslovakia, the present-day Czech Republic. The only info I have on the Battle of the Bulge is what I read in 2nd Div. History books and books written about the Battle of the Bulge.

Sincerely,

L.E.S.

Letter dated January 13, 2001

I was in Company K 9th Regt 2nd Div, the same as your Dad. Continued on with Co. K through Normandy and then to the Battle of Brest and got wounded there on Sept. 16. In October, I rejoined Co. K is located in the Ardennes Forest in Belgium. The German 12th Panzer Div started an attack on Dec. 17 and, on Dec. 18, broke through our positions and were overran (run)—the whole Co. K was reported missing in action on Dec 17. All were either killed or taken prisoner. I was in a group of 8 guys taken prisoner. The Co K Morning Report is dated Jan 4, 1945, stating the Company was being reorganized at Elsenborn, Belgium, so that is probably where your father joined Co. K. I guess your dad took my place. Sorry, I couldn't help more. Good luck in your search. – F. Roger

Letter dated January 15, 2001

Thank you for your letter, but I'm afraid I am not much of a help to you. I joined K Company 9t Inf. Reg, 2nd Division, as a replacement around March 1, 1944. K Company went into Normandy at Omaha Beach on D-Day plus one. I was very fortunate to last until July 28, 1944, *when I was wounded at the St. Lo breakthrough. I was sent to a general hospital in England and remained there until the end of October. After that, I was assigned to limited duty in Germany and France until I was shipped home in December 1945. According to your letter, your dad went through many offensive actions. I know for sure he had a very tough time - especially being an infantry replacement. Good luck to you in your search. I hope you are successful in finding out more army background information.*

Best Regards,

J.R. Paulson

Letter dated February 19, 2001

Dear Pedro:

For six weeks in January and February, I was in the same squad and platoon with Pete Ramirez. We knew each other, performed guard duty, marched together, and did some firing of weapons together, but in early combat, you knew the guys you dug holes with most intimately. Some nights, we stayed (in) abandoned houses, and we all slept on our overcoats, blankets, or what was available. Your father was a good soldier, and I say that because we all (most) followed orders from above. I do not recall all of Company "K" becoming prisoners. Many did; at least six from the weapons platoon survived all of December. Many were wounded and killed, and some had frozen feet. A few, like me, were replacements. Some were experienced, some were not.

Primarily, the division crossed the Rhine on March 21st on a pontoon bridge near Remagen. They had fought defensively on the west bank of the Rhine. After crossing, the resistance was sporadic; sometimes, it was tough, and other times there was no opposition. Remember, there were always mines. The Division fought with the 9th Armored and the 69th Division. More later.

Sincerely,

E. Howard

My dad was awarded the Purple Heart, along with the Good Conduct, Victory World War II, American Campaign, and European-African-Middle Eastern Campaign medals. He was honorably discharged at Camp Fannin in Tyler, Texas. When he returned to the United States after the war in Europe ended, he was briefly stationed at a base in Alabama. Recalling his brief stay there, he expressed sadness at the way African Americans were treated in Alabama. My father never uttered racist remarks nor displayed bitterness toward other ethnic groups. *"Todos somos humanos,"* he would say – "we are all humans." The only times I heard him openly criticize others was when he saw blatant unethical or immoral behavior. I believe that his experience during World War II molded him into the person he became: a compassionate, benevolent, and loving human being and a wonderful father with a deep reverence for life. He cared deeply about his family, his neighbors, his community, and his country. Of all the people I've encountered in my lifetime, his conduct, his service to others, and his compassion for all life influenced my own personal and professional life. My dad received an honorable discharge from the Army at Camp Fannin in Tyler, Texas, on January 28, 1946. A year-and-a-half later, in

July 1947, he married Ester Longoria. Two-and-a-half years into their marriage, they started a family with their first son, who was named after my uncle, my Dad's brother, Ernesto.

As an adult, I asked her why I was two months premature. She recalled my older brother Ernesto standing with her in a corral, watching my Dad milking a cow. Ernesto approached the cow from the rear, placing him at risk of getting kicked by the bovine. My mother hurriedly picked him up to move him out of harm's way. She concluded that picking up my brother, who was a bit heavy, caused her to go into labor. I was delivered in Falfurrias at Bartlett Hospital by Dr. Glenn Bartlett. I was born two months premature in Falfurrias, Texas, on October 19, 1951.

The hospital was a wooden house-like structure, probably more like a clinic than a full-fledged hospital. My mother also recalled that since I weighed two pounds, the nurses fed me with a very small bottle. Somehow, milk spilled onto the crib bedding, which I assume resulted from the nurses propping the small bottle as best they could with a small towel when they had to tend to other patients. The spilled milk attracted ants into the crib. "*Ya te comian las hormigas,*" (the ants almost ate you) was my mother's introductory sentence every time she would talk about my birth. Upon hearing my mother say this, I would roll my eyes back in anticipation of the story I had heard so many times before. It wasn't until I was a freshman in college that my mom added more to the story, that made me realize how close I came to my life ending soon after my birth. The doctor advised my parents to take me to a hospital capable of prenatal care located in Kingsville, Texas, 60 miles from my parents' home in Encino. My mother told me that she and my father would drive the 60 miles to go see me at Kingsville, where I spent my early weeks of life in an incubator. I'm sure the trip took longer to complete back then as the speed limit was 55 mph or possibly slower, and the highways were narrow, 2-lane conduits. My mother recalled that my maternal grandmother Maria advised her not to go see me as frequently. My grandmother had lost quite a few babies as a young mother, and there were no doctors or hospitals in Encino. During the 1920s and '30s, the only way residents in the ranching community of Encino got around was by horseback and wagons pulled by mules. Twenty miles to a doctor in Falfurrias was a long journey for the residents of Encino. Based on my grandmother's experience, premature babies did not live very long. My parents not giving up on me gave me a whole new perspective on the story. My parents' love and devotion led me to realize that I am here on Earth for a reason. When my parents brought me home, my mother recalled that she could fit me in a shoebox as I was very small. She also covered her nose and mouth with a bandanna so as to limit my exposure to germs.

My first home at Encino was a white one-story house that my dad's cousin, Marcos Cantu, built for my father in 1947 before my dad married my mother. The house was very simple: no bathroom, two small bedrooms, a living room, a kitchen, and a dining room. The windows had to be propped open with a wooden dowel. A small, 1-room wooden bath house also doubled as a laundry room. The house was located on a narrow strip of land 75 feet wide and one mile long. It was bounded on the east by US Highway 281 and to the west by the Southern Pacific railroad tracks. The highway was and still is a major corridor extending north 1,875 miles from Brownsville, Texas, near the U.S. border with Mexico, to the Canadian border 77 miles northeast of Minot, North Dakota. Marcos was a phenomenal carpenter and woodworker. In 1956 or early

1957, my dad hired Marcos to build my parents a new and slightly larger house with a bathroom, three bedrooms, a living room, a dining room, and a family room. Ernest, Ariel, and I grew up in that house up until we moved out after graduating from high school. Marcos, a master carpenter and woodworker, built many of the houses in the Encino area. Years later, during my college years, he showed me boxes filled with wooden toys he had made, some with wheels that, when pulled across a floor, levers attached to the wheels initiated a movement of other wheels, arms, legs, or wings on the toy. Before he married my mom, my dad lived with his father, Brijido (*Bree-hee-tho*). Brijido was married to Maria Garza, who was 14 years younger than him. Maria died young, at age 46, in Corpus Christi in September 1946, three months after my dad returned from his service in the Army. With no doctors close by, life expectancy was very short due to little to no medical care. My grandfather Brijido died six years later, in Nov 1952, when I was one year old. My parents were quite frugal when I lived at home. Ernesto and I received only one toy each year during Christmas. Although the toys we received were made of steel, they were eventually rendered useless by Ernesto and me, and we had to wait almost a year to get new toys at Christmas.

To my Dad, strangers were friends he had not yet met. His compassion and ability to interact with friends and strangers led him to serve his community for 16 years as a county commissioner. His unwavering trust in others eventually caused him to lose his ranch in the mid-1970s. A decline in cattle prices and subsequent severe reduction in income caused my dad to take out loans at several area banks. He then attempted to sell the ranch to pay off the loans; however, he did not contact a real estate agent, and being the trusting individual he was, he dealt directly with the buyer. The result was a legal quagmire lasting almost ten years. My dad's interactions with people from different backgrounds and ethnicities made a life-long impact on me. I recall only one incident that was more out of ignorance than outright racism and one incident of overt racism.

During my career with the U.S. Fish and Wildlife Service, the Assistant Field Supervisor and I were showing a biologist from the Bureau of Reclamation (USBR) small isolated tracts of thorny brush remaining along the Rio Grande in South Texas. The USBR biologist looked at the river and then at me and asked, "Pete, when did your parents cross the river?" Momentarily stunned by the question from a college-educated individual, I asked myself how Dad would have responded to this. "My family was here in the 1740s; when did your family cross the Atlantic?" I answered. There was no response from the college-educated individual.

In August 2011, a man left a disturbing voice message directed to me on our answering machine, "Take you and your family back to Mexico, where you came from." The threatening tone of the voice message shook my wife, Julie, to the core. I saved the message and later played it back to my son and daughter without telling them the content of the message beforehand. "Why is he saying that about us, Dad? He doesn't even know us," my son responded. "You have a Spanish surname," I replied and advised him and my daughter to respond, not with anger but with a concise reply that their family roots extended back to the Mayflower on their mother's side and that my family had been in Texas when it belonged to Spain. Unfortunately, my son was the target of racist taunts five years later as he was paying for his lunch at a fast-food restaurant in Fort Collins; a man seated at a nearby table and wearing a red MAGA (Make America Great Again) hat worn by some supporters of Donald Trump who was running for president at the time, heard the cashier say "Thank you, Mr. Ramirez." The Trump supporter growled, "Go back to Mexico, where you came from." My son attempted to tell the man that our family's roots extended back to the 1600s and 1700s, but the adult bully would not hear any of it and kept repeating his taunts. My son was deeply affected by this incident and did not want to return to work the next day. When he described the incident, he told us that two customers present at the restaurant overheard the conversation and summoned security. My wife and I comforted him and also told him that if he did not go to work, the racist would win. He took our advice and showed up for work the next day.

"Nothing in all the world is more dangerous than sincere

ignorance and conscientious stupidity."

– Dr. Martin Luther King, Jr.

My father served as County Commissioner from 1956 to 1973 and was well-respected in and outside Encino. He went out of his way to assist residents of our community.

There were numerous times that he transported Encino residents suffering from cancer to the M.D. Anderson Cancer Treatment Center in Houston, a distance of almost 300 miles on two-lane highways that took four or five hours to reach. He would return the patients to Encino on the same day. Never a day went by at our home without several visits by his constituents seeking his help and advice. His compassion for others and service to his community left an indelible impression on me. My Dad's compassion towards economically disadvantaged persons and families in our community influenced my political views and my interpersonal relationships with persons of different ethnicities from various parts of the country, as well as the world. At some point when I started thinking about my future, I, too, wanted to give back to my country and my community like my father but had not zeroed in on how.

"La educacion, nadie se los quita." Translation: "An education, no one can take (that) away from you," advised my Dad and my mother drilled into my brothers and me. My parents knew that their grade-school education was not enough. During day trips to the Lower Rio Grande Valley to visit distant relatives from my mother's side of the family I

would look out from the back seat of our family's car and see farm laborers harvesting vegetables and picking cotton. Both my parents were born and raised in their parents' homes located within their grandparents' ranches. They walked to their one-room schoolhouses close to their family's ranches until they reached the eighth grade. Given the importance they placed on our education, I wondered why they both had not continued to the high school located 20 miles to the north in Falfurrias, the Brooks County seat, a decision they regretted. Years later, I learned from Micaela De Luna Perez, wife of my mother's cousin, Enrique Longoria, that during the 1940s, students in southern Brooks County had to either rent a room at a boarding house or stay with a relative in Falfurrias.

My parents' families could not afford to send them to high school, and their only mode of transportation was by horse or mule-driven wagon. My father remained at the Las Cuatas Ranch to help my grandfather with ranch work, and my mother stayed at home to help her mother with housework as well as cultivating and harvesting crops in their fields. They both emphasized the need to get a good education and implored us to make good grades and try our best. They did not want their sons to face the same hardships they did. I dreaded the times my parents attended a parent-teacher night at my elementary school because they did not speak English very well, although that was true of most parents from my community. My Dad spoke English better than my mom, but that was probably due to the time he spent in the Army during the war when he had to speak English with his fellow soldiers. When I was in grade school, I believed that I and others like me could never go to college because we were not smart enough. That was the mindset at the time, so I assumed I would grow up to be a rancher like my dad.

Most of the farming in the Encino area was done five to six miles to the southwest in the area where my mother grew up, locally referred to as "*la mesa.*" There, the loamy soils were more conducive to growing crops compared to the sandy soils at Encino. At the age of 12, I decided to emulate my older brother by taking a summer job picking cotton at *la mesa* to earn some spending money. My mother packed a lunch for me, and I rode with adult relatives who were traveling to the same ranch to pick cotton. Farmers who could not afford mechanical cotton pickers resorted to manually picking cotton in the 1960s. Farm laborers walked through the fields, removing the mature cotton fibers by hand and placed them in large sacks, which they dragged behind them. This was difficult work, as the bags could weigh up to 100 pounds when full, and the sharp spikes on the plants left their fingers bloody and sore. Manually picked cotton was placed in a six-foot-long sack made of durable cotton holding 40 to 45 pounds of cotton. The sack had a strap that went over the cotton picker's shoulder. I probably weighed 60 pounds, so picking and dragging 40 pounds of cotton became a futile effort on a very hot and humid day. Exhausted and weak at the end of the day, I earned a paltry five dollars for one day's work, spending the following day at home recovering from heat exhaustion. I only worked one day and experienced firsthand what my mother had gone through as a child. It was not until I was in middle school that I learned that college was possible and that I was smart enough to attend a university.

I came to fully appreciate my Dad's compassion and service to others in September 1967, when Hurricane Beulah made landfall near Brownsville, some 70 miles to the southeast, with winds up to 109 miles per hour. The hurricane dumped almost 30 inches of rain in Encino in seven days, a little over the average annual amount of 28 inches. Depressions in the sandy soil filled with rainwater and became *lagunas* (ponds). Prior to Beulah, South Texas had experienced a decade-long drought. In some areas, residents built their houses in or near these natural depressions. With no discernible drainage, the heavy amount of rainfall quickly filled the depressions. The largest truck that could make its way on flooded county and private roads was the county dump truck. My Dad, a county commissioner, drove one of the county's dump trucks located in Encino to evacuate residents from their flooded homes, check on their welfare, and provide food to residents isolated by flooded roads. Dad, along with help from my older brother, kept that up for several days. I stayed home to help my mother and keep her company. As county commissioner, my father tapped his connections with a local oil well service company employee to procure large pumps to dewater residences in flooded areas. The pumps moved water out of the flooded depressions that impacted homes and roads. I don't remember my father sleeping very much during that time as he moved from one crisis to the next. My father's compassion and service to others left an indelible mark on my soul. Like my dad before me, I, too, felt the desire to make a difference and make the world, at least my part of it, a better place; I just did not know how I could do that. One or two years later, one of my Dad's cousins who worked at the Tepeguaje Ranch brought back issues of *National Wildlife* magazine published by the National Wildlife Federation, a non-profit wildlife conservation organization founded in 1936 by Jay N. Darling, chief of the U.S. Bureau of Biological Survey. Through this magazine, I developed an interest in wildlife conservation. The seed was planted; wildlife conservation became my calling.

Our house was located on a live oak-covered strip of land approximately 80 feet wide and extending west one mile from U.S. Highway 281. Our house was approximately two miles east-northeast from my Dad's ranch. As a child, I spent most of my time outdoors, not by choice but due to the admonishment of my mother, who did not want me or my older brother messing up the house. The large, gnarly live oak trees adjacent to our house served as our climbing gym and our "imagination" station. Their highest branches were our refuge when we pushed the envelope of my mother's patience, and we feared physical punishment. Sometimes, I spent more time in our nearest neighbor's house with the Rodriguez family during the day than I did in my own home. Walking distance to the Rodriguez family's house was almost the length of a football field. Victoria 'Toya' Rodriguez was my second mom, and she always welcomed my older brother and me into her home. The Rodriguez family of six lived in a three-room shotgun house. Their shotgun house was about 12 feet wide and three rooms deep, consisting of a kitchen and two bedrooms. The exterior wooden walls and the cedar shingles on the roof were all that separated the occupants from the elements. When it rained, Victoria placed pots to collect the rain leaking through cracks in the cedar shingles. A separate 1-room outbuilding served as a bathhouse and a laundry room. During infrequent cold snaps during the South Texas winters, the family heated their house with a make-shift heater in the kitchen consisting of a galvanized washtub approximately 32 inches in diameter and 18 inches in depth and filled with sand. The washtub was set on bricks to suspend the tub above the wooden floor. Coals from a wood fire were brought in and placed in the tub to heat the house.

The patriarch of the family, Pedro Sr., worked as a ranch hand at the Coyote Ranch and later at the Skipper Ranch and La Escondida Ranch. 'Toya' was a wonderful woman who raised a family of six sons and one daughter who worked their way out of poverty as adults. The Rodriguez's house sat in a shallow depression downslope from our house. The slope was almost imperceptible given the generally flat topography of the area but enough to collect water during heavy rains, which occurred infrequently. Intense rainfall from Hurricane Beulah flooded Rodriguez's home and forced them to move to another house two-and-a-half miles to the north at La Escondida Ranch. A few months later they moved to a small house in Encino. I mostly played with Rene and Mario who were the closest to my age. During my teen years, I also interacted with their older brothers, Pedro (Pete) and Reynaldo (Rey). After the flood forced them to move, I continued to interact with them as my older brother Ernest would drive me up to their home, or Rey would drive to our home. They all have remained life-long friends that I consider my "brothers."

My father's ranch exposed me to a variety of domestic animals: cows and calves, sheep, goats, horses, chickens, and the family's pet dogs. On occasion, my father would bring a cow and her newborn calf to the corral located 100 feet behind our house. There were two instances where he brought only the newborn calf home, and my older brother and I would bottle-feed the calf. At home, I grew up with pet dogs that most families, including my own, had for security. The dogs kept wild animals such as raccoons, coyotes, and skunks from venturing near the residences. In addition to bottle-feeding calves, I also would care for baby cottontails and jackrabbits that my Dad's cousin Adan (Adam), whom we addressed as *tio* (uncle), would bring us to tend to. Tio Adan lived and worked as a ranch hand in the Encino Division of the King Ranch. He was tasked with managing the milk cows and delivering milk to the families that lived on the King Ranch. I assume that Tio Adan encountered young cottontails or jackrabbits during his work and perceived the young rabbits as "orphaned" and needing care. My fascination with wildlife took root when my Tio Adan would "rescue" a small rabbit, place it in a shoebox, and ask my brother or me to care for the "orphan." Tio Adan meant well, but that was the worst thing to do, as the young animals were not orphans. Young animals are rarely abandoned by their parents. Every evening, without fail, *tio* Adan and his wife Sofia (*tia*) would drive the four miles from their house in the King Ranch to visit our family as well as some of their other relatives. During their daily visits, *tio* Adan would tell us *cuentos* (stories) of growing up in the Encino area and his work as a ranch hand in *la Kineña* (Kee-neh-nyah), the King Ranch. His cuentos provided an oral history of life in Encino; regretfully, given my young age, I did not have the wherewithal or resources to record his cuentos. My brothers Ernesto, Ariel, and I were their surrogate children as they did not have children of their own. My beloved *tio* died of a heart attack on February 23, 1971, at the age of 58, when I was a freshman in college. His death profoundly affected me as his passing was my first experience of losing a family member whom I deeply loved and cared for. I took a flight home to attend his funeral and openly cried as his casket was lowered into the earth at the Las Cuatas Ranch cemetery. His wife Sofia moved out of their house in the

King Ranch and into their three-room house located about one mile south of my parents' home. During my trips home from Nacogdoches and later from Corpus Christi, I would visit with her up until she passed away in a nursing home in 1985.

Hurricane Beulah not only broke a prolonged drought in the area, but it and other tropical storms that followed temporarily changed the environment in my Dad's ranch. Heavy rains from Beulah filled the small, less than a-quarter-acre stock pond in my Dad's ranch and expanded it into a 12-acre lake. Months after the deluge, I walked the perimeter of the lake. Evaporation had reduced its size, although it was still quite large. As I walked along the shoreline, I noticed several fish skeletons almost 12 inches in length. "There are large fish in the laguna," I mentioned to my older brother Ernesto. He was skeptical at first until he saw the fish remains along the shore of our hurricane-created lake. We both wanted to confirm the existence of fish in the lake; however, we did not own any fishing gear as the nearest places to fish were over 50 to almost 100 miles away. Our second cousin, Tomás, did his own fishing tackle since he and his dad were avid hunters and anglers.

We told Tomás about our suspicions and invited him to bring a fishing rod and lures to find out. Tomás caught several large-mouthed bass and bluegill sunfish. My brother and I purchased fishing licenses, rods, and lures a few days later, and so began my love for sport fishing. My brother and I wondered how the fish managed to wind up at the lake. We assumed the fish were transported by the flood waters generated by Hurricane Beulah. The nearest pond stocked with fish that we knew of was located at the Tepeguaje Ranch, approximately two-and-a-half miles to the northwest. Eventually, evaporation reduced the lake to its original size. Ten years later, my Dad experienced the same fate as his family had several generations before him; a decline in livestock prices and financial hardship forced him to sell his ranch.

My interest in hunting and fishing morphed into an interest in biology thanks to David Smith, my high school biology teacher, a bespectacled and lanky individual who wore black framed glasses, a white shirt, and slacks. I already had developed an interest in science years before as I had a deep-seated curiosity in how things worked, everything from portable gas-powered water pumps in my dad's ranch to how the plywood in my mom's kitchen cabinet was made. I took apart several radios that no longer worked just to see the internal components. Biology was a required course during my sophomore year in high school. I remember my first year of biology, which involved dissecting the requisite slew of organisms, ranging from a roundworm to a large bullfrog, all reeking of formalin[2]. We assumed that Mr. Smith grew up in the Trans-Pecos area of West Texas as his college *alma mater* was Sul Ross State University in Alpine, Texas, north of Big Bend National Park, although I don't remember ever learning where he grew up. He had a litany of sayings. When a student peered through a microscope and wondered aloud what the multicellular item on the slide was, Mr. Smith would matter-of-factly reply, "That's a wild gyrookus," or "You're not just ah-woofin'." The biology classroom was my respite from my other classes, save for my journalism class, which was my other favorite one. The combination biology lab classroom was a miniature zoo with *aquaria* filled with multi-colored fancy-tailed guppies and terrariums inhabited by snakes. Other inhabitants in the classroom included a smattering of

---

[2] Formalin is a 40% solution of formaldehyde in water.

class clowns, me included, that added a touch of levity to this science course. I looked forward to this class as well as the journalism class.

During my sophomore year in high school, I read a newspaper article in the *Corpus Christi Caller* that mentioned the wildlife management department at Texas A&M University. It was then that I began to consider a career in wildlife management. Never having heard of such a discipline, I read whatever I could find in my high school library about this topic or a subject close to it. Four television shows also influenced my career path: *Lassie, Mutual of Omaha's Wild Kingdom, Wide World of Sports* and *American Sportsman*. The TV episodes of *Lassie* from 1964 to 1968 featured Robert Bray as Corey Stuart, a US Forest Service ranger. *Mutual of Omaha's Wild Kingdom* featured zoologist Marlin Perkins and his sidekick, Jim Fowler, also a zoologist. The show focused on wild animals, primarily in Africa and South America, in their natural habitat. Given my interest in wildlife as well as hunting and fishing, the *American Sportsman* also had some influence as the series featured skiing and other winter sports in addition to hunting and fishing.

Growing up in South Texas with little to no topographic relief and no snow, I developed a deep curiosity for mountains, snow, and "real" winters. My fifth-grade teacher, Mrs. Agnes Dorow, also piqued my curiosity about the American West, specifically our national parks. Mrs. Dorow and her family spent the previous summer visiting national parks out west. She brought a View Master stereoscope and reels to class. The reels were thin cardboard disks containing pairs of small transparent color photographs on film, the equivalent of 35mm color slides but much smaller. I viewed images of national parks in the View Master and was captivated by the Rocky Mountain landscapes, the wildlife, and the green conifer forests. I was determined to visit those beautiful, pristine places someday.

I took advanced biology during my senior year under Mr. Smith, where he introduced me and my classmates to ecology at a time when pollution of the environment was becoming a newsworthy topic. Environmental catastrophes during the late 1960s piqued my interest – the Torrey Canyon oil spill off the coast of Cornwall in March 1967, the Santa Barbara oil spill off the coast of California in January

1969, and the Cuyahoga River in Ohio catching on fire on June 1969 from oil and chemical pollution. I browsed my high school's library for books on wildlife. I read *Silent Spring* by Rachel Carson, a book on the demise and eventual extinction of the passenger pigeon, as well as environmental articles on *Life* and *National Geographic* magazines and other periodicals in the library. I learned about the toxic effects of pesticides on birds and other wildlife and how abundant wildlife species, such as the passenger pigeon, with an estimated population of at least three billion birds, could be wiped off the face of the Earth forever.

Under Mr. Smith's tutelage, I conducted my first biological field study. I sampled fish in several lagunas in the vicinity of Falfurrias and identified them to genus and species. The field study consisted of collecting fish using a seine net. The seines varied in length from 15 feet to longer with a depth or width of five feet or more and were made with either monofilament lines or braided nylon. Each end of the seine was secured to one- to two-inch diameter poles four to six feet in length. I held one of the poles, and one of my classmates held the other. One of us would wade into the laguna, stretching the seine out as we went. Once the full length of the net was extended, my classmate on the shore would follow and wade into the pond. We would walk parallel to the shore, each of us holding the bottom of our poles slightly ahead of the top of the pole and keeping the weighted line on the bottom. After pulling the seine for a minute or so, we lifted the bottom of the net and held it slightly above the water to examine our catch. If we felt that we had an adequate catch, we would walk the seine towards the shore, where we would then segregate the fish by species and count the number collected.

We would save a few of each species and transport them back to the classroom to identify the genus and species. My first field study was not, by any means, a scientific study but more of an inventory of fish species inhabiting each pond. My study was awarded as an outstanding project for the Falfurrias High School Science Fair. I was hooked on field biology. To this day, I wish I had been able to contact Mr. Smith to thank him as he instilled in me a passion for field biology and a life-long commitment to protecting wildlife and our environment. Unfortunately, Mr. Smith moved on some years after I graduated from high school, and I never learned of his whereabouts, but not because of a lack of trying.

Chapter 2: Leaving the Nest

Attending a university was a giant leap for me both academically and culturally, as I was not an honor student in high school, and I graduated with a high B. I was not involved in clubs or other activities until my senior year when I served as sports editor for the school newspaper *'Hearts Delight'* named after a local flower, the hearts delight (*Abronia ameliae*), restricted to the loose sandy soils of the South Texas Sand Sheet (STSS) that occupies an area of approximately 2,600 square miles (4,200 km^2) of predominantly loose, sandy soils, and active and relict dunes that includes Brooks County. I grew up in a ranching community that was over 95 percent Mexican American with a community-wide social perception that we were not as smart as Anglos. The fact that most adult residents in Encino only made it through grade school fed that perception. I learned later from Michaela Longoria, wife of my mother's cousin, Enrique, that attending high school during the 1940s and prior required students to live in a boarding house at the county seat 20 to 30 miles from home. Most, if not all, residents could not afford to send their children to high school. My mother and father remained at their family ranches after completing the eighth grade as there was plenty of work to maintain the ranches and grow and harvest their own food. The girls cleaned the house, assisted with cooking, sewed and made their families' garments, and washed, ironed, and mended clothes. The boys learned at an early age how to ride horses, rope calves and steers, helped with building and mending fences, hitched mules to wagons and farm implements such as plows, and helped with the weeding and harvesting of crops. Many of the older residents did not speak English or did so with a limited command of the language, probably a result of being culturally as well as physically isolated from towns and cities where English was the prevalent language. The few Anglos that lived in our community worked for the oil companies at the local oilfields or as foremen of the large ranches. Some, especially the ranch foremen, were bilingual out of necessity to communicate with the Mexican American ranch hands.

Up until the seventh grade, I pictured myself as a rancher like my father and his father and grandfather before him. I would sketch drawings of my future ranch's layout: the ranch house, barns, and corrals. My dad knew that his and my mother's grade-school education was not enough, and both regretted not completing their education. They both emphasized the need to get a good education and implored my two brothers and me to make good grades and try our best. They did not want their sons to face the same hardships that they experienced. In grade school, I believed I and others like me could never go to college because we were not smart enough. It was not until I was in middle school that I learned that college was possible and that I was smart enough to attend a university. During my senior year in high school, Texas A&M University at College Station was the only academic institution in Texas offering a degree in wildlife management. I mentioned that to my small cadre of friends, and one of them responded, "A&M is too hard; you will flunk out." The implication was that I was not smart enough because of my ethnicity. I thought about that and looked at other university catalogs in my high school guidance counselor's office. The cover of one college catalog in particular caught my eye; a beautiful stand of pine trees lined each side of a street leading towards the university administration building. I reached for the catalog, paged through it to find the biology curriculum, and learned that Stephen F. Austin State University (SFASU), located in Nacogdoches, Texas, offered a major in "biology with a wildlife emphasis."

Nacogdoches is considered the oldest town in Texas, established in 1779 by Don Antonio Gil Y'Barbo. At that time, Texas was part of New Spain. Although Nacogdoches has Spanish and Mexican roots, Nacogdoches and Texas became inhospitable to native Tejanos after Texas won its independence from Mexico in 1836 as racism gained a foothold in the new republic. Growing up in the rural ranching community of Encino, most of the residents of that small community and the surrounding ranches had lived there for several generations, comprising over 90 percent of the population in the southern half of Brooks County; thus, my exposure to overt racism did not occur until my sophomore year in high school during a church-sponsored trip to a Catholic Youth Conference in Miami Beach, Florida. I traveled on a charter bus with other students from Falfurrias High School as well as from other high schools within the Corpus Christi diocese. Our first stop during the long journey was to grab snacks and fast food and refuel the bus at Baton Rouge, Louisiana. Our group included one

African American student. A few of the 18-year-old senior students entered a nearby tavern knowing that the legal alcohol drinking age back then in Louisiana was 18. The group quickly filed out of the place, informing the rest of us waiting outside that the bartender told them, "We will serve you but not him," as he pointed to the one African American student in the group. I was proud of the group for walking out and denying the establishment their business. The second incident was at a department store in Miami, where I accompanied a small group into the store to buy souvenirs. After completing our shopping, we stepped outside, and a store security guard immediately stopped the African American student in our group, searched the paper bag the student was carrying, and took him back into the store. The rest of us followed, asking the security guard why the student was detained, and learned that the security agent suspected the student of shoplifting. The student told the security guard that he paid for the item as he was led back into the store. The cashier vouched that the student had indeed paid for the item. The student told us that he opened the package containing the souvenir he had purchased while he was in the store. A store employee must have observed him with the item in his hand and assumed he had not paid for it. Those two incidents from a long time ago are burned into my memory.

During my freshman year at SFASU in 1970-71, I heard stories of what Nacogdoches was like only two years prior, with businesses posted with signs proclaiming "No Mexicans Allowed." SFASU is 444 miles from my hometown of Encino, and back then a 7-hour drive. A week or so before the start of my first semester, my parents drove me and my two brothers to Nacogdoches. En route to Nacogdoches, we stopped for lunch at a restaurant in a small East Texas town just north of Houston. I can only describe the ambiance as karma, an unspoken feeling emanating from the waitress taking our order that conveyed the message, "You don't belong here." Several decades later, at the Ouachita River in southern Arkansas, I felt the same karma, only much stronger from a man standing near the boat ramp as my wife's brother-in-law, Michael, and I returned from an early morning duck hunt at the Felsenthal National Wildlife Refuge. After securing the Jon boat on the trailer, Michael drove his vehicle and boat trailer up the boat ramp, stopping momentarily to let me into his vehicle. As Michael drove, I focused on the man standing near the boat ramp.

"Let's get out of here now," I implored in a frightened tone. "Why?" asked Michael, perplexed at my urgency to leave. "I can't explain it, Michael, only that I felt some threatening karma from that man." Michael reassured me that the man was probably upset that we were at his favorite hunting or fishing spot.

Leaving home and my family was something I was compelled to do, given my career choice. I knew that pursuing a career in wildlife conservation could mean living away from my family, my friends I grew up with, and my hometown. My parents, two brothers, and I spent the night at a local motel in Nacogdoches. The next morning, I moved into my dormitory room. I said my goodbyes to my two brothers and hugged my mother and father, all the while choking back tears and trying to conceal my fears and sadness. Strong familial ties made it extremely hard for me to leave my family and my hometown. I kept telling myself, "I have to do this if I want to achieve my goal." Watching my family drive away was emotionally excruciating. I thought, "What have I done?" I did not know anyone as I was the only student from my high school attending SFASU. I registered for classes a few days later and upon submitting the paperwork to pay tuition, the person receiving the payment looked at my paperwork and informed me that tuition totaled over $700. Tuition and fees at that time averaged between $300 and slightly over $400. I was stunned, and after asking why tuition was so high, the person stated that it was for out-of-state tuition. For a brief moment, I felt like running away and going home because I felt that I was being judged by my surname. "I have to do this," I told myself. "I am a resident of Texas," I responded. I later learned that I was one of five Mexican American students on a campus of over several thousand students. My roommate and the residents in my dorm wing accepted me; however, some of the dorm residents from East Texas had never interacted with Mexican Americans and had preconceived, stereotypical notions common during that time. "I thought all Mexicans wore large sombreros, had dark, black hair and thick mustaches," was one comment I received. "How would Dad have handled this," I asked myself. "*Mejor que haiga un loco y no dos*," he would say. Translation, "Better one crazy person than two." In other words, don't stoop to their level. I took the approach of giving them a brief summary of my and my family's history.

Being so far from home, I sought students who had something in common with me. Music was my connection with residents in my dorm wing. Several residents played guitar, and although I did not have a drum kit, I resorted to playing a tambourine. We had several jam sessions in the stairwell of the dorm, which provided great acoustics. Before the Christmas break, our dorm group of musicians decided to walk to all the residence halls on campus and sing Christmas carols. We started our rounds, going dorm to dorm, standing outside the residence halls singing three or four carols, and walking to the next one. At some point, a campus police car followed our progress. It was obvious what we were doing, so the campus cop either wanted to listen to our performances or ensure we were not up to some nefarious act like instigating a panty raid. After we serenaded the last residence hall, we approached our own dorm and saw the campus cop driving onto the parking lot. Someone in our group suggested singing a Christmas carol to the campus cop. As we began to sing Silent Night, two or three in our group kneeled on one knee and extended their arms out during some of the verses. "I hope the campus cop has a sense of humor," I thought, hoping that the members of our group who took a knee would not be reprimanded by the officer. My other connection was through my Roman Catholic faith. During my freshman year, I became involved with the Newman Center, a student center for Catholics. Through my involvement at the Newman Center, I met additional students, including the few Mexican American students attending the university. I volunteered for various activities at the Newman Center. One activity involved assisting 12-year-old Danny, an African American who has cerebral palsy, with exercises, mostly sit-ups. Danny lived in a predominantly black neighborhood on the west side of Nacogdoches. A student from the Newman Center would transport Danny to the center for his exercises. At the end of my senior year at SFASU, I drove to Danny's house, trying in vain to suppress tears as I walked up to the front porch where he was sitting. I told him I had completed college and was leaving SFASU. I will always remember his smile and his cheerful attitude.

I overcame my initial fears of college being "too hard" and excelled in biology and forestry courses. It was not easy, and I spent many hours each day studying and preparing for exams and working on homework assignments. My freshman and sophomore years included required courses such as English literature, history, US government, math, physics, chemistry, and biology.

I slogged through most of those courses except my biology classes, geography, US government, and electives that I enjoyed. During the spring semester of my sophomore year, I changed my minor from journalism to forestry. I enjoyed the forestry courses, especially the introductory course taught by the dean of the forestry school. The highlight of that course was touring the Temple Industries sawmill plywood mill. I finally got to see firsthand how plywood was manufactured. Most of the biology and forestry coursework entailed the memorization of scientific names, biological and ecological concepts, and species identification, among a plethora of other information. I spent many long hours studying for tests, working on assignments, and writing research papers.

I spent many hours at the university library studying for tests, interspersed with short breaks, perusing magazines such as *National Wildlife* and *National Geographic.* During one of those breaks, I read the *National Geographic* magazine article *"Stalking the Mountain Lion – to Save Him"* by Dr. Maurice G. Hornocker two years earlier.

Hornocker's article focused on his ground-breaking research on mountain lions in the Idaho Primitive Area that later became the Frank Church River-of-No-Return Wilderness Area. By that time, I was interested in predator ecology and the conservation of predatory species such as hawks and eagles, wolves, and mountain lions. After reading the article, my goal to do research on predators took root. Little did I realize back then that I would be studying and working under the mentorship of Dr. Hornocker two years later. The hard work paid off with my acceptance into graduate school at the University of Idaho, thanks to the recommendation of my forest wildlife management instructor, John Stransky. In addition to teaching the wildlife management course at SFASU, Stransky was employed by the research branch of the U.S. Forest Service and conducted wildlife studies at the Stephen F. Austin Experimental Forest. I applied to several land grant universities in western states, including the University of Idaho, where Maurice was the leader of the University of Idaho Cooperative Wildlife Research Unit. I thought, "It would be great to work under someone like him," although, at the time, I never thought it would be possible to work under someone of his stature. When I was accepted to graduate school at Idaho, I learned that Dr. Hornocker would be my major professor.

During my junior year at SFASU, my desire to experience the mountains out West led me to apply for summer employment with the U.S. Forest Service. I was offered a job as a forestry aide at the Bighorn National Forest in north-central Wyoming. This proved to be quite the adventure for a 21-year-old from South Texas driving solo for over 1,600 miles and far from friends and family. My only companion was Tanya, my year-old border collie-lab retriever mix dog I adopted during my junior year at SFASU. Although I could have planned a shorter route from South Texas to north central Wyoming, the route north entailed driving through the Texas Panhandle, a country flatter than a pancake. I planned my route further west, driving from Encino to Eagle Pass, Texas, and continuing northwest toward Del Rio, stopping at Langtry, Texas. Why Langtry, Texas? The only reason to stop and visit this isolated town on US Highway 90 was to visit the Judge Roy Bean Visitor Center. Viewing the movie *The Life and Times of Judge Roy Bean,* starring Paul Newman as Judge Roy Bean prior to my trip, prompted me to see and learn more about the real-life judge in this out-of-the-way place. During the late 1800s, Roy Bean served as the only judge for several hundred miles in this parched, God-forsaken place of Texas. Following my brief visit, I looked west across the Rio Grande towards the Mexican state of Coahuila and saw mountains for the first time in my life. From Langtry, I continued northward across New Mexico, driving east of the Sacramento Mountains to Roswell, where I spent the night.

The next day, my route led me east of the snow-capped Sangre de Cristo Mountains. As I approached Raton, my drive took me up Raton Pass, a first for this "flat-lander" from South Texas. I stopped at the summit of Raton Pass, elevation 7,834 ft., and soaked up the view of the mountain peaks to the west in Colorado. I was awe-struck by the beauty and ruggedness of the landscape. Interstate 25 (I-25) paralleled the front range, greeting me with a peak after snow-capped peak that reached for the sky. I reached Fort Collins by mid-afternoon and took the one exit onto Mulberry Street. The gateway into Fort Collins at that time was pretty stark. Downtown Fort Collins was not much to look at, and Old Town Square did not exist until 12 years later. I obtained a room at the Travel Lodge motel across from the Colorado State University campus. The tree-shaded campus provided a visual respite from the almost tree-less area from the interstate westward into the city of 64,000 people. I drove around the campus and took in the rural houses with horse pastures immediately west of the university. "I'd like to live here someday," I thought as I considered this area close to the mountains and a two-day drive from my hometown in South Texas. This was the farthest I had driven solo and away from home. My excitement at seeing the Rocky Mountains during my drive through Colorado dampened my thoughts of home, my family, and my hometown friends. I expected a similar landscape in Wyoming and encountered rolling grassland and a sagebrush sea instead. The Laramie Mountains stretched from just west of Wheatland northwestward towards Casper. At 15 to 20 miles distance from the interstate, they appeared like hills to me. The treeless terrain caused me to miss the live oak and mesquite trees back home as homesickness crept into my soul.

As I approached Buffalo, Wyoming, the sight of the snow-capped Bighorn Mountains dampened my thoughts of home. Cloud Peak dominated the mountain range at

13,171 feet in elevation. Forty minutes later, I rolled into Sheridan and checked into a motel. As soon as I got settled into my room, I phoned my parents as I did every evening that I was on the road up to Wyoming. The next day, I drove west up and over the Bighorn Mountains and was amazed at the amount of snow above eight thousand feet in elevation.

As I made my way west on Alternate Highway 14, a thick blanket of snow and four to five-foot snow drifts made the Forest Service road leading to the Medicine Wheel Ranger Station impassable. The day after I arrived at Lovell, WY, the location of the Medicine Wheel Ranger District office, I decided a distraction from the isolation of my motel room and thoughts of home was in order. I drove back to the mountains and stopped at a picnic area at the foot of the Bighorns to view Five Springs Falls. While there, I encountered two couples and a two-year-old girl. The two-year-old's parents asked if their daughter Christie could pet my dog, Tanya. I obliged, and as Tanya licked her face, her parents saw the Texas license plate on my truck and asked if this was my first visit to Wyoming. "Yes, I'm up here to begin working at the Medicine Wheel Ranger District," I replied. We exchanged introductions, and one of the adults asked if I knew anyone in the area. "I don't know anyone up here. This is the farthest I've ever been away from home," I answered.

Christie's parents, Bob and Barbara Carlton, informed me that they lived just west of Lovell and invited me to stop and visit them anytime I drove down the mountain from the ranger station to buy groceries and supplies at Lovell. The second couple, Pedro and Nancy Hernandez, lived in Billings, Montana. Pedro and Bob were childhood friends who grew up together in Hardin, Montana, 50 miles east of Billings. I learned that Bob worked with the Federal Aviation Administration (FAA) at a radar facility at the summit of Medicine Mountain, five road miles from the ranger station where I would spend my summer. The radar facility was one of many such sites operated throughout the United States to track commercial and private aircraft using the airspace to prevent mid-air collisions. Bob, Barbara, and Christie became my surrogate family away from home. I would stop by and visit them on a Saturday or Sunday drive down to Lovell to buy groceries.

My first days on the job entailed working at the ranger district office in Lovell, as the ranger station was located at almost 9,000 feet in elevation, which was still snowed in during the first two weeks of June. Since most of the Forest Service roads were still impassable, my work with another co-worker included repairing the telephone wires leading up to the ranger station from Lovell. The telephone lines extended from Lovell up the Bighorn mountains to the ranger station and were not maintained by the telephone company. Repairing the telephone lines involved using climbing spurs attached to our work boots and lower legs. We also mended the fence enclosing the horse pasture near Lovell, where the Forest Service horses spent the winter. After the access road was plowed, the seasonal staff and I settled in at the ranger station cabin. We shared a small cabin with a recreation aid and a fire guard, both seasonal workers. On occasion, one or two of the trail crew staff would stay in the cabin, although they usually spent their nights camping out on the trails they managed. The Forest Service kept four horses at the ranger station for the trail crew and the range conservationist to use. The mountains, the dry, cool montane climate, and the wildlife proved intoxicating. "I want to live and die in the mountains," I thought to myself after the first week on the job. I worked with Mike Steigerwalt, a forestry student from Pennsylvania State University. Together, we walked many miles surveying the perimeters of timber stands proposed for logging and collecting data for the district's forester to estimate the quantity of timber available for harvest at the proposed stands. We measured the diameter and height of trees at several sampling plots within the proposed stands. Most of the time, we walked on deadfall logs that, in some places, were strewn on the forest floor like matchsticks spilled on a kitchen floor. We used the fallen logs as pathways, walking three or four feet above the ground. The sharp stubs of broken branches on the deadfall gnawed at the knobby soles of our boots. By the end of the summer, the soles of my boots were worn smoothly. After completing the surveys, we assisted crews with marking trees for selective cutting in the proposed timber sale areas.

I spent weekends fly fishing for trout along Porcupine Creek with Mike. Trout fishing was nothing like fishing for large-mouthed bass and bluegill sunfish at my Dad's ranch. Fortunately, Mike was a good teacher in the art of trout fishing. That summer, I realized the addition I had made to my mental 'bucket list' when I was in the fifth grade, and my wish was to visit Yellowstone National Park. One of the trail crew members who lived near Powell, Wyoming, offered to guide Mike and me to Yellowstone. Jeff guided us to Cooke City and the northeast entrance to the park; however, we did not venture much farther to view other areas of the park. Needless to say, I vowed to return and visit that spectacular park again and did so four years later after completing graduate school and field work in northwestern Montana. I visited Old Faithful and the geyser basin.

During the spring semester of my senior year at SFASU, I was accepted into graduate school at the University of Idaho, thanks to the recommendation of my forest wildlife management instructor, John Stransky. In addition to teaching the wildlife management course at SFASU, Stransky was employed by the research branch of the U.S. Forest Service and conducted wildlife studies at the Stephen F. Austin Experimental Forest. After completing my undergraduate degree in biology and a brief stay with my parents, I packed all my belongings into my pickup truck and headed back to Wyoming to work as a range technician at the Medicine Wheel Ranger District during the summer. Bob and Barbara graciously allowed me to store most of my personal belongings in their basement. I worked with Walter van Poollen, the other range technician. Walter was a student at Colorado State University and was bilingual, with Dutch as his second language. Our tasks as range technicians included sampling transects in grazing allotments to determine grazing use and impact. Other work included fire suppression at a small lightning-caused fire within the Medicine Wheel Ranger District, packing camping gear into the Little Bighorn Canyon, and other duties as assigned. The pack trip into the Little Bighorn Canyon entailed using horses to transport the Range Conservationist, Walter, me, canvas tents, and other assorted camping gear down the Little Bighorn drainage into the canyon. After we set up the camp, we rode our horses to the trailhead approximately two to three miles from the Montana-Wyoming border. Vehicular access from the ranger station to the trailhead at the mouth of the Little Bighorn Canyon required driving east over the mountains and down to Ranchester, Wyoming, then north on Interstate 90 to Wyola, Montana, a 2-hour drive, followed by 16 more miles to the trailhead. We met Roger Williams, the district ranger, accompanied by several men from Lovell at the trailhead. The camping and fishing trip was a goodwill gesture by the ranger district to the city of Lovell. I never asked about the details of how or why these men were selected, but apparently, it was an annual event. Walter and I exchanged our horses for the Forest Service vehicle that Roger drove to the trailhead. Walter and I said our goodbyes and drove back to the ranger station. When we arrived at the ranger station, we called Arlene, the district office administrative clerk, to inform her of our safe return. She laughed and said she had received several phone calls from residents living near Wyola reporting that a couple of hippies had stolen a Forest Service truck.

Walter and my personalities clicked not just during work but during the off-hours as well. Walter and I developed a good relationship with the district forester, Larry Gash, to the extent that we were comfortable joking with him in a harmless way. At the end of one particular workday, after I refueled the Forest Service vehicle, I returned to our cabin to find Larry sitting at the kitchen table. I greeted Larry and followed with small talk about my work day. Larry then brought up the subject of the Lovell

Mustang Days parade. The Mustang Days event at Lovell was held during the last week of June and included a parade, a rodeo, and other entertainment for the locals and tourists. "If Walter wears the Woodsy Owl costume at the Mustang Days parade, will you wear the Smokey Bear one?" Larry asked. "Sure, I'll do anything to see him as Woodsy the Owl," I replied. Larry was pleased and informed me that the costumes would be shipped from another Forest Service office in time for the Mustang Days festivities.

The Forest Service used the Woodsy Owl icon or cartoon to raise awareness of protecting the environment. Woodsy Owl's slogan was "give a hoot, don't pollute." Walter was nowhere within earshot or even in the cabin, as I recall. Later that afternoon, I relayed my conversation with Larry to Walter. "That sneaky.... Larry asked me if I would wear the Woodsy Owl costume if you wore the Smokey Bear one," Walter half laughed and half snorted. As Mustang Days approached, Larry received the Smokey Bear costume; however, the Woodsy Owl costume was missing in action somewhere in a national forest in California, Oregon, or Washington where it was last used. The morning of the parade, I donned the costume and climbed onto the Forest Service pickup truck bed.

As the pickup truck slowly made its way along the parade route on the main street, I waved to the spectators, especially the children, with one hand and steadied myself with my other hand, holding a shovel and using it as a crutch. At the end of the parade, I was helped off the pickup truck bed and interacted with the children. No words were spoken; however, the children were beside themselves at seeing Smokey Bear. By that time, the summer ambient temperature rose, and the Smokey Bear costume morphed into a sauna-like environment. Fortunately, the interaction with the children ended before the threshold for heat exhaustion was reached. Once out of sight of spectators, especially the kids, I quickly shed the costume and drank lots of water. Walter came up to me, expressed disappointment at not being able to dress up as Woodsy Owl, and added that it would have been fun for him. I replied that it was fun except for the sauna-like conditions inside the costume.

During my two summers at the Medicine Wheel Ranger District, I learned of several caves, including Horse

Thief Cave, in the foothills between the Bighorn River and the Bighorn Mountains. I became interested in spelunking during summer breaks from high school when I accompanied my parents on trips to the Hill Country northwest of San Antonio and visited several commercial caverns. Walter and I obtained general directions to Horse Thief Cave and informed our co-workers, as well as my friends, the Carltons, of our plan in case they would have to contact search and rescue if we did not return one or two hours before dark. We made our way on gravel roads, searching for the large natural opening of Horse Thief Cave, and after two or three failed attempts, we spotted the large entrance. The cave opening immediately led to a large 700 square-foot 'room,' big enough to hold several heads of horses; hence the name as horse rustlers in the late 1800s and early 1900s used the cave to hide horses as they stationed lookouts near the cave entrance to see when someone approached their hideout. We entered the large room and made our way through a narrow passageway. Walter and I each carried water bottles, two flashlights, extra batteries, and a roll of red surveyor's tape. I placed short lengths of red surveyors' tape or flagging along our route to help us navigate our return to the surface. The passageway narrowed to a point where continuing on required that we belly crawl.

Not knowing what to expect, we decided to play it safe and exit the cave. As summer drew close, I bid farewell to my friends, the Carltons, and the mountains that ignited my desire to live and die in a montane environment. My dog Tanya and I headed towards Moscow, Idaho, and the University of Idaho by way of Yellowstone National Park. I was enthralled with the views of the Grand Canyon of Yellowstone and Tower Falls. I spent the night camping near Gardiner, Montana, and completed the drive to Moscow, Idaho, the next day.

Chapter 3: University of Idaho

After I completed my summer job at the Medicine Wheel in late August, I looked forward to the next phase in my life: graduate school at the University of Idaho. I planned my trip to Moscow, Idaho, and included driving through Yellowstone National Park to visit sites that I had not seen during my previous visit the summer before. The next day, I drove westward through Montana, where, 30 miles west of Butte, Montana, along Interstate 90, I was puzzled by the turquoise waters of Silver Creek that wound through a barren floodplain devoid of any vegetation. Little did I realize at the time that the turquoise color resulted from heavy metals present in mine tailings from copper mines in Butte and Anaconda and deposited along the stream by past flood events. During the 1990s, some of my future colleagues in the U.S. Fish and Wildlife Service (FWS) spent a significant portion of their careers on the remediation of this stream and other contamination from the copper mines and smelters.

I drove Highway 2 into Idaho and reveled in the beauty of the Lochsa River as it churned its way through spruce-fir and cedar-hemlock forests. The Lochsa River and the highway merged with the Clearwater River, which continued west to Lewiston. I expected the landscape of northern Idaho to be similar to my only reference, a photo I had seen of the Sawtooth Range in central Idaho. At Lewiston, I drove up Lewiston Hill, a sinuous stretch of Highway 95 with 64 curves and switchbacks and a climb of 2,000 feet. Upon reaching the top of Lewiston Hill, I saw rolling grain fields instead of rugged mountains. I would be remiss if I didn't state that I was extremely disappointed. I arrived in Moscow, Idaho, late in the day and spent the night in a local motel. The next day, I drove to the University of Idaho campus and the Forestry, Range, and Wildlife building to meet with Dr. Ernie Ables, who was designated as my major professor. I would be working on a small mammal study related to wolverine research led by Dr. Maurice G. Hornocker, leader of the U.S. Fish and Wildlife Cooperative Wildlife Research Unit. The study area was located in the Flathead National Forest south of Glacier National Park in Montana. Cooperative Wildlife Research Units (Co-Op Units) were jointly supported by the Fish and Wildlife Service, the Wildlife Management Institute, the state wildlife management agency, and land grant universities of participating states. The Co-Op Unit's objectives were to train students for technical positions in the field of wildlife management and ecology. The Coop Units also provided research and technical assistance to participating states and federal agencies in tackling important wildlife problems. I was familiar with Dr. Hornocker's work with mountain lions through an article he published in National Geographic magazine two years prior. The research done on mountain lions and other predators by Hornocker and others at the University of Idaho compelled me to apply to graduate school there. I thought, "It would be great to work under someone like him," although at the time I applied, I did not expect to work under someone's supervision of his stature.

During my first meeting, Dr. Ables informed me that he would not be my major professor as he had recently been promoted to associate dean of the College of Forestry, Range, and Wildlife. "You will be working directly under Maurice Hornocker," Dr. Ables informed me. He asked me where I was staying, and I replied, "At a local motel." He then immediately offered his home until I found a place to rent. "I have a dog," I added. Dr. Ables accepted my dog

Tanya and me into his home. He and his wife, Juanita, were very gracious. Prior to the start of classes, I spent my days looking for a place to live, and each day, I would return to the Ables' residence dejected. Juanita and Ernie would reassure me each time that I could remain at their home until I found a place to live. Eventually, after several weeks of searching, I secured a temporary home 10 miles east of Moscow in the small logging community of Troy, Idaho. I lived in Troy through the fall semester and a portion of the spring semester. I commuted to campus each weekday with two other graduate students who lived in Troy. At the end of the fall semester, I planned to travel home to visit my family in South Texas. Since I had Tanya with me, I had to find someone willing to care for her during my absence. By this time, I was comfortable addressing Hornocker by his first name.

I informed Maurice that I planned to visit my family and needed someone to care for Tanya. He suggested I talk to Esther Louie, the Co-Op Unit secretary, and added that Esther and her husband, Wayne Beymer, lived on 80 acres of forested land near Deary, Idaho, 20 miles east of Moscow, along with their dog Metro. Esther and Wayne agreed to care for Tanya at their home, and I was able to visit my family during the Christmas break. Upon return, I reconnected with Tanya and visited with Esther and Wayne. Six months later, in June, Esther and Wayne drove six to seven hours from their home to my field camp in the Flathead National Forest in Northwestern Montana, where I began fieldwork for my Master's thesis, further cementing my love for them, resulting in a life-long friendship.

My fall semester courses included statistics, sampling techniques, classification of forest communities, and a course on the fundamentals of research. I wrote up my research study plan and sampling techniques for the fundamentals of the research course. I struggled with statistics, especially when the course delved into calculus in some of the statistical tests. I did not take calculus at SFASU as it was not a required course for biology majors. A graduate teaching assistant conducted the statistics lab and assisted students with statistical problems. During one lab, the statistics professor attended the lab. I was struggling with one particular problem, so I raised my hand for help. The professor approached and stood behind me. "I don't know if I did this problem correctly," I asked him. "What do you think?" the professor replied. It came across as very condescending to me. I sat there in silence, thinking, "If I knew the answer, I would not be asking you for help." A feeling of helplessness flooded me. Later that afternoon, the teaching assistant helped me work through some of the calculus problems and continued to help me, allowing me to get through statistics with a 'B' for my final grade. Even though I thanked him after he helped me with statistical problems involving calculus, I wish I could remember his name and thank him again years later. On one particular day, I walked into the front office of the Wildlife Department and Co-Op Unit and engaged in a conversation with Esther. My voice must have conveyed anxiety or trepidation and prompted Maurice to summon me into his office.

I walked toward his office, which was located across from the front office. Without saying a word, Maurice led me to a filing cabinet in his office. He opened a file drawer, reached in, and pulled out a folder. Again, without saying a word, he opened the folder and showed me his transcript from undergraduate school. His grades were similar to my grades from undergraduate school. With that seemingly small gesture, Maurice restored my confidence. "I can do this," I thought to myself.

I took the 'Big Game Management' taught by Dr. James "Jim" Peek during the spring semester. Most of the students, if not all, had Bachelor of Science degrees with majors in wildlife management. Their knowledge of wildlife management issues was much better than mine, as I only had two wildlife management courses at Stephen F. Austin State University. Dr. Peek had each student in the class review and comment on published scientific journal articles. During these discussions, I often felt out of place and did not belong there, as most of my classmates had better knowledge of wildlife management issues than I did. They were more articulate in their discussions than I was. Even though I interacted with students from various parts of the country, I never forgot where I came from and who I was. I always kept my connections with my friends back at home and, most importantly, my immediate family.

I learned so much during my two years in graduate school; at the time, it seemed like a long time, but it went by fast. Since I was one of only a few Mexican Americans in northern Idaho and the University, I found that students would ask me about my culture. I had a classmate from Northern New Mexico by the name of Pat Aguilar. He would tell me all about Northern New Mexico, its history, and its culture. He grew up in a small village of Peñasco, north of Santa Fe and south of Taos, nestled up in the foothills of the Sangre de Cristo Mountains. Through our conversations and listening to Pat talk about where he grew up, I wound up educating myself regarding my family's history and culture. Growing up in South Texas, when I did, the prevailing social norm was to reject the language and the culture. Outside of our small ranching community, we were made to feel that it was un-American. Listening to Pat talk about New Mexico, I sensed an acceptance of the culture where he grew up. After graduate school, I visited Northern New Mexico. I was so impressed with that area and the pride that people had in their culture. That's not to say that we in South Texas were not proud. *We were!* However, our culture and identity were suppressed for the most part in school and in society outside of our small, rural, ranching community.

At the beginning of the spring semester, one of the graduate students in the carpool moved from Troy to begin his PhD field research in what is now the University of Idaho

– Taylor Wilderness Research Station in the heart of the Frank Church River of No Return Wilderness Area. The other graduate student moved to Moscow. The end of the carpool meant driving 10 miles to and from campus every day in my pickup truck that burned through a tank of gasoline every nine days. As a research assistant, I earned $3 per hour; with the increased cost incurred driving myself from Troy to Moscow, I found myself flat broke at the start of the last week of the month. Fortunately, Larry Hoffman, a forestry graduate student who was renting an apartment in Moscow, needed a roommate as his former roommate, a wildlife graduate student, departed for his field study in Southern Idaho. I spent the remainder of the spring semester in Moscow. I spent seven-and-a-half months on campus completing my requisite coursework before moving to Hungry Horse, Montana, to begin fieldwork on my small mammal study in the Spotted Bear Ranger District of the Flathead National Forest.

Chapter 4: Up The South Fork

Maurice hired Howard Hash as a research associate in charge of the Wolverine Project field operations and Gary Koehler, who had completed his master's degree under Maurice. Howard had obtained his wildlife graduate study at the University of Idaho, owned his own airplane, a Cessna 180, and had experience as a bush pilot flying over and landing in backcountry airstrips in mountainous terrain. Gary had recently completed his master's research study of pine marten in the Selway-Bitterroot wilderness area. His experience living and working in the backcountry as well as live trapping pine marten, was an asset in the Wolverine Project. Gary and Howard began preparing for the winter trapping of wolverines during the summer and early fall. I spent that first summer living in a small camp trailer, trapping small mammals, and determining the habitat types seven days a week, four weeks a month, with occasional trips to Hungry Horse and Kalispell to buy groceries and other supplies. A U.S. Forest Service house in the small town of Hungry Horse, located three and a half miles downstream of Hungry Horse Dam, served as one of my homes during my fieldwork for my master's degree thesis in the Flathead National Forest. Hornocker procured temporary use of the house from the Forest Service for the Wolverine Research Project. I stored what meager belongings I owned, primarily books, vinyl record albums, cookware, and dishes, in the basement of the Hungry Horse house. I typically bunked at that house whenever I made the 60-mile trip from Spotted Bear or my camp trailer near my study area into Kalispell to buy groceries and other provisions. Planning and construction of the Hungry Horse Dam between 1948 and 1953 necessitated the construction of housing for government and contract workers due to the remote location of the dam site. Hungry Horse Dam impounded 34 miles of the South Fork of the Flathead River and created Hungry Horse Reservoir with a surface area of approximately 23,800 acres and 170 miles of shoreline. The reservoir is bounded on the west by the Swan Range and on the east side by the Flathead Range. Great Northern Mountain, elevation 8,705 feet in elevation, dominates the Flathead Range directly east of the reservoir. The portion of the Swan Range west of the reservoir rises to slightly over 7,400 feet in elevation. Years after the Hungry Horse Dam was completed in 1953, the Bureau of Reclamation transferred the houses and other buildings to the U.S. Forest Service. The administration building became the headquarters for the Hungry Horse and Spotted Bear Ranger Districts.

I conducted my fieldwork during the summer months of 1975 and 1976. Before Hornocker's wolverine study, biologists assumed that wolverines required extensive tracts of undeveloped or roadless montane forest. Two years of radio-tracking data flipped that assumption on its head, as wolverines were tracked moving through clearcuts. Hornocker wondered if clearcuts provided any food for wolverines in the form of small mammals. My graduate study entailed collecting data on the diversity and relative abundance of small mammal species in clearcuts of known-age and comparing it to that in uncut forested areas.

I trapped small mammals in uncut forested sites, one-year partial cuts, five-year clear-cuts, 15-year clearcuts, and subalpine basins at or above timberline. Subalpine basins are dominated by grasses, sedges, and low shrubs such as huckleberry and false huckleberry, also referred to as Mensisia.

False huckleberry shrubs created thickets, with some so dense it made walking through them difficult and, at times, impassable. I often had to place my feet on the shrubs' stems to walk through the thickets. Snow covered the study area at the tree line and higher elevations during the month of June. Howard and I hauled the Co-Op Unit's 10-12 foot camp trailer up the Quintonkin Creek drainage on the west side of Hungry Horse Reservoir and 40 miles upstream of Hungry Horse Dam. I'd make trips to the Spotted Bear Ranger Station to use their showers and use their phone to communicate with Howard. The Quintonkin and Sullivan Creek drainages had intensive logging between 1960 and 1975 and provided a diversity of known-aged clearcuts as well as uncut forested areas for my research project. Gary Koehler assisted me during the first summer of fieldwork. He had completed his master's degree studying pine marten in the Selway-Bitterroot wilderness area in Idaho. Gary live trapped pine marten during winter and small mammals, primarily rodents, in the wilderness area during summer. Hornocker hired Gary to work on the Wolverine Project, assist with the live trapping operations, and help me set up my small mammal fieldwork. We shared our field camp with Gary's dog, Rascal, a Siberian husky, and my dog, Tanya. Howard and I initially sited the camp trailer five miles up the Quintonkin Creek drainage near Posey Creek. After we moved our gear into the camp trailer, Gary and I scoped out the clearcuts and forested areas in the Sullivan and Quintonkin Creek drainages. A week later, we moved the camp trailer to a much nicer and forested site adjacent to the confluence of Sullivan and Connor creeks in the Flathead National Forest.

Gary and I planned a small mammal sampling scheme and decided on 30 trap stations with two snap traps per station on three transects with stations 30 feet apart. We trapped small mammals with snap traps and the larger Columbian ground squirrels with live traps. The live traps were approximately 24 inches long, six inches wide, and seven inches in height. Twenty live traps were placed 30 feet apart along two of the sampling transects. I set the snap traps and checked them at each sampling site for a total of three trap-nights.

I ran the live traps for four consecutive days at each sample site. I flagged a 125-meter-squared circular plot to measure the percent ground cover, identify the plants, and determine the habitat type. I worked on two sample sites during each trapping session. The live traps were collapsible and folded flat with a footprint of 24" by 13" for easier transport and storage. When transporting traps to the next sample sites, I would stack the folded live traps and place them on the cargo rack above the rear fender. The weight of 40 stacked live traps above the rear wheel made driving the motorcycle a challenging endeavor. Back then, the Forest Service constructed earthen berms across some forest roads to restrict car and truck access to sensitive areas like subalpine areas. Riding the trail bike up and over these berms with the weight of 40 traps over the rear wheel caused the motorcycle to flip up and backward on two of those crossings. After getting thrown off the bike the second time, I learned to walk the trail bike up and over those berms. Snap traps were transported in cardboard boxes to and from the sample sites. One box was strapped to the handlebars of the motorcycle, and the second box to the rear cargo rack. To set traps in subalpine forested habitats and open subalpine basins above timberline, I strapped ten live traps and a box full of snap traps onto my pack frame and hiked up two miles from the road to the sample sites. Rusty menziesia, also known as false huckleberry, a 3 to 6-foot tall shrub, dominated the understory of the subalpine fir forested sites just below the timberline. Shrub density was so thick it made walking extremely difficult, having to part overlapping branches to make our way through and walking on or over low branches. Setting snap traps in this habitat type was just as difficult. The live traps were set in the open subalpine basins, which made it much easier.

Except for the two 'bike rodeo' incidents and having the chain break on one of the trail bikes, most of the fieldwork was uneventful: riding a Honda Trail 90 motorcycle to the sampling site, checking traps, and recording data (species captured, number of each species captured); reset the traps or move them to the next site; ride back to the Connor Creek campsite; fill out field data sheets – two copies of each data sheet, and write a narrative account of the day's field activities. With fieldwork and data documentation completed, I would spend the remainder of the day working on a term paper for one of my graduate classes, reading a book, or trying my luck with my fly rod. I reveled in spending every day out in the field, even in light rain showers. There were a few times I got soaked riding the motorcycle in the rain. Although most days were uneventful, wildlife sightings would add a brief moment of awe to an otherwise mundane day. As I zipped along the forest roads to and from my sample sites, I kept an eye out for bears. I never saw a grizzly bear, but I did encounter black bears. On one occasion, I did come close to a black bear sow with two cubs. The bears were upslope, approximately 20 to 30 yards from the road. I stopped the motorcycle and watched the bears to see what they would do. The mother bear let out a huffing sound, and the cubs quickly climbed up a lodgepole pine. The bear then moved further into the timber, and I continued down the road. Other wildlife I observed included elk, mule deer, porcupines, coyotes, badgers, red-tailed hawks, osprey, golden eagles, and bald eagles.

Typical small mammal species captured included Columbian ground squirrels, deer mice, yellow-pine chipmunks, western jumping mice, shrews, and red-backed voles.

Columbian ground squirrels are burrowing animals and occur in the Northern Rockies in Western Montana, Idaho, and eastern Oregon and Washington, extending northward into the Canadian Rockies in southeastern

British Columbia and western Alberta. This species prefers open habitats such as alpine and subalpine meadows and clearcuts. They feed on vegetation, insects, eggs, and carrion. I documented higher densities of Columbian ground squirrels in clearcuts and open subalpine basins where grasses and sedges were most abundant. I observed them along all the roadsides in the study area. Roads serve as pathways for these ground squirrels to colonize new clearcuts. Columbian ground squirrels emerged from hibernation in the clearcuts, which were mostly snow-free in mid-April, as well as in the snow-covered subalpine basins above 6,400 feet in elevation. The ground squirrels dug their way out of the four- to six-foot thick snow remaining on the ground at these higher elevations. I observed ground squirrel burrows in snowpacks four to six feet deep in subalpine basins at 6,400 feet in elevation.

Now and then my routine would be changed by unexpected events. One sunny July day, as I was checking my live traps located in a 15-year-old clearcut, I encountered a striped skunk in one of them. I returned to camp and asked Gary for ideas on how to free the skunk. We tossed around several options and settled on draping a tarp over the live trap to shield us from the mustelid's chemical defense system. We drove to the Spotted Bear Ranger Station and asked a Forest Service employee if they had any old tarps we could have. We surmised that if we borrowed the tarp, they would most definitely not want it returned. They gave us a moldy old tarp and transported it to the trap site to free the skunk. Our plan involved one of us holding the tarp up so that it would provide a shield from the skunk's spray, slowly approaching the trap, and draping the tarp over the live trap. After arriving at the site, it was obvious that the skunk could not move around in the trap. The narrow confines of the trap would only allow this mustelid to back up to exit the trap once we opened the trap's door. One of us held up the tarp so that the other could cut a hole in the tarp, allowing the lucky person holding the tarp up as a shield to view the trap and the skunk. A skunk's defensive spray is composed of seven major volatile components, two of which include thiols, also known as "mercaptans, and acetate derivatives of these thiols. Two of the thiols, (E)-2-butene-1-thiol and 3-methyl-1-butanethiol, comprise a sulfur and hydrogen atom bonded together and are responsible for the strong and repellent odor. Somehow, Gary drew the short straw, although I do not remember having any straws at that moment. Gary held the thiol defensive shield (TDS, aka moldy canvas tarp) in front of him, each hand extending upward and outward, holding a corner of the TDS. He slowly inched his way toward the trapped skunk, taking two steps toward the live trap. The skunk tried to shift its body to position its rear end toward Gary, but its efforts proved futile. The wire mesh live trap was 7 inches wide, 7 inches tall, and 20 inches long, large enough for the skunk to enter into the trap and small enough to restrict the mustelid's movements. The process was a dance between the animal and the human, two steps by Gary and an attempted move by the skunk. This continued for what seemed like hours but took only a few minutes. What seemed like an eternity to me and probably to Gary and quite possibly the skunk, Gary was close enough to drape the tarp over the trap quickly. The skunk tried in vain to raise its tail, thus removing any impediment to the chemical spray and allowing the vile liquid to reach its target. The skunk engaged its defensive spray even though it could not raise its tail and point its rear end toward the approaching threat. We waited a few minutes, hoping that the acrid smell would dissipate. It didn't; the thiols burned our eyes and throat even though

Gary and I did not get sprayed. We attempted to hold our breath, but doing so only caused us to breath in a mouthful when we had to take a breath. My body reacted to the noxious odor by retching repeatedly in an attempts to expel the smell that would gag a maggot. Not knowing if the skunk had an additional round of spray, we discussed how to open the trap door to release the skunk without getting sprayed. When an animal entered the live trap and walked on the trigger pan towards the back third of the trap, the animal's weight on the trigger pan would close the trap door. The door would drop from the top of the trap, and a door lock frame would prevent the trapped animal from pushing the door open to escape. To open the trap door, one would have to push the door lock frame and raise the bottom of the trap door. Gary held his breath and wiped the tears out of his eyes, and with a small stick, pushed the door lock frame to open the trap door. "Pedro! Get me a longer stick!" I frantically searched for a longer stick. "Hurry!" Gary pleaded with a sense of alarm, frosted with a layer of impending doom, "It's starting to walk out!"

"It's a clearcut," I answered as my eyes desperately searched for a longer stick. The skunk was more interested in fleeing than firing off one more salvo of the chemical irritant. We left the trap and the tarp at the site and are planning to retrieve them later after the stench has subsided. A day or so later, we recovered the trap and dumped the tarp in a trash can at the ranger station.

CHAPTER 5: GRIZZLY COUNTRY

During the last day of June, I drove up to West Glacier and met up with Evelyn "Evie" Merrill, a wildlife graduate student at the University of Idaho, and Frank Singer, a university alumnus. Singer conducted research at the park, and Evie worked at the park collecting data at campgrounds to determine factors influencing bear interactions with visitors hiking in Glacier National Park. Evie invited me on a weekend trek up the Camas Creek drainage to survey backcountry campgrounds. Evie's summer job entailed surveying backcountry campgrounds in the park and recording if food and trash were stored correctly and secured to prevent depredation by black bears and grizzly bears. Always willing to hike and explore the backcountry and wilderness areas, I accepted the invitation. Later that evening, I packed food and other gear into my backpack. I was aware of the risks and precautions I'd have to take to avoid confrontations with bears, especially grizzlies. Days after completing the hike, I was glad I had not read the book *Night of the Grizzlies* by Jack Olsen; more on that later. We started our hike at 9:30 am near Lake McDonald Ranger Station at the upper end of Lake McDonald, hiked up one mile, and stopped at an open brush field where we stopped and sat to enjoy the view of Lake McDonald and Great Northern Mountain. After 10 or 15 minutes, we hiked another mile, followed by climbing up 1,900 feet then down to the Camas Creek drainage and Trout Lake. We reached Trout Lake at 12:30 pm. We stopped along the lake shore, munched on candy bars, and drank some water. Following our 30-minute rest stop, we hiked the trail along the southeastern shore of the lake for about a mile-and-a-half and continued to Arrow Lake another mile-and-a-half upstream. Steep slopes and peaks surrounded the U-shaped drainage carved out by glaciers. We crossed two snowslides and noted their approximate locations—there was no GPS for civilian use back then. We encountered bear scats on the trail and observed areas that had been dug, probably by bears.

We encountered five or six hikers on the trail, which felt crowded to me after spending a month at my campsite at Connor Creek with little to no visitors. Evie and I reached the Arrow Lake campground at 3 pm. "I feel like a Winnebago RV pulling into a campground," I commented as

I viewed one backpacking tent pitched at the campground. The campground was located at the lower end of Arrow Lake, where we pitched our tent and hung our food bags and backpacks high up in a spruce tree. After we set up our camp, we continued hiking up the drainage to Camas Lake, a distance of three miles. We forded the icy cold waters of Camas Creek as it flowed out of Arrow Lake. I took off my hiking boots and socks, pulled my pant legs over my knees, and waded across. Midway across the stream, my toes began to get numb from the frigid water. After crossing, I stood shivering on the opposite bank as Evie forded the stream. After our feet warmed up and dried, we put our socks and boots on and resumed our trek upstream. We observed several bear diggings and scats on the trail and came across an avalanche chute strewn with many trees felled by the torrent of snow and piled on the chute like spilled matchsticks.

Further up the trail, we reached another stream crossing where we used a log and a large rock to bridge to the opposite bank. As I walked on the log, it shifted and I did some log birling for a few seconds. Fortunately, I managed to keep my balance and stay dry.

Upon seeing grizzly bear tracks on the trail, I began to talk loudly and sing songs. I think I sang every song I ever heard on the radio. Further upstream, about one mile from Camas Lake and the Camas Lake campground, we had to cross Camas Creek again, except this reach was a raging torrent. I walked upstream to find a shallow place to cross. I found what seemed like a suitable place to cross. We took off our boots and socks and grabbed some alder branches to use as hiking poles to steady ourselves in the rapid current. I crossed the stream first and could feel the current trying to push my feet downstream. I held on to the pole and inched my way across the fast-flowing water. I slowly crossed so as not to risk losing my precarious footing. I then waded into a deep section of the stream where the water came up to my hips. I almost lost my balance with the push of the strong current. I pushed myself upright using the wooden pole for leverage. Upon reaching the bank, I motioned to Evie to stay put so I could find a better crossing, but my search was in vain. Evie was determined to cross and successfully did so. I looked at her, standing on the bank, wet and cold, shivering with the cold. She was the first woman I knew who could hike seven miles with a heavy backpack, leave it at our campsite, continue hiking an extra three miles, wade across icy, fast streams, and not complain or turn back.

After recovering from the ice-cold stream crossing, we lost the trail and walked through an alder thicket. As we made our way through, I kept hoping we would not come face to face with a grizzly bear. We made our way across a snowfield peppered with glacier lilies. Upon reaching the campground adjacent to Camas Lake, we noticed only one tent at the site. Evie mentioned that the campground reservations list showed that all the campsites were reserved. Evie collected data for the campground-grizzly bear study. She recorded the number of tents at the campground and noted if food was properly stored in food bags and hung out of reach on trees.

After she completed her task, we hiked down the drainage and headed back to Arrow Lake. We chatted briefly with two backpackers who mentioned they had seen a bear with two cubs. We resumed our hike down, taking a shortcut to Camas Creek down a steep slope and through some thick alder. Upon reaching the creek, we found a shallow crossing that made fording the stream much easier; however, a dense stand of alder and yew greeted us on the other side. Navigating through this tangle of branches forced us to walk on, and over an obstacle course of branches. Our hiking boots did not make contact with the ground as we pushed ourselves through. After what seemed like hours, we finally made it to a clearing and found the trail leading to Arrow Lake and our campsite. The sun inched its way behind the ridge as we sat and rested for a few minutes. I lifted my gaze up the opposite slope and spotted a large bear at the bottom of a snow field about one-quarter of a mile from us. It was an impressive animal, even at that distance. As we walked along the trail, the bear's blond silver-tipped hair and hump above its shoulders clearly marked the animal as a grizzly. Two cubs accompanied the bear.

We continued our hike to Arrow Lake, whistling and singing as loud as we could, and sighted another grizzly 100 yards up the slope across from Camas Creek. We added more songs to our vocal repertoire. We crossed Camas Creek at the same spot where I tried log birling on the hike up. This time, the log won and rewarded me with wet boots, socks, and feet. The next morning, after breakfast, Evie collected data from Arrow Lake, followed by our trek back to the trailhead and civilization. During the hike, I kept talking about eating a banana split at the Lake McDonald Lodge. With each mile, I described in detail the ingredients of the banana split and how delicious it would taste. After two days of hiking, we each ordered a banana split and ate our best-tasting reward. The restaurant at the lodge was filled with neatly dressed tourists, a contrast to our appearance after hiking almost 20 miles in two days.

A week after our hike, I purchased the paperback book "*Night of the Grizzlies*" and read author Jack Olsen's detailed description of two separate and fatal grizzly bear attacks that killed two young women on the same night in 1967. One of the attacks occurred in the campground at Trout Lake. Michelle Koons and four of her friends camped at Trout Lake. At 4 am, a grizzly bear approached their campsite. Koon's friends unzipped their sleeping bags and climbed up trees. The zipper on Koons's sleeping bag jammed, and the bear dragged the young girl approximately 300 feet away from the campsite. I never saw a grizzly bear in my study area; however, I did, on a couple of occasions, see scat and tracks. I borrowed Gary's .357 magnum revolver and practiced shooting a target at close range and climbing up trees. Capsaicin-based bear spray was not available until the 1980s. I did have a heart-thumping moment while walking through a dense stand of huckleberry shrubs in a subalpine basin. My senses ramped up to hypersensitive as the shrubs offered bears a cornucopia of huckleberries. As my eyes scanned the basin, I flushed a spruce grouse a few feet ahead of me. The rapid rumbling sound of the bird taking flight triggered an instantaneous flood of fear coursing through my nervous system until I saw the grouse in flight less than a second later.

CHAPTER 6: LIFE IN THE BACKCOUNTRY

The Spotted Bear Ranger station, located about 60 miles upstream of Hungry Horse, became the Wolverine Project's field research base. Two Forest Service gravel roads led to the Spotted Bear Ranger Station, one on the west side of Hungry Horse Reservoir and another on the east side. The ranger station included housing for Forest Service employees. Typically, depending on the weather and the amount of snow, the Forest Service vacated the ranger station in early to mid-December and returned in early to mid-April after the access roads adjacent to the reservoir were plowed open. During the first two winters of the wolverine study, project staff stayed in the cabin of an outfitter's camp near the ranger station.

During my first summer on the project, Maurice acquired a surplus two-bedroom mobile home from Rapid City, South Dakota, used as temporary housing for victims of the 1972 flash flood that devastated that city. In mid-June, the mobile home was set up adjacent to the Diamond R Ranch, a hunting and fishing outfitters facility adjacent to the Spotted Bear River and one-third of a mile from the ranger station complex. Howard constructed a snowshed over the mobile home, extending the roof at one end. This provided a place to store a winter season's supply of firewood. Gary assisted Howard with installing a wood-burning stove in the mobile home. Howard replaced the existing electric refrigerator with a propane-powered one as electrical power was not available.

While preparing the mobile home for the winter, Howard, Gary, and I spent one evening in it. After supper and an evening of conversation, each one of us crawled into our sleeping bags. Later that evening, I heard a scuffle and loud cursing from the bedroom opposite the mobile home. I crawled out of my sleeping bag to investigate and called, "Is everything okay?" Howard yelled out, "A damned mouse just crawled over my face!" Later that evening, we heard scratching sounds from within the walls of the mobile home. Needless to say, all three of us did not sleep soundly that night. The next morning, we surmised that a rodent or rodents had infiltrated our base camp. We discussed the rodent invasion over breakfast and reached a consensus: the rodents had to go. We assessed what little data we had based on the acoustical signature and intensity of the wall scratching and assumed that, in all probability, a bushy-tailed wood rat crawled into the space between the interior and exterior walls of the mobile home. I volunteered to drive to my camp at Connor Creek and retrieve some traps to remove the unwanted residents.

That morning, I drove to Connor Creek and retrieved a couple of live traps, and took them to the base camp at Spotted Bear. I set the traps inside the mobile home and baited them with peanut butter. The next morning, a captive bushy-tailed wood rat gazed at me from within the trap, its eyes shining like onyx beads. I placed the trap and its prisoner in the back of my pickup truck, planning to release the wood rat somewhere along the road back to Connor Creek. After driving a few miles from Spotted Bear, I pulled over to the side of the road, removed the live trap from the back of my pickup truck, placed it on the ground, and released the wood rat. As soon as the trap door opened, the wood rat gained its freedom and scampered underneath my pickup. I looked underneath my truck and saw no sign of the rodent. Assuming the large rodent had sought freedom in the forest away from his human captor,

I placed the empty trap in my truck and drove to my camp at Connor Creek. A few days later, I opened the hood of my pickup truck to check the oil. I noticed a mass of grass and other detritus jammed under the air filter housing. For a brief nanosecond, my initial thought was, "What the ….!" followed by the realization that when I released the wood rat from the live trap, the animal climbed up onto the truck chassis, surviving the twenty-mile trip to my Connor Creek campsite. After I arrived at the campsite, the wood rat must have busied itself, constructing a nest on top of the engine block and underneath the air filter. A day or so later, I opened the hood of my truck to check the oil, and I saw bits of dried grass protruding from underneath the metal canister containing the air filter. I removed the air filter canister, grabbed a stick, poked at the nest to make sure the nest was vacant, and removed the unwanted squatter.

As colder weather settled in, I trapped Columbian ground squirrels until the second week of September, when the ground squirrels gradually went into estivation. I found that adult male ground squirrels became dormant at an earlier date in the fall than the adult females and immature ground squirrels. I continued running snap traps to sample smaller rodents until the snow in mid-October made it impractical to trap. I moved the camp trailer from Connor Creek to our base camp at Spotted Bear and settled into the mobile home. I continued to live in the mobile home at Spotted Bear through the winter of 1975-76, live trapping wolverines and on through the summer of 1976, continuing fieldwork for the small mammal study.

Absent running water in the mobile home, I obtained water from the Spotted Bear River, located approximately 300 feet from the base camp. A ten-gallon stainless steel milk can serve as our water storage container. Since the mobile home lacked functional plumbing, the bathroom served as a storage room. The bathtub remained functional for bathing. I would heat water on the kitchen stove and a second water container on the wood-burning stove. I'd pour the hot water into the bathtub and add cold water to bring the bathwater to a comfortable bathing temperature—each of the two bedrooms provided two metal cots with mattresses and sleeping bags for warmth. Coleman lanterns powered by white gas provided light.

As colder temperatures and snow brought my small mammal trapping to a close, Maurice asked if I would like to assist with live-trapping wolverines during the winter. I accepted without any hesitation. Maurice informed me that my dog Tanya would not be able to stay with me during the trapping season. Initially, I was dismayed at having to part with my canine companion. However, once we began running the traplines, the reason for Maurice's decision became very apparent. Running the traplines, I would be absent from Spotted Bear every other night, and Tanya would be tethered to a dog run. I decided to take Tanya to my parents' home in South Texas. In early November, I embarked on a marathon drive of slightly over 2,300 miles in two days.

The first day I departed from Hungry Horse was at 3 am, and I planned to drive as far as I could on the first day. I drove south towards Missoula along the highway on the eastern side of Flathead Lake. It was snowing, but for all appearances, the road surface was wet. The car ahead of me did not appear to have any traction problems, so I assumed the road was not icy. Little did I realize that although the highway appeared wet, black ice robbed my tires of friction, and my truck began to skid. I struggled to steer my truck out of the skid to no avail. When I saw my truck headed off the highway and off a steep slope, I did the only thing I could to keep the vehicle from rolling over; I managed to point the front end down the slope. As my truck bounced down the steep slope, I saw a snow-covered road and some houses at the bottom. My mind raced with thoughts of crashing into someone's home. Fortunately, that did not happen. Upon reaching level ground, the truck tires slammed into the ground. I managed to drive my pickup truck onto the snow-covered road and quickly realized that one of my front tires was flat. The impact caused the seal between the tire and the rim to break. I stopped to change the tire; however, the jack sank into the snow when I attempted to raise the truck to change the tire. I walked to a nearby house and reluctantly rang the doorbell as it was very early in the morning, probably close to four am. A woman answered the door, and I explained that I had run off the road and had a flat tire. I quickly asked if she had a board I could use to place under the jack. A few minutes later, she handed me the board. I could jack up my truck, change the tire, and continue my journey. I drove for almost 24 hours and stopped at a rest area south of Raton, NM, a total distance of 1,365 miles. I slept for two hours inside the camper shell-covered pickup bed and then resumed my journey south. Sixteen hours later, after driving 960 miles, I arrived at my parent's home on a rainy night. I knocked on the door and surprised my mother when she answered the door as she was not expecting me until the next day. *"Mijito!"* she exclaimed as she opened the door to let me in. I gave her a hug and headed straight to my bedroom. I slept continuously through the night and the following day. When I recovered, I swore I would never do a drive like that again.

I spent two weeks at home with my parents and my younger brother, as well as friends that I grew up with. The reunion filled my heart with joy as I made the most of my time with my family and friends. While there, I bought several bags of oranges and grapefruit during a shopping trip to the Lower Rio Grande Valley. On my return to Hungry Horse, I stopped at the residence of the lady who provided me with the board that enabled me to use the jack and change my flat tire. I thanked her for helping me and presented her with a bag of oranges and a bag of grapefruit.

I returned to Hungry Horse from my trip to Texas quite exhausted but looking forward to a week-long trek into the Bob Marshall Wilderness Area. My previous backcountry hiking included my two-day backpacking trek in Glacier National Park with Evie and a weekend hike into the Cloud Peak Wilderness Area in the Bighorn National Forest in Wyoming. I unpacked my gear and proceeded to pack gear for the trip into the Bob Marshall wilderness area to assist Howard and Gary with distributing live traps in "the Bob" and stocking U.S. Forest Service guard station cabins with food and firewood for the winter. Maurice and Howard had obtained permission from the Forest Service to use the cabins during the winter to run the wolverine traplines. The plan was for Gary and his brother Tim to run the traplines on cross-country skis.

The guard stations were used principally for short stays by a few Forest Service employees, completing routine tasks such as fire patrol, trail maintenance, and construction. The guard stations included Black Bear, Salmon Forks, and Big Prairie, which are located between 10 and 15 miles apart along the trail following the South Fork of the Flathead River. The Black Bear Cabin is located

9 to 10 miles from the Meadow Creek trailhead on the west bank of the South Fork Flathead River at 4,268 ft. above sea level. The cabin was constructed in the 1920s with the logs joined by full logs joined with full dovetail notches. The Salmon Forks cabin is located approximately 8 miles upriver from the Black Bear cabin near the west bank of the South Fork of the Flathead River and upstream from the confluence of Big Salmon Creek. The Salmon Forks guard station was established in the late 1930s. The cabin was constructed in 1963, prior to the enactment of the Wilderness Act of 1964. The Forest Service initially established the Big Prairie cabin area as a district ranger station, and some buildings were constructed as early as 1916. The Forest Service included the Black Bear, Salmon Forks, and Big Prairie cabins in the Bob Marshall Wilderness and the Spotted Bear ranger station in the National Park Service's National Register of Historic Places in 2015. We were to deploy and assemble wooden live traps along the trail between the Black Bear and Salmon Forks cabins and another set between the Salmon Forks and Big Prairie cabins. I was looking forward to the trek into the Bob. It would be my first multi-day trek into a wilderness area. I drove up to our Spotted Bear base camp and met with

Cameron Lee, an outfitter guide with the Wilderness Lodge at Spotted Bear, at five o'clock the next morning to drive to the Meadow Creek trailhead and head into the Bob.

The next morning, I loaded my backpack into Lee's pickup truck and followed him to the trailhead in the Wolverine Project pickup loaded with unassembled wooden traps and food. A pack string of horses led by Lee transported the 20 wooden traps and food to the Black Bear and Salmon Forks cabins in the Bob Marshall wilderness area.

The wooden traps were constructed by Howard, who was a master of all trades and excelled in all of them: carpentry, auto and snowmobile mechanics, automobile body repair, shoeing horses, fly-tying, fly fishing, hunting, and so much more. The five panels for the wooden box traps and the sliding metal door and frame were packed flat. Gary, Howard, and I would assemble the traps after they were deployed at each trap site along the trail. We packed the horses with the traps and food and headed up the trail into the Bob, my first trip into the heart of a wilderness area. After I returned from my long-journey from Texas, I only had time to pack for my trip into the Bob and did not have time to go to the grocery store and purchase food for my hike into the Bob. During the morning of my hike into the Bob with Lee, I did not eat breakfast or did I pack a good lunch. I packed some cookies and an orange that I brought over from Texas. I followed Lee and the pack string up the South Fork trail. After lunch I began to tire as my backpack weighed down on my shoulders. I wanted to stop and rest but did not want to fall behind. Six hours later, we arrived at the Black Bear cabin, and I met with Gary and Howard. Gary accompanied Lee to the Salmon Forks cabin, deploying ten of the traps along the way. Gary spent the night at the Salmon Forks cabin, where Howard and I would join him the next day. Howard fixed supper, and after cleaning up, I crawled into my sleeping bag and quickly fell asleep.

The next morning, Howard rode his horse, leading the project's two mules, Toby and Topper, and I followed on foot behind the pack string. The trail was pocked with small craters made by the hooves of horses that had previously trod through the mud a few days prior. The freezing temperatures hardened the craters, making the walk extremely difficult. To make matters worse, it started to rain sometime during our journey. After walking half-way to Salmon Forks, my left leg began to ache. I was better prepared for this hike and had two candy bars, cheese, and sausage for lunch. We reached our destination by mid-afternoon. The cabin at Salmon Forks was a small, one-room abode, but it was comfortable. We took the horse and mule to the corral and fed them as snow began to fall. We returned to the cabin, cooked supper, and cleaned up afterward. I crawled into my sleeping bag following discussions with Gary and Howard on the next day's tasks. The ache in my leg persisted during the evening. Having spent two weeks in Texas with my family, my thoughts drifted to my family and friends back home. I missed them all and wished I was in the mountains of Northern New Mexico instead of Montana so that I could be closer to them. I thought of the distance as almost 100 miles south of the Canadian border and my hometown 64 miles north of the US-Mexico border. The following day, we cut firewood with a crosscut saw, which was my first experience using this tool. The metal saw made a pleasant ringing sound as it cut through the wood. We cut enough wood to last during the winter and stacked the wood in a small shed behind the cabin.

We rose early the next morning, packed the mules, Toby and Topper, with the wooden live traps and food, and headed up the trail to Big Prairie. Howard led the pack string while Gary and I followed. The landscape was much different from the extensive forested areas from the Meadow Creek trailhead to Salmon Forks. We traversed open meadows with scattered stands of Ponderosa Pine. As we neared Big Prairie, I looked back and over my shoulder at the open meadow offering a magnificent view of Scarface Peak, a jagged, snow-capped outcrop of limestone jutting up to 8,282 feet in elevation. I grabbed my camera and captured the image on film. We arrived at the Big Prairie cabin at mid-afternoon. Gary and Howard took care of the mules and horses, and I stored the food in the cabin. Morning at Big Prairie greeted us with a temperature of 7 degrees Fahrenheit. We cut firewood to last the winter and transported the logs on the mules to the wood shed about 500 yards away. The next day, we distributed the live traps along the trail on the way back to Salmon Forks, arriving at the cabin late in the afternoon. Morning breakfast at Salmon Forks consisted of seven-grain cereal, the third time on the menu. I dreamed of bacon and eggs as the seven-grain hot cereal was beginning to wear on me. Weeks later,

Gary confessed that he packed the food and neglected to pack a more diverse menu. I did not eat seven-grain hot cereal for months afterward. Howard and Gary distributed live traps along the trail from Salmon Forks half-way up to Big Prairie. I remained at Salmon Forks and cut firewood with the crosscut saw. Later that evening, the full moon cast the reflected sunlight onto the snow-covered landscape, creating a dazzling effect.

On the seventh day of my wilderness experience, we distributed live traps between Salmon Forks and Black Bear. The following day, Gary and Howard distributed the remaining four traps along the trail, and I stayed at Black Bear cutting firewood. During the afternoon, four hunters approached the cabin. They informed me that they were going to wait for the outfitter guide, who had stayed back to round up his mules. Later that afternoon, Howard and Gary returned to Black Bear. As darkness approached, the guide and his pack string had not arrived, so Howard invited the four men to come into the cabin and join us for supper. Three of the four men were from Chicago, and the fourth was from Plentywood, Montana. They entertained us with lots of amusing stories, especially the older man from

Montana. Later in the evening, the guide arrived, and four men rode out with him in the dark.

After nine days in the wilderness, I was ready for a hot shower and the comforts of civilization. We hit the trail early as heavy snowfall made it imperative to drive two vehicles and a horse trailer on snow-covered roads from the trailhead back to Hungry Horse. We reached the Meadow Creek trailhead by mid-afternoon and Hungry Horse at nine o'clock that evening. I took a badly needed bath, which felt wonderful. Since I had ventured home in November, I could not afford the option to spend Christmas with my family in South Texas. I opted to visit my friends in Billings, Montana, and Lovell, Wyoming. While at Billings, I spent Christmas at the home of Pedro and Nancy Hernandez. Although I missed spending the holiday with my family, Pedro and Nancy made my Christmas quite memorable. I met Nancy's relatives and the Hernandez family, including Pedro's mother, Lupe (Loo-Peh). Lupe served me *chorizo* (Mexican sausage, frijoles (beans), tamales, and homemade tortillas, just like my mom would have.

CHAPTER 7: WINTER IN THE BACKCOUNTRY

Gary Koehler and I began running traplines from Spotted Bear in mid-December. Given Gary's previous experience running traplines on cross-country skis in the Selway-Bitterroot Wilderness, driving a snowmobile never made it into his 'bucket-list' of things to do during his lifetime. Given his cursing at the snowmobile whenever it got stuck or had mechanical problems while running the trapline, I assumed this was his first time operating a snowmobile as it was mine; but then again, he grew up in northwestern Washington, although his hometown receives more rain than snow on average. Howard ran two trap lines along Forest Service roads, each approximately 18 miles, on the east and west sides of Hungry Horse Reservoir. Maintenance crews kept those portions of the roads cleared so that logging trucks could extract timber from the forest. Howard sited the traps along unplowed roads extending from the east and west side roads up creek drainages. Howard would drive up the plowed portions of the Forest Service Roads, unload the snowmobile from the small trailer towed by a pickup truck and then snowmobile up the drainage to check the traps or traps if there were more than one. I ran two traplines with a total of 28 traps from our base camp at the Spotted Bear Ranger Station. The traplines totaled approximately 24 miles and were run on snowmobiles from our Spotted Bear Ranger Station base camp. The first trapline, the Elam Line, ran along the west side road from the Spotted Bear airstrip to Elam Creek, a distance of six miles. On the day I started from Spotted Bear, I first ran the live traps along this line. I then would return to Spotted Bear to refuel the snowmobile and then proceed to run the second line along the road west of the South Fork south to the Meadow Creek Gorge trailhead near the north boundary of the Bob Marshall wilderness, a distance of approximately 11 to 12 miles, then west-southwest along the road up the Bunker Creek drainage for another 6 miles. Typically, two to three hours of daylight remained after running the second trapline up Bunker Creek. A tent camp approximately three miles upstream of the confluence of Bunker Creek and the South Fork of the Flathead provided refuge at the end of the day.

The tent camp included a wooden deck or floor raised one to two feet above the ground, four-foot-high plywood walls, and a canvas wall tent suspended over the deck and walls by a wooden frame and rafters. Clear plastic sheeting covered the tent roof and side walls to allow snow to slide off the roof. A wood-burning stove provided heat, a camp stove cooked our meals, and camp gas-fueled lanterns provided light. Metal cots with mattresses and sleeping bags kept us warm at night. We stored non-perishable food consisting of oatmeal, pancake mix, coffee, instant chocolate, and an assortment of canned vegetables, soups, chili, and stews in a metal trash can with the lid secured to prevent rodents and other animals from stealing our food.

During the daily trapline runs, we would record the number of predator tracks observed along the road and collect predator scats in small plastic bags. Scat analysis provided data on the food habits of predators inhabiting the study area. Most of the tracks observed and scats collected were from coyotes, although on occasion, we would record tracks of other predators such as lynx, mountain lion, pine marten, weasels, and wolverines. We would check the condition of the bait in the traps and replace desiccated bait with relatively fresh bait when necessary. A closed trap door would raise our hopes for a wolverine capture; however, most were weasels and pine martens. A wolverine capture was cause for celebration given the amount of trapping effort involved to live trap and radio collar one wolverine. Tracks showed that some wolverines approached the trap but did not try for the bait inside the trap. Some wolverines, such as the female wolverine that Howard named "No Nose," were trap-prone and recaptured several times. No Nose was first captured as a subadult during the previous year in 1975. The female wolverine had its muzzle torn away. Maurice and Howard initially assumed the wolverine was injured in a fight with another wolverine. During the study, they discounted this after snow tracking and radio tracking of wolverines indicated "no intraspecific strife of any kind." In their final scientific publication of the Wolverine study in the *Canadian Journal of Zoology*, Maurice and Howard stated that the injury was probably inflicted by a mountain lion.

Routine daily chores at Spotted Bear included preparing and eating breakfast; packing survival gear and snacks into backpacks; feeding Tanner, a black and tan cougar hound; and loading gear into the snowmobile sled. Maurice brought Tanner to Spotted Bear in mid-December, hoping to use the hound to trail and tree a cougar and radio-collar the large feline. He was interested in comparing cougar movements with radio-collared wolverines. Unfortunately, Tanner and Maurice only had one opportunity to hunt cougar during the remainder of the project, which was unsuccessful. The sled carried cross-country skis, my backpack, fuel containers, an axe, a shovel, and survival gear. Upon arrival at Spotted Bear, after running the trapline from Bunker Creek, we would fire up the wood-burning stove to heat the mobile home, followed by refueling the snowmobiles and performing needed maintenance. Depending on how the end of the day progressed regarding the amount of time running the traplines and doing snowmobile maintenance, we can either prepare supper or fill out the appropriate datasheets.

There were several to fill out in duplicate, including animals captured in the live traps, predator tracks observed along the trapline, daily narratives, minimum and maximum ambient temperatures, and general notes on snowfall.

Once the data was recorded, I would write letters to my family and friends.

Howard and his Cessna 180 fixed-wing aircraft were our lifeline to the outside world during the winter trapping season. Howard was a "jack-of-all-trades" and a master of all: auto mechanic, auto body repair, two-cycle (snowmobile) engine repair, carpentry, and bush pilot. His expertise in backcountry mountain flying and his penchant for flight safety made him the perfect choice as field project leader for the Wolverine Project. During the winter trapping season, Howard attached skis to his airplane, enabling him to land at the Spotted Bear airstrip, approximately three miles from the Spotted Bear base camp. Before landing at the airstrip, he circled his airplane over the Spotted Bear camp to summon us to the airstrip. We would jump on our snowmobiles and ride to the airstrip. Once there, we would maneuver the snowmobiles back and forth over the length of the airstrip to pack the snow down, thus facilitating Howard's landing and takeoff. While we packed the snow on the airstrip, Howard would use that time to radio-track wolverines. Once we landed, we were rewarded with mail, groceries, and other supplies, such as snowmobile parts.

When we captured a wolverine, a radio collar, as well as equipment for immobilizing the mustelid, was flown in by Howard. During the summer and fall of 1975, he would fly over my field camp at Connor Creek, and we would drive to the airstrip to connect with Howard. Mail flown in by Howard kept us in touch with family and friends. During the summer and fall, I telephoned my parents during my overnight stays at the Wolverine Project house at Hungry Horse. Telephone calls during the winter trapping season were less frequent, and I relied on letters to keep in touch with my parents.

During my first winter season, I snowmobiled approximately 45 miles per day. Excluding a week off for Christmas and two days back at Hungry Horse in March, I ran the trapline seven days a week for 108 days. I grew to hate the snowmobiles, especially after logging over 4,200 miles in the noisy contraptions during my first winter trapping season. I towed a sled packed with survival gear, including cross-country skis and poles, a snow shovel, an axe, lunch, backpack, and bait for the live traps. The sled also served to transport a live trap with a captured wolverine to our base camp at Spotted Bear, where we would immobilize them, mark them with ear tags and numbered tattoos, record body measurements, and fit them with a radio collar. The Bombardier snowmobiles made during the 1970s were not the sleek, lightweight models currently available. They were so heavy and noisy that we had to wear hearing protection earmuffs, similar to headphones, but without the music. I added extra foam to my earmuffs to further reduce the sound. The project kept four snowmobiles at Spotted Bear during the winter trapping season: three single-track snowmobiles and a double-tracked snowmobile with one front ski instead of two. Gary nicknamed the double-tracked snowmobile "40-Acres" based on the song "*Give Me Forty Acres (To Turn This Rig Around)*" by the American country music group The Willis Brothers. I was not familiar with this song, but the moniker was very appropriate as the two-track snowmobile was not only extremely heavy at 550 pounds. It was also a beast to turn around, hence the moniker. The Alpine was a workhorse with dual 15-inch-wide rubber tracks. The other three single-track snowmobiles were 265-pound Ski-Doo Scandics.

Joseph-Armand Bombardier (pronounced Bom-bahr-dee-ay), from Valcourt, Quebec, built his first snowmobile in 1922. The 1970s Bombardier Ski-Doo had a sprocket-driven track and a wheeled track suspension. Snowmobile manufacturers must have heard Gary's and my loud cursing of the snowmobiles every time they broke down significantly when a component of the wheeled track suspension system broke, and we had to replace it. Manufacturers reconfigured the snowmobile track and suspension systems years later. The snowmobiles we used had a wheeled track suspension consisting of four sets of bogie (bow-gee) wheels, each set with four bogie wheels about 5 to 6 inches in diameter. The bogie wheels supported and guided the track and provided proper tension and alignment for the track to rotate smoothly. Depending on the snow conditions and the ambient temperature, snow would accumulate in the space within the oval track loop and eventually cause the track to stop turning. The remedy involved tipping the snowmobile on its side, grabbing the axe we packed along with other survival gear in the sled, and using the flat side of the axe to pound on the bottom of the track to loosen up the packed snow within the track suspension system. Unplugging the track would take 30 minutes to an hour. There were times when I felt like using the sharp edge of the axe on the snowmobile, but then reality would immediately take over my thought process, and I would curse the machine instead. Several beatings were followed by taking the end of the axe handle and jamming it into the packed snow to break it further and remove enough of it from within the track assembly to allow the track to propel the snowmobile once again.

During the first winter season, Gary spent December and January running the traplines with me out of Spotted Bear and the Bunker Creek camp. The following month, Gary and his brother Tim skied into the Bob Marshall Wilderness to run the traplines there. I enjoyed working with Gary during the summer, fall, and the first two months of winter as he would make light of stressful and frustrating situations, such as recurring mechanical problems with the snowmobiles. Regardless of how much trouble the snowmobiles gave us, Gary and I would always laugh at the situation. We joked about the snow machines, whether we were lifting them up and out of a depression in the snow to free the darned machines or trying to figure out why they would not start. We disliked the machines so much that we contemplated ideas for getting rid of those cantankerous contraptions every evening. Splash gasoline over the snowmobile and accidentally drop a lighted cigarette on it. I suggested this idea to Gary about 50 times until he reminded me that we didn't smoke. "Good idea to start?" I asked sarcastically. Wiring up the throttle to full power and running the snowmobile off a cliff with Gary jumping off at the last minute. I always volunteered Gary for this idea.

Parking the snowmobiles in the path of an avalanche chute, then climbing up the slope at a distance from the avalanche chute, hopefully triggering the avalanche to bury the snowcats with six feet of snow. We could never come up with a safe method of triggering the avalanche without becoming victims ourselves. Sometimes, the snow buildup would cause a bogie wheel assembly to break, or some other part would fail, requiring a replacement. We would call Howard to purchase one at Kalispell or Whitefish, and he would bring us the replacement bogie wheel assembly during his next weekly flight to Spotted Bear. Replacement of the bogie wheel assembly sometimes took a whole afternoon as it required tipping the snowmobile on its side and removing frozen chunks of snow adhering to the wheel assembly, a time-consuming process. Since we operated the snowmobiles every day in all types of weather and snow conditions, we carried a tool kit, spare electrical wires, spark plugs, and other odds and ends to enable us to make quick repairs on the trail or at the Bunker Creek camp.

Snowmobile incidents often exceeded the laughter threshold. One January morning at Bunker Creek camp, Gary snowmobiled up the Upper Bunker trapline, and I stayed at the tent camp washing dishes, storing food items in a secure container, and splitting firewood into kindling for our next stay. Just when I thought this would be a productive day running the trapline back to Spotted Bear, the events that transpired suggested an omen of things to come for the next two winters. As I busied myself at the tent camp, Gary walked back to camp, the victim of snowmobile failure. We both rode back up the Upper Bunker trapline and attempted to get the snow machine to start. For over two hours, we tried every troubleshooting technique we learned from Howard. *Nada, zero, zilch, nothing.* We both rode the one working snowmobile to the Spotted Bear airstrip. Our plan was to retrieve 40-Acress parked at the airstrip so that Gary could use it. We arrived at the airstrip late afternoon, and things progressed from bad to worse. We could not get 40-Acress to roar into life. Humor as an antidote ceased earlier that day, replaced by much cursing ripping through the cold winter air. We finally resuscitated 40-Acress; however, the snowmobile 'curse' was not done with us yet, and my snowmobile would not start. Gary rode 40-Acress down the westside road to check the traps while I stayed and dealt with the recalcitrant snow machine. After 30 minutes, I managed to get it started, and I hightailed it for the Spotted Bear camp. Two days later, we had two to three feet of powder snow on the road to deal with as we made our way from Bunker Creek camp to Spotted Bear. A tow bar installed on the front end enabled us to run 40-Acress and the Scandic snowmobile in tandem to bust through deep powder snow. Both Gary and I got stuck three times each. We cussed, heaved, and moaned as we struggled to move the quarter-of-a-ton 40-Acress out of the ditch. To add insult to injury, we had to replace the drive belt on the monster snow machine later that day. Humor was scarce that day at the Spotted Bear Ranger District. Snow continued to fall the next day, so I packed the airstrip with 40-Acress, and Gary snowmobiled down the westside road to check those traps. The remainder of the day was a rerun of the previous one: snowmobiles got bogged down in the deep snow, we dug the machines out, removed the ice, and packed snow from the bogie wheel assemblies, repeat.

We started running the traplines from Spotted Bear during the second week of December, during which I received a quick introduction to backcountry snowmobiling and running a trapline. Our first excursion required transporting two live traps to locations on Cedar Creek Road, an uphill grade with one foot of powder snow. I quickly veered off the road, and the snowmobile got stuck in the loose snow. I unhooked the sled carrying the two live traps from the snowmobile to make it easier to free the machine. Gary came over to assist in spite of both our efforts, we could not get the snowmobile out. After much pushing and pulling, we finally got the machine out onto the road. We laughed and joked in the face of adversity. I traveled up the road a bit and got stuck again. Laughter and jocularity evaporated, and loud cursing descended like a dark cloud. We got both of the snowmobiles stuck a third time. After freeing both snowmobiles, we made it to the sites where Howard instructed us to set the live traps. It was quite an experience for me, having spent the first two decades of my life not knowing what real snowy winters were like—quite the initiation for what became a recurring event running traplines the rest of the winter season.

One week later, low temperatures dipped below zero. Howard instructed us to pull the sliding doors off the traps during subzero temperatures as those conditions would not bode well for an animal confined in a metal barrel live trap. We also pulled the doors off the traps before our upcoming departure for a week off during the Christmas holiday. I ran the trapline along the west side road and pulled the doors off the live traps. As I rode up to one of the trap sites, I noticed the trap door was down. At first, I presumed wind gusts had moved the trap enough to cause the door to shut. As I approached the trap, I noticed tracks near the trap. I knocked on the side of the barrel trap and heard a deep, rumbling growl. I looked closer at the nearby tracks and thought they looked like Wolverine tracks. I banged on the trap again and again and received a deep, rumbling growl. I let out a *"yii-hah"* as jubilation flooded my entire being. This was my reward for all the hard work I did in undergraduate school and the past two semesters at the University of Idaho. I was working on predators; I was ecstatic!

I resumed checking the remaining live traps and pulled the trap doors as quickly as I could. I returned to the trap site with the captured wolverine, loaded the trap onto the sled, and high-tailed it to Spotted Bear. Upon arriving, I excitedly told Gary that we had a wolverine. Gary jumped on a snowmobile and rode to the ranger station to call Howard on the telephone. "It ain't every day you catch a wolverine," I wrote in my journal later that evening.

Howard flew into the Spotted Bear airstrip the next day, bringing a radio collar and all the necessary gear to immobilize the wolverine. Howard peered into the live trap and informed us that we had captured "No Nose." Howard named the female wolverine "No Nose" as it had its muzzle torn away. Maurice and Howard initially assumed the wolverine was injured in a fight with another wolverine. They discounted this after snow tracking and radio tracking during the study, which indicated "no intraspecific strife of any kind."

In their final scientific publication of the Wolverine study in the Canadian Journal of Zoology, Maurice and Howard stated that the injury was probably inflicted by a mountain lion. No Nose was first captured as a subadult during the previous year in 1975. She was trap-prone and recaptured several times, as were a few other wolverines captured during the course of the research project. I developed a fondness for "No Nose," given her survival instincts despite her injury and propensity for getting captured, especially during the second winter of live trapping. During the daily trapline runs, we would record the number of predator tracks observed along the road and collect predator scats in small plastic bags. Scat analysis provided data on the food habits of predators inhabiting the study area. Most of the tracks observed and scats collected were from coyotes, although on occasion, we would record tracks of other predators such as lynx, mountain lion, pine marten, weasels, and wolverines. We would check the condition of the bait in the traps and replace desiccated bait with relatively fresh bait when necessary. A closed trap door would raise our hopes for a wolverine capture; however, most were weasels and pine martens. Tracks showed that some wolverines approached the trap but did not try for the bait inside the trap. A wolverine capture was cause for celebration as we averaged one wolverine initial capture per month.

During our Christmas week off, I drove to Montana and spent Christmas with Pedro and Nancy Hernandez in Billings, Montana. Pedro and Nancy made my first Christmas away from home quite memorable. I met Nancy's relatives and Pedro's parents and brothers. His mother "Lupe" fed me chorizo, frijoles, tamales, and tortillas, just like home in South Texas. After I visited with Pedro and Nancy, I drove to Lovell, Wyoming, and visited with Bob and Barbara. I returned to Hungry Horse two days after Christmas and constructed a doghouse for Tanner. The next day, Howard drove Gary and me to Spotted Bear, and we baited all of the live traps. Howard and Gary returned to Hungry Horse on New Year's Day, and I remained at Spotted Bear to run the traplines. Subzero temperatures greeted me on the first day of 1976. I bundled up with two pairs of long underwear, a wool shirt, wool pants, three pairs of wool socks, two pairs of mittens, a balaclava over my head, a scarf wrapped around my neck, and my winter snow boots.

I ran the trapline along the upper westside road, and No Nose greeted me on my first day of the year with her familiar growl inside one of our live traps. I snowmobiled back to Spotted Bear to refuel, warm up, and retrieve the radio telemetry receiver. I rode back to the trap containing No Nose to check that her radio collar was transmitting prior to releasing her. Two days later, I recaptured No Nose approximately 16 miles 'as the crow flies' from the previous capture and probably 20 miles at the very least, traversing several drainages and ridges. Impressive! Analysis of radio telemetry data by Maurice and Howard following the completion of the research project showed females traveling a maximum of 24 miles in three days and male wolverines traveling a maximum of 40 miles.

Gary returned to Spotted Bear the next day during the afternoon to join in the fun and excitement of running traplines on a snowmobile. The next morning, we started late due to a broken bolt in the sled hitch. After repairing the hitch, we ran the traplines and arrived at the Bunker Creek Camp at 2:30 pm. We cross-country skied the remainder of the afternoon. The following morning, Gary rode up the Upper Bunker Creek trapline, and I remained at the tent camp washing our breakfast dishes, splitting firewood, and sweeping the tent camp floor. To my surprise, Gary approached the camp site on foot as his snowmobile quit running. We both rode up in my snowmobile to work on Gary's snowmobile. We tried replacing the fuel filter and the coil, as well as a variety of other troubleshooting to start his snowmobile, to no avail. We gave up after two hours, leaving the snowmobile where it had died. We both ran the traplines on one snowmobile and stopped at the Spotted Bear airstrip at 3:30 that afternoon, where, 40-Acress, the twin-track Alpine snowmobile was parked. Gary attempted to start 40-Acress, but we were 'snake-bit.' When it rains, it pours, but in our case, when it snows, it dumps. After several attempts, 40-Acress roared to life 30 minutes later, followed by my snowmobile calling it quits. Thirty minutes after Gary left to check the remaining trapline, I succeeded in starting my snowmobile and high-tailed it for our base camp at Spotted Bear.

"The first week of the year foreshadowed what followed for the rest of the winter: running the traplines on snowmobiles. If it ain't one thing, it's five or six," I wrote in my journal on Feb 12, 1976. Forty Acres was running hot so I phoned Howard from the ranger station telephone and advised him of the situation. Howard advised me to use the Scandic snowmobile even though the assembly on the front set of bogie wheels was broken. I went ahead and ran the trapline to Upper Bunker on the Scandic. Rain in the morning made the snow wet and sloppy, causing the snowmobile's track to clog up. I stopped nine times on the way to Upper Bunker to remove the snow from within the track.

In spite of mechanical problems with snowmobiles and wrestling the heavy machines out of deep powder snow, the anticipation of capturing a wolverine motivated us every day. Seeing a closed door on a live trap made me feel like a kid viewing his Christmas gifts under the Christmas tree begging to be opened. I hoped for a wolverine every time I approached a closed live trap, and more often than not, the captive was a weasel or a pine marten. Eleven days after capturing No Nose, we captured a beautiful male wolverine. Ten days later, we captured another male wolverine. During January and February, we captured a wolverine every 10 to 14 days. On the last day of February, I checked the Upper Bunker Creek trapline and noticed the door to one of the live traps was closed. I stopped the snowmobile and walked towards the trap, hoping that I had captured a wolverine.

I knocked on the live trap, hoping to hear the deep growl of a wolverine, but that familiar sound did not resonate within the metal barrel. I opened the trap door slightly, and instead of a feisty wolverine, I saw the thirty-pound male wolverine that Howard had nicknamed 'Growly' lying on his side and breathing slowly. Hoping that Growly was only napping, I grabbed a stick and poked at his side. Growly did not stir, and I realized this was serious. I loaded the trap with Growly onto the sled and rode back to Spotted Bear, hoping that Howard could fly into Spotted Bear and transport Growly to a veterinarian. I stopped periodically, got off the snowmobile, and quickly checked on Growly. He breathed slowly and seemed oblivious to his surroundings. As I rode towards Spotted Bear, I felt a sense of dread for Growly. This was the seventh time I had captured this wolverine, and after his second recapture, I felt that Growly was having difficulty surviving this winter.

Multiple captures in steel leg-hold traps in prior years led to broken teeth as he fought the cold metal for freedom. Most of Growly's canines and incisors were broken and worn down to the gum line. Three of his four paws had toes missing. Encounters with steel traps in previous years transformed a 38-pound healthy male wolverine into a 20-pound scavenger. Two local fur trappers ran their traplines within the South Fork of the Flathead drainage during the first two winters (1972-1973 and 1973-1974) of the research project and captured Growly as well as other wolverines. Repeated captures of radio-collared wolverines by these trappers forced Maurice to request the Montana Fish and Wildlife Commission to temporarily close the South Fork of the Flathead River basin to commercial trapping as the capture of radio-collared wolverines by fur trappers meant the loss of valuable data for the research project. The commission granted the request and closed the entire South Fork drainage area to commercial trapping during the last three winters of the research study.

With Gary and Tim running the traplines in the Bob Marshall Wilderness, Maurice hired a person to assist with trapping at Spotted Bear beginning in mid-February. The relationship started on shaky ground as I was used to working with Gary over the past seven-and-a-half months. Gary and I clicked in terms of our work ethic and our personalities. We were both able to read the situation and dive in, help, and do what was needed at the moment. Three days into the new hire's stay, I wrote in my journal that he was a nice guy but would not jump in and lend a hand when I was struggling to free the snowmobile stuck on the trail. Looking back, I should have taken the time to teach him instead of expecting him to dive in and help. This was the first time I encountered this type of relationship with a coworker, as previous ones just read the situation and dived in to help. I should have been more patient with him; however, we only had two months left in the season to trap wolverines and averaged capturing and radio-collaring one wolverine per month. I expected him to learn and adapt as quickly as I did, given that I had no prior experience living and working in the backcountry with no operating and troubleshooting snowmobiles. This was my first lesson in conflict resolution, and we ended up splitting the work.

I ran the trapline from Spotted Bear to Bunker Creek, and he ran the trapline along the road on the west side of the South Fork of the Flathead River and Hungry Horse Reservoir. This shorter trapline enabled him to run that entire trapline from Spotted Bear. In late February, Gary and Tim skied from the Salmon Forks cabin to the Bunker Creek camp, arriving at 7 pm that evening. I laughed for the first time since the day they skied into the Bob Marshall wilderness earlier that month. I transported them on the snowmobile to Spotted Bear, although I did not write in my journal how I managed to do that, as the Scandic snowmobile could only accommodate two persons. Maybe one of them rode in the sled. At Spotted Bear, we continued trading stories throughout the day and into the evening with much-interspersed laughter. Gary and Tim returned to Bob Marshall the next day, and I was sad that I was not going with them.

On the first Friday of March, I flew out with Howard to become reacquainted with civilization after five weeks of living the life of a wolverine trapper in the backcountry. The next day, I crammed as much as I could: shopping, doing my laundry at a laundromat, eating pizza, and watching a movie at a movie theater in Whitefish. I also had a ski shop mount cable bindings on my cross-country skis. While waiting for the ticket booth at the movie theater to open, I walked to a pay phone at a restaurant near the theater and telephoned my parents. The sound of their voices flooded me with melancholic joy, missing them and my friends as they talked of events back home. After the movie, I returned to the project headquarters at Hungry Horse, laid down, and rested after a busy day. My shins ached at the end of the day as my body was accustomed to walking on snow, not concrete sidewalks, asphalt, and other hard surfaces. Record albums played on my stereo filled my few evenings at Hungry Horse with music. I missed making music with the garage band I played drums with when I lived back home. That evening, I listened to my record collection until two in the morning.

The Spotted Bear trapline bonanza of Wolverine captures in January and February ended with Growly's capture on the last day of February. On March 7, I observed wolverine tracks at three trap sites along the westside road but no captures. I assumed the same wolverine approached those three traps and, for some reason, chose not to enter.

In early March, I followed wolverine tracks meandering through the timber, leading to several tree wells. Tree wells are holes around the base of a spruce or fir that form when snow accumulates around the base of a tree but not under the lower branches or around the trunk.

The depth of tree wells progressively increases as the snowpack height increases. Several of these tree wells were three feet deep. Skiing through the dense timber was challenging and could be hazardous. Falling head first into a three-foot deep tree well risked head injuries as well as making it very difficult to extricate myself from the hole with my skis on. The wolverine then followed a logging road leading to 10 to 15-year-old clearcuts. The wolverine tracks led straight through the cleared area and did not meander. Once, the tracks crossed the clearcut and led into mature timber, where the tracks meandered through the forest and entered several tree wells. In one tree well, I observed rodent tracks and small blood stains on the snow next to the Wolverine tracks. I interpreted this sign as a wolverine predation of a rodent in the tree well. I decided to set some snap traps in tree wells to document rodent activity in tree wells. My observations of coyote, pine marten, weasel, and wolverine tracks this winter indicated that these predators inspected tree wells in their search for a meal. I captured nine red-backed voles and one deer mouse during eight trap nights.

In mid-March, Howard asked me to deliver a radio collar to Gary and Tim in the Bob Marshall wilderness area. I rode my snowmobile from the Bunker Creek camp to the trailhead at Meadow Creek Gorge. The temperature that morning was 4oF. Once I crossed the snow-covered pack bridge across the South Fork of the Flathead, I felt free and euphoric. The snow-covered trail drew me into the wilderness like a magnet. Three miles in the trail was washed out by a mudslide. I removed my skis to hike downslope towards Mid Creek, where I stopped to drink some water.

Further up the trail, an icy snowslide blocked my path. I once again took off my skis and cautiously walked over this obstacle; to slip meant a fast slide into the river one hundred feet below. I made it across and continued to Black Bear. I made several more stops for water and lunch. Two days later, while at Spotted Bear, I wrote the following in my journal: "After I ate my lunch, I resumed my trip to

Black Bear cabin. The peace and tranquility were soothing to the soul. I felt very close to God being alone in the wilderness." Upon reaching a segment of the trail where I could see the cabin across the river almost half a mile away, I strained my eyes, hoping to see a wisp of smoke from the chimney, a sign that Gary and Tim were there. There was no smoke, so I continued along the trail. I reached the pack bridge, crossed the South Fork, and made my way to the cabin. Gary and Tim were not there. I started a fire in the wood-burning stove, made myself comfortable, and napped for about an hour. I started supper at 6 pm and kept hoping Gary and Tim would show up as I missed their company, but that was not the case. I later learned they were running the trapline between Salmon Forks and Big Prairie. The following morning, I cooked pancakes for breakfast on the wood-burning stove, packed my gear, and headed back to the Meadow Creek Gorge trailhead.

The hard-packed snow made for a fast glide. One or two miles down the trail, I lost my balance and fell forward, causing the toepiece on my cable bindings to come off the right ski. I screwed the toepiece back on the ski and skied another mile before the toepiece came off again. I took my skis off, fastened them to my backpack, and hiked out as the snow was hard-packed. By mid-afternoon, the temperature warmed up, and the snow softened. My boots sank six inches with every step. The hike out became slow and tiresome. After two miles, my ankles hurt, and I was exhausted. It took me two hours to walk the remaining one-and-a-half miles to the snowmobile. By the time I reached the snowmobile, I was ready to lie down and not go any further. To add insult to injury, the snowmobile refused to start, and I could not walk an extra three miles to the Bunker Creek tent camp. I cursed and moaned and finally got the recalcitrant machine started and made my way back to Spotted Bear.

Increasing warm temperatures and zero captures of wolverines signaled the upcoming end of the trapping season with each passing day. A few pine marten captures in March raised my hopes for a wolverine that went unfulfilled. Each day became drudgery, especially when snowmobiles quit running or got stuck in the wet, slushy snow. On the second day of April, Howard landed at the Spotted Bear airstrip, and I received instructions to deliver a radio collar and other supplies to Tim and Gary at the

Black Bear cabin in the Bob. The next day, I skied from the Meadow Creek trailhead up to Black Bear.

The snow was hardpacked and icy. About 3 miles upstream from the trailhead, the two read screws on the ski's cable binding's toe piece came off. After three minutes of unsuccessfully trying to secure the screws back on, I decided to walk to Black Bear. I fastened the skis to my backpack and proceeded up the trail. I arrived mid-afternoon at the pack bridge leading to the Black Bear cabin. The smokeless chimney informed me that Gary and Tim were not at the cabin, so I hiked down from the pack bridge to the river bank. I took a drink of some cold river water, sat on the bank, took my boots and socks off, and enjoyed the warm sun. The sight of a bald eagle soaring over the river completed my reverie. Fifteen minutes later, Gary and Tim appeared, skiing down the trail toward the cabin. I hurriedly put my socks and boots back on and headed towards the cabin. Once there, I opened the cabin and the storm shutters. I looked out the window facing the trail and saw Gary and Tim approaching with big smiles on their faces. Joy flooded me as well; I had not seen them in over a month and missed their company. Gary brewed some tea, and Tim went to the river to fetch water. We moved some chairs from the cabin, placed them on bare ground under a pine tree, sat down, and drank our tea. Gary and Tim read the mail that I had brought up for them. I also surprised them with a can of beer packed in for them. Tim later helped me glue my ski binding's toe piece back on the ski. After filling up with dinner and having no room for the dessert that Tim prepared, we spent the evening trading stories accompanied by much laughter. I had a great time. The next morning, we greeted the day at 5 am, and Gary ignited the kindling on the wood-burning stove. We feasted on Tim's apple cobbler for breakfast. After helping Tim wash dishes and packing my gear, I reluctantly departed for Spotted Bear at 8 am. Colder temperatures during the evening and morning provided me with hard-packed snow and an easy hike all the way to Mid Creek. One mile past Mid Creek, I put my skis on as the sun's warmth softened the snow. I arrived at the Meadow Creek Gorge trailhead at 1 pm.

One week later, the warm temperatures in the high 60s devoured the snow. Wolverine trapping ceased on April 13th. At the Bunker Creek tent camp, we loaded up the sled and snowmobiles with as much food and gear, including mattresses and sleeping bags, as we could fit, knowing that bears emerging from hibernation would wreak havoc if we left any food behind. We loaded live traps onto the larger aluminum sled and hauled the live traps to Spotted Bear on a follow-up trip that day. That same day, the Forest Service plowed the road on the east side of Hungry Horse Reservoir. My last entry for the 1975-1976 trapping season read: "Now the air is filled with noise; the generator's incessant rumble fills the air day and night. Traffic moves up and down the roads. I will miss the peace and solitude I experienced this winter." A total of nine wolverines and two fishers were captured at all the traplines between January and April of 1976. Two wolverines and one fisher were recaptured; the remainder were initial captures. Each wolverine capture required 497 trap days.

I made up for my Christmas absence with my family by visiting them in April 1976 after we wrapped up trapping that spring. That April, after visiting my family, Gary and I drove to Moscow. As we approached Moscow, Gary asked if I would like to visit with his friends, Clem and Mary, university alums. As we neared Clem and Mary's home,

Gary asked me to speak only Spanish when introduced to his friends, and he would tell them that I did not speak English. I told Gary, "I will nod, smile, and tell them, "Mucho gusto. If they ask you where I'm from, tell them I'm from San Carlos de Bariloche, Argentina." When we arrived, Clem and Mary hugged Gary and exchanged pleasantries. All went according to plan, even when Mary asked Gary, "How do you communicate with Pedro? You don't know any Spanish, Gary?" "Oh, I've learned some Spanish words, so we manage," Gary replied. Mary and Clem led us into their home, and the conversation flowed between the three. I sat silently and just smiled. After what seemed like 15 or 30 minutes, Mary said something that just begged a response from me, and to this day, I can't remember what she said. I found an opening to reveal the ruse. "That's bullshit," I cut into the conversation in a slightly raised voice. Mary's eyes were the size of saucers as she rapidly looked at Gary and shouted, "Gary, you sonofabitch! What if we had been talking about him!" We all laughed hysterically.

In mid-June, I resumed small mammal trapping in clearcuts and uncut forested sites at higher elevations just below the timberline. I completed the small mammal trapping on July 10th. Maurice asked me during one of his winter visits to Spotted Bear if I would consider working on the project the following winter. I didn't hesitate and enthusiastically replied, "Yes." I returned to Moscow in late July to analyze the data from my small mammal study and complete a final draft of my thesis by October, an ambitious task for three months. I hoped to return to Hungry Horse in late October or early November and join Howard and Gary in deploying live traps in the Bob Marshall wilderness.

Chapter 8: Lifelong Friendships & Lessons Learned

Prior to departing Montana for Idaho, I had asked Esther and Wayne if I could camp out at their place near Deary, Idaho, while I looked for an apartment in Moscow. Esther and Wayne worked at the university and lived a spartan life in a small one-bedroom house. I left most of my belongings at Hungry Horse since I expected to return later during the fall. The cap-covered back of my pickup truck served as my bedroom during the night, with a sleeping bag and pad as my bed. During the day, when not commuting to Moscow with Esther and Wayne, I would drive twenty miles to the university to work on my thesis. Later in the afternoon, I would search for apartments that did not require a long-term lease. Several weeks of searching proved unsuccessful and I wound up camping at Esther and Wayne's place during my stay in Idaho. At the university, I shared an office with Bill Krohn, a doctoral student at what used to be a dormitory. Initially, all my thesis work involved organizing my field data recorded on hard copy data sheets, a time-consuming task given that personal computers were in their infancy during that time and largely unavailable. Statistical analysis followed and all were done with pencil and paper. I met and made many new friends through Esther and Wayne. Often times, my thesis work at the university meant working long into the evening. Esther and Wayne introduced me to Kemper McMaster, a fisheries graduate student. Kemper offered the couch at the house he rented in Moscow whenever I stayed late working on my thesis. During my overnight stays at his place, Kemper cooked bacon, grits, and eggs for breakfast the following morning. Grits for breakfast in Idaho were an uncommon menu item, but not for Kemper, who grew up in South Carolina. The smell of bacon cooking served as my alarm clock.

Wayne grew up in the San Francisco area, and Esther was raised in San Francisco's Chinatown. Esther's parents were Chinese immigrants, and she was the first generation of her family born in the U.S. My stay with them became a cultural exchange of sorts. I learned about the Chinese American culture, and Esther and Wayne learned about mine. During the fall, Esther's father shipped Esther mooncakes and Peking duck. I asked Esther why the cakes were called "moon cakes." She explained that moon cakes were a traditional dessert to celebrate the fall harvest. She then grabbed a knife and sliced the cupcake-sized treat, and in the middle was a yellow-orange "moon." Esther read the puzzled look on my face and told me the "moon" was made by baking and egg yolk within the cake. She divided the moon cake into three pieces, then handed one piece to me and one to Wayne, and kept the third piece for herself. It was delicious. Wayne worked as a plumber at the university and was very well-read.

A boundless curiosity and knowledge of diverse topics allowed Wayne to engage in deep conversations with just about anybody. I found myself looking up information on Mexican traditions in the university library and asking my friends and family back home after Wayne would ask me what some of those traditions meant and how they came about. Wayne and Esther's hospitality extended to several fisheries and wildlife graduate students. Their 80-acre parcel of forested land provided a welcomed retreat from the stresses of graduate school. The graduate students gave their place the moniker "the Beymer Farm." Esther and Wayne kept two horses named Charlie and Willow; two white-fronted geese, Albert and Victoria; their dog Metro; and a cat named Jenny. During my stay, I met a few of their neighbors, several graduate students, and other folks who frequented the Beymer Farm.

As the pages of the calendar flipped, I spent long days crunching numbers to determine if small mammal densities were statistically different between the different-aged clearcuts and the uncut forested areas. I purposely reworked the calculations two to three times to make sure there were no errors—data interpretation and writing my thesis followed by long nights and Southern breakfasts at The House of Kemper. During the thesis-writing phase, I spent some of my time writing at Esther and Wayne's house while they were away working at the university. My desire to join Howard and Gary in the Bob Marshall wilderness to set up live traps in November and run the traplines out of Spotted Bear motivated me to work long hours to complete my thesis. Walks in Esther and Wayne's forested "back forty" were my antidote to writer's block. I did manage to include some days for other activities. I helped one of Esther and Wayne's neighbors pick up and load bales of hay into a farm truck, followed by unloading the bales and stacking them in the neighbor's barn—another memorable outing involved trout fishing at Elk Creek west of Deary with Bill Krohn. Once we arrived at Elk Creek, we donned our waders and grabbed our fly-fishing gear. "I'll fish upstream, and you fish downstream," Bill said. I watched Bill in his chest waders walk upstream along the creek. I proceeded downstream in my hip waders, although my waders extended only to my mid-thigh. Dense willows along the creek banks made casting difficult. I continued to fish downstream wherever the willows offered clear access to the creek and space to cast a fly. Willow branches extended their fingers, catching my fly with almost every cast. Fly fishing became a futile effort. The tributary streams flowing into the South Fork of the Flathead River had spoiled me the year before with guaranteed fishing success, so my patience at Elk Creek was wearing thin. The dense willows made it impossible to fish from the bank, so I had to wade into the stream, which was fairly shallow. At one point, my patience cracked like thin ice as I unknowingly waded into a deep hole. Cold water rushed into my waders as I struggled to keep my balance. I managed to wade out of the hole and onto the bank. Once on dry ground, I took off my waders and drained the water. My jeans were soaked, and I was cold. I walked back upstream, and as I approached Bill's vehicle, I saw him walking towards me with a big smile and one hand holding up a stringer with several trout. "How'd you do, Pete?" Bill asked. "It sucked!" I replied with a scowl on my face. I did get over my frustration on the drive back, though. Recalling that time, I count my blessings for the lifelong friends I made during my two years and seven months in graduate school. I've kept in touch with Bill, Kemper, Gary, Esther, and Wayne ever since. It is interesting how bonds form from shared experiences and hold firm over the years.

During the last two weeks or so of August, I overheard a graduate student talk about a 3-day backpacking trip in the Eagle Cap Wilderness in northeastern Oregon and climbing up Sacajawea Peak, the highest peak in the Wallowa Mountains at 9,838 ft in elevation. I grilled the students with questions about the hike, the trail, and the climb. The more I learned about it, the more I wanted to do that hike and climb that peak. I discussed the hike with Evie, and she, too, was interested in backpacking in the Eagle Cap wilderness. Later that day, I mentioned the hike to Wayne and Esther, and they, too, were interested in participating. As the plan unfolded, Esther and Wayne's neighbor, Tom Witt, expressed an interest. Unfortunately, Esther had a conflict and couldn't accompany us. Our party of four, including Evie's dog Tahjene, departed for Joseph, Oregon, and the Wallowa-Whitman National Forest at 5:30 pm on Friday, September 3rd.

After we crossed the Grande Ronde River and the Washington-Oregon border, I heard a thumping sound emanating from the rear of my pickup truck. The sound intensified as we continued down the road until it got so bad that I decided to stop and camp after we found a suitable place and check the truck during daylight the next morning. I drove slowly until we saw a place to pull over off the highway. We grabbed our backpacking gear, crossed a fence into a cow pasture, and made camp among a stand of ponderosa pine. I kept thinking about the problem with my truck as we cooked hamburgers and roasted corn on the cob over an open fire. After dinner, we extinguished the fire and slept under the stars. The moon was full, accompanied by a sky peppered with bright stars. I went to sleep, hoping and praying that the vehicle problem was not a major one.

The morning light greeted us while we packed our gear and didn't bother with breakfast. We climbed into my truck and drove for a mile, and the problem became even worse. I pulled over, and all of us climbed out of my truck. Tom looked underneath the rear tire and axle and saw a large bulge on the sidewall of the tire. I breathed a sigh of relief that it was not a problem with the axle of the wheel. I was a poor graduate student and could not afford a major repair job on my truck. We changed the tire and arrived at the U.S. Forest Service Ranger Station at Joseph at 7:30 am.

We obtained a backpacking/camping permit for Ice Lake, a beautiful alpine lake at the foot of the Matterhorn, the second-highest peak in the Wallowa Mountains at 9,826 ft in elevation. We started our trek at 9 am at the Wallowa Lake State Park trailhead and followed the West Fork of the Wallowa River upstream for two-and-a-half miles. We stopped at a spot with wild raspberry bushes and ate some raspberries. Tahjene kept us entertained by chasing red squirrels. We crossed the river over a rustic wooden bridge and began our steep ascent up to Ice Lake, a climb of 2,346 feet and 20 switchbacks. Having missed breakfast, my stomach was complaining, and so were my feet. We elected to stop for lunch and ate cheese, summer sausage, cookies, and candy bars. We soaked up the warmth of the sun for about an hour prior to resuming our hike up to Ice Lake. The switchbacks seemed never-ending, but soon, the trail leveled out, and we could see Ice Lake, its cold blue waters shimmering in the bright sun. We make our way to a forested bench on the south shore of the lake. We found a suitable campsite, spread our sleeping bags, and slept for an hour. Our supper consisted of canned tuna, macaroni, and instant chicken soup. After supper, the three of us climbed up the south ridge and enjoyed the view. I reveled in being in a wilderness area once again.

After a granola breakfast and instant coffee, we started our ascent to the Matterhorn and Sacajawea Peak at 8 am and reached the summit of the Matterhorn at 10:30 am. We sat for about 30 to 45 minutes and enjoyed the view of Eagle Cap Peak, numerous alpine lakes, the Blue Mountains to the west, and the Seven Devils in Idaho to the east. From the Matterhorn, we traversed slowly along the steep ridge leading to Sacajawea Peak. We stopped for lunch at South Hurwall Peak, slept for about an hour, then resumed following the sharp ridgetop to Sacajawea Peak.

We reached the summit at 2:30 pm and opened the metal box containing the summit register, a notebook signed and dated by persons reaching the summit. The four of us signed the register and read some of the entries. One memorable entry made a day or so before ours included the name and age of a woman and a brief account of her ascent. The 65-year-old lady wrote that she and her husband climbed Sacajawea Peak every summer for many years. She made the climb for her husband, who had passed away earlier in the year. I stared at her note and said, "I hope when I'm that old, I will still be able to do what she has done." We placed the notebook back in the metal box, closed it, and placed it back securely. We watched a mountain goat running down a scree slope and then up an almost vertical rock face to the northwest of the summit. After absorbing the view, we made our way down a scree slope to Ice Lake and our camp site. We moved our camp after supper, and judging by the clouds, we pitched the rain fly. The three of us, plus Tahjene, slept under the rain fly. Somehow, I wound up at the edge of the rain fly, and our concern about the rain was justified. It did rain during the evening and water dripped onto my sleeping bag. I didn't get much sleep that night. Cold temperatures greeted us the next morning, with fog draped over Ice Lake like a shroud. We packed our gear and hiked back out to civilization.

In September and October, I raced to complete my thesis so that I could accompany Howard and Gary to the Bob Marshall Wilderness in November. I turned in the first draft of my thesis to Maurice and my graduate committee for review. I walked the hallways of the Forestry, Range, and Wildlife Sciences (FRWS) building with a sense of relief, yet my brain felt like mush. My classmates broke my zombie-like state as I walked down the hall with invitations to the Capricorn Bar, a popular hangout on Main Street, Moscow, for university students. I did not drink alcohol at that time, and if I frequented a bar, I was probably the designated driver. Live music at the Capricorn and not the alcohol prompted me to accept their invitations. I danced the night away to the music of Dusty and the Saddle Pickers. In between dances, I would sit at the large table where my classmates held court; I cracked jokes and acted goofy, all the while quenching my thirst with a pitcher of water. The next day, several of the students joked that I had gotten drunk on a pitcher of water.

As the last few weeks of October approached, I received comments on my first draft from Maurice and two of my committee members. Comments from the third committee member were all that remained for me to complete a final draft and head to Montana. Whenever I encountered that committee member walking the hallways of the FRWS building, I would ask him if he had completed the review of my thesis. As the end of October approached, my inquiries became increasingly frequent. I realized I would not receive the third review by the end of October, so I departed for Hungry Horse to help Howard and Gary prepare for the winter trapping season.

Chapter 9: Live Trapping Wolverines

In November, I assisted Howard and Gary in preparing gear for our excursion back into "The Bob" to stock the cabins with food and plenty of firewood to last through the second winter of live trapping. Howard constructed new live traps to replace the wooden box traps of the previous winter. The wooden box traps had a small quarter-inch hole on the top panel, allowing a cable to extend from the traps' interior to a metal pin holding the trapdoor open. Bait was attached to the end of the cable inside the trap so that when a wolverine pulled on the bait, the cable would free the trapdoor to slide shut. One persistent wolverine held captive in one of the wooden traps saw daylight in the small hole and chewed on that small hole until it was large enough to allow it to escape. Howard constructed the new live traps from chain-link fencing material and a metal frame. We distributed and assembled the new traps as we had the previous year.

Since we were not running traps in December, I looked forward to spending Christmas with my family in

South Texas. While there, I recall my dad asking me to show "pictures" of Montana and its wildlife to his cousins who still lived on the ranch where my great-grandfather, grandfather, and father grew up. "They have never seen anything like that," my father pointed out. My dad and grandfather grew up in Las Cuatas Ranch, about one mile west of Encino. Las Cuatas (the twins) was likely named for two nearby *'Lagunas'* (Playa Lakes) located just east of the ranch. These depressions collected water during heavy rains or tropical storms, forming two to three acres of Lagunas. The seasonal water source for livestock and possibly for the ranch families may have determined the location of the ranch houses nearby. The Las Cuatas Ranch residence complex consisted of wooden houses and sheds. Two houses served as living quarters (bedrooms), a separate building for the one-room kitchen, a bathhouse, and an outhouse. I assume the buildings were constructed in the late 1930s or 1940s. The kitchen was physically separated from the living quarters as wood-burning stoves were used for cooking in the kitchen. I remember my father's aunt, Maria Rita Longoria Ramirez, baking biscuits in the wood stove during one visit I made when I was five years old. My father's cousins living at the ranch included

Lucas, Emma, Rosendo (Chendo), Eufracia (Pacha), and Macario (Macarito). The men worked as ranch hands at the larger ranches in the Encino area. Macarito was the only one who knew how to drive and chauffeured his brothers and sisters. For local trips along the county road, Lucas and Chendo rode in a wagon pulled by two mules. They used this wagon at least through the mid-1970s.

I showed my Dad's five cousins images of elk, deer, pine marten, wolverines, and other wildlife as well as the snow-covered mountain landscapes of northwestern Montana, using a slide projector that I borrowed from my older brother. They were fascinated as they probably had never ventured farther than San Antonio, 200 miles to the north, and spent most of their time in Brooks County. Just about every time I showed an image of a wild animal, my Dad's cousins would ask, "*se comen?*" (can you eat them?). To them, wild animals were a source of food.

The family, as did my Dad, grew up during the Great Depression, so I understood the reason for their inquiry and mindset. During my week-long visit, the reality of my parents' financial survival hit me like a plunge into icy cold water. My mother informed me that my father was probably going to lose the ranch. I asked my father about that, and I learned that my parents were having financial difficulties, so my father took out a loan to pay bills and provide subsistence. Unfortunately, the only collateral he had was his ranch. The lender eventually called him on the loan and threatened foreclosure, so my father found a buyer for his ranch. My father suffered the same fate as had past generations of ranchers in South Texas during the late 1800s and throughout the 1900s. Cattle ranching and ranch owners fell victim to cyclical droughts, forcing them to sell their land to better-educated and business-savvy buyers. My father tried to reassure me that everything would work out fine; however, that did not assuage my fears of losing the land that had been in my family for three generations. For the first time in my life, I saw and felt the vulnerability of my parents. As their child, I always felt that they were invincible; however, I now felt helpless even though I had a burning desire to help them, but I did not know how. Upon my return to Montana, I immersed myself in the Wolverine Project, realizing that my time on this research project was drawing to a close with an uncertain future for me and my parents.

I spent the 1977 winter season running the trap lines solo as Maurice felt I could do so based on my prior winter's performance. Given that I was working and living solo at Spotted Bear, Maurice, and Howard procured a shortwave radio from a communications network based in Boise, Idaho, for backcountry residents living year-round in privately-owned inholdings within the Frank Church River-of-No-Return Wilderness in central Idaho. I used the shortwave radio at Spotted Bear to contact the network in Boise, and the dispatcher would relay my message to Howard by telephone. Most of my message consisted of grocery orders, snowmobile parts, and notifying Howard of Wolverine captures. A high-pressure ridge stalled offshore of northwestern Washington threw us a curve ball by causing a significant reduction in snowfall in our study area. The reduced snowfall probably caused wolverines to remain at higher elevations to procure food and not have to venture down the slope to our traplines.

On the last day of December, a meager six inches of snow covered the road, enabling Howard to drive Gary, Tim, and me to Spotted Bear. The start of the 1977 trapping season on New Year's Day greeted us with a morning temperature of -12°F (-25°C) with the mobile home windows covered with frost. After a breakfast of eggs, bacon, and hash brown potatoes, Gary and I attempted to fill a milk can with water from the Spotted Bear River. We encountered a thick layer of ice on the surface of the river, prohibiting us from harvesting water from the stream. Gary and I resorted to plan B and rode snowmobiles to the South Fork bridge for water. From the bridge, we lowered a bucket down with a rope to scoop a bucket full of water out of the river and filled the milk can. The following day, the temperature dropped to -22°F (-30°C). Gary and Tim loaded their backpacks onto the large aluminum sled. Gary and Rascal rode on the sled along with all that gear, which required him to get off the sled and push the snowmobile and sled on the uphill grades. We reached Bunker Creek camp at 3 pm and spent the remainder of the afternoon cross-country skiing.

During the night, the three of us added more firewood to the wood-burning stove during shifts. After a Sunday breakfast of pancakes, we loaded gear onto the larger aluminum sled, and I transported Gary, Tim, and Rascal to the trailhead at Meadow Creek Gorge. I rode the snowmobile back to Spotted Bear in the subzero temperature, freezing my exhaled breath and lining my parka hood with frost. I arrived at Spotted Bear at 10:30 am and checked the outdoor thermometer, -14° F. I loaded the wood-burning stove with firewood and ignited the kindling. After the fire got going, I held the indoor thermometer 10 feet from the stove; the temperature climbed to 17° F. I tried cutting up bait for the traps, but the frozen meat shattered into tiny pieces when I struck it with the axe. I hacked at the meat until I had a whole quarter cut up. Later that evening, I worked on revisions to my thesis based on edits provided by Maurice and two of my committee members.

Three days later, I decided not to bait the traps due to the extremely freezing temperatures, so I baited the traps the following day. The single-digit temperatures froze the water in both the metal milk cans in the Bunker Creek tent. I placed both cans near the wood-burning stove, loaded the smaller milk can on the sled, and transported it to the creek to get water. I had to chop through the 2-inch thick layer of ice with the axe to get water. Extreme cold temperatures continued through the first week of January.

My morning routine during subzero and single-digit temperatures at the Bunker Creek tent camp involved crawling out of my sleeping bag, starting a fire in the wood-burning stove, hopping back into bed, and then waiting for the temperature inside my canvas shelter to warm up.

It usually took 30 minutes for the camp to warm up. One early evening in mid-January, I walked out of the tent camp and looked up at the cloud-covered sky, hoping the skies would clear so that Howard could fly into Spotted Bear with plenty of mail from my family and friends. The camp lantern light sifted through the tent canvas, giving my shelter a warm golden glow reflected in the white snow. As I stood there looking at the tent glow, I marveled at how a simple structure such as this tent with a wooden floor and frame provided me a refuge from darkness and cold. A microenvironment separated from the harshness of winter by a thin sheet of fabric, yet offering all the requirements for survival: plenty of firewood, a warm stove, a place to dry out, food to eat, and a warm bed to sleep in.

Subzero temperatures continued a week later, with three degrees below zero at Bunker Creek camp and a much-reduced snowpack. Nine days into the season,

Murphy's Law, "If something can go wrong, it will," paid me a visit with vengeance as I prepared to run the trapline. After packing all the gear onto the sled, I yanked on the snowmobile's starter rope and was greeted by silence instead of the engine's screeching roar. After three or four yanks, I removed my parka and mittens, figuring I was overdressed for troubleshooting the snowmobile. I grabbed the tool kit from under the snowmobile seat, removed the spark plug, and reconnected it to the spark plug wire. I positioned the connected spark plug's metal end to the exposed metal on the snowmobile and yanked on the starter cord to test for a spark. As I pulled on the starter cord, I kept my eye on the spark plug and saw a spark. The spark plug was good. Next, I changed the electrical coil. Nothing! I replaced the spark plug wire. *Nada*! Changed the fuel filter. Zilch! Sputter, sputter.

My hands were getting cold working in the subzero weather. I restarted the fire in the wood-burning stove, contemplating a stay at least until noon. In troubleshooting the problem, I brushed one of my fingers on a sharp metal edge on the snowmobile, resulting in a small incision. The blood dripping from the incision fell on the cold metal and immediately froze. I went back inside the tent camp, washed my hands, and put a band-aid around my finger. I put another log in the wood stove, anticipating a lengthy stay. After working on the snowmobile for almost 2-and-a-half hours with negative results, I concluded I would have to ski back to Spotted Bear and contact Howard for assistance. As it was noon, I decided whether to ski back to Spotted Bear or the next morning. I decided to go for it, packed some crackers, cheese and candy into my pack, and a small axe in case I had to spend the night out and build a fire. I put on my cross-country skis and left Bunker Creek camp at 12:20 pm.

I reached the turnoff to the Meadow Creek Gorge trailhead, a distance of three miles, in forty minutes. I had a good glide on the packed trail created by the snowmobile. I estimated that I'd make it to Spotted Bear by five or 6 pm. I kept up a good pace; sweat came down my hair and formed an icicle on my forehead. Fortunately, the temperature warmed up as the day progressed. Somewhere along the road to Spotted Bear, I stopped to drink water from a small spring that had not frozen, and then I ate a candy bar. It took me two-and-a-half hours to reach Jungle Creek, approximately 10 miles from Bunker Creek camp. When I reached Addition Road, one mile from the footbridge leading to Spotted Bear, I began to lose my energy and tire. I could not kick as hard and get a longer glide on my skis. My objective was to reach a footbridge crossing the South Fork of the Flathead River with the trail leading directly to the Spotted Bear Ranger Station. This route would save me an additional two miles if I returned to Spotted Bear on the road. I was concerned that I would not be able to find the trail leading from the road to the footbridge in the dark, as there was no sign marking the trail. The last mile to the trail was the longest. I took the trail to Spotted Bear and took my skis off to walk across the bridge. Once I crossed the footbridge, I put my skis back on and approached our base camp. Tanner greeted me with his deep barking and howling. I was so glad to see and hear him as I skied into the base camp; when I arrived, I walked over to his dog house and embraced him. After I entered the mobile home, I built a fire in the wood-burning stove. It seemed to take forever to warm up the house, and my hands were very cold. I drank six cups of hot chocolate and four glasses of Tang, an instant breakfast drink.

Monday morning at Spotted Bear, I started the remaining snowmobile and checked the traps along the westside road. I stopped to replace the hanging bait at the live trap site near Tin Creek. A piece of bait, typically road-killed deer, was attached to a pole near the live trap to entice wolverines to the site and, hopefully to bait inside the trap. I shut the snowmobile off, grabbed a chunk of meat from the sled, and walked over to the trap site to replace the hanging bait. After replacing the bait, I started the snowmobile, and down the road I went, stopping at the next live trap site and replacing the bait. Wolverine tracks led to the trap; however, the trapdoor had not been tripped. "Probably, No Nose," I thought to myself. No Nose was trap-prone and knew where to find an easy meal. After baiting the trap, I proceeded to the next trap site. The trap door was closed, and again I assumed it was No Nose. I slowed the snowmobile as I closed in on the trap site, and the engine quit. "I'm positive I did not push the engine kill button on the snowmobile handlebar," was the first thought on my mind. Murphy's Law, "If anything can go wrong, it will," came down on me the day before like a clod of snow falling from a tree. Another of Murphy's laws was descending on me like a torrent of snow down a steep slope, "Things tend to progress from bad to worse." I walked over to the trap, and sure enough, it was No Nose. I released her, and she bolted out of the trap and headed down the slope. I tried to restart the snowmobile, and once again, I was faced with a futile effort: yank on the starter cord and received only sputters from the engine. Yank, sputter, repeat. Isn't the definition of insanity doing the same thing over and over again and expecting different results? My self-diagnosis was correct all along; the snowmobiles were driving me crazy. I had no tools either, as they were all in the snowmobile I had left behind at the Bunker Creek tent camp. What a fix! I tried to start the snowmobile for an hour and a half. I cursed, I prayed, I yelled, and I even tried to make light of my dire situation by laughing. Once again, I put my cross-country skis on, and as I was about to leave, a Forest Service truck pulled up.

It was the second week of January, and the road from Hungry Horse to Spotted Bear was still passable. One does not equate the word drought with winter, but, in essence, that was the status of my second winter at Spotted Bear, with very little snow. The Forest Service employee gave me a ride to the airstrip where 40-Acres was parked, dropped me off, and proceeded to the ranger station. My plan was to start 40-Acres and return to the Spotted Bear camp. I knew 40-Acres was ailing due to a busted bogie wheel; however, I reasoned that 40-Acres could limp back to camp, that I could do some repairs, and that all would be good with my snow-covered world.

I was about to lift the cowling sheltering the "life-giving metal organ" of this industrial-sized snowmobile when it dawned on me that 40-Acres was missing a clutch bolt. Things were definitely progressing from bad to worse. I put my skis back on and skied back to Spotted Bear. I spent the afternoon sourdough baking bread and sourdough cinnamon rolls. The wonderful smells emanating from the oven worked wonders for reducing my stress and frustration. Later that evening, I contacted Howard over our shortwave radio and informed him of my situation.

The next day, Howard drove the project Ford 4x4 pickup truck to Spotted Bear. The previous winter, he would have had to fly into the Spotted Bear airstrip. Steve Wirt, a friend of Howard's, accompanied him. Howard picked me up at the camp and drove Steve and me to the airstrip to repair 40-Acres. After completing that task, we traveled down the west side road and managed to get the Scandic snowmobile started. Howard engaged his "jack-of-all-trades and master-of-all" mode and concluded that the snowmobile needed a complete electrical rewiring operation.

We passed by the trap where No Nose was captured the day before, and true to form, No Nose was recaptured. We released the scavenging mustelid after we checked her radio collar. We returned to Spotted Bear at 2 pm that afternoon, refueled the snowmobiles, reloaded the sled with the requisite gear, and headed up to Bunker Creek. We reached Bunker Creek camp at 4 pm. Howard and Steve remained at the Bunker Creek camp, and I headed for Upper Bunker to check the live traps.

When I returned, the Scandic snowmobile I had abandoned on Sunday was up and running. "What was the problem with it, Howard?" I asked. I was glad to see the machine operating as much as I hated it. "Well shoot, all it needed was a new spark plug," Howard replied with his North Carolina southern drawl and added, "All the spare ones in the snowmobile won't fire under compression." We headed back to Spotted Bear as the sun was setting. The snowmobile I was riding on was shorting out and losing power. "Why me?" I thought, "I must be cursed." We finally made it to Spotted Bear at 6 pm. Three days later, Murphy's Law decided it was not done with me at Spotted Bear.

After eating lunch, I repaired electrical wires on the snowmobile and discovered a broken motor mount bolt. I removed all the bogie wheels and the rear axle to access and remove the broken motor mount bolt. Replacing the motor mount bolt took four hours. As if mechanical problems were not enough, weather conditions contributed to the "joy" of snowmobiling. Twelve inches of powder snow greeted my morning two days later at the Bunker Creek tent camp. After loading the sled with my requisite gear, I revved up the snowmobile and immediately got stuck.

I left the sled at the Bunker Creek camp and loaded my backpack, skis, snowshoes, and shovel on the snowmobile to facilitate plowing through the deep powder. It took me one hour to make it out of the camp site after getting stuck twice. Once I managed to make it onto the road back to Spotted Bear, the snowmobile plowed through the deep snow at times, pushing the powdery snow up over the windshield and onto my face, making it difficult for me to see the road. I got stuck numerous times and had to shovel snow from the front and sides of the snowmobile. All that digging resulted in a crater three to four feet deep and three feet wide. I would then put on the snowshoes and break trail for about 50 to 75 yards. I lost count of the number of times the snowmobile bogged down in the deep snow, although my estimate was at least 15 times. My lower back began to ache from all the shoveling. The next day, the snowmobile bogged down nine times. I would turn off the snowmobile, put on snowshoes, walk 200 to 300 yards up the road, and back to the snowmobile to break trail, repeating the process every time the snowmobile got stuck in the deep snow. It was a tough two days, but I didn't complain. I welcomed the snow, hoping that wolverines would make their way from higher elevations and visit the traps. Breaking the trail on snowshoes was a nice break from riding on the noisy snowmobile. I could hear chickadees chirping and snow clods falling from the snow-covered trees.

The anomalous winter season decided to pile on adversity the very next morning; instead of deep powder snow, fog, and rain made for a challenging day of snowmobiling. The rain covered my goggles, froze, and coated the lens with ice, restricting my vision. The rain turned the snow into the consistency of wet cement. I had to stop several times, tip the snowmobile on its side, and pound the bottom of the track with the axe to remove the packed snow within the bogie wheel suspension system. Rain continued the next day, confirming that this winter season was unlike the previous one. The next day, while running the Elam trapline from Spotted Bear, the snowmobile veered off into a tire rut and tipped, thus throwing me off onto the hardpacked snow. After a few seconds of wondering what happened, I looked over the snowmobile and saw its left ski askew. The pin attaching the snowmobile's left ski to the suspension spring was broken. I used wire to reattach the ski to the spring and slowly rode the snowmobile back to Spotted Bear. I repaired the connection with a replacement pin and resumed running the trapline. I took most of the trials and tribulations in stride even though I ran the trapline solo and did not have Gary along to laugh in the face of adversity.

The much-reduced snowpack in January allowed for vehicle access to Spotted Bear through most of January. Forest Service staff drove up to the Spotted Bear Ranger Station on January 5th, Howard on the 11th, and three men from the Kalispell area on the 22nd. By mid-January of the previous winter, deep snow limited access to Spotted Bear to snowmobiles and small airplanes with skis. Snow depth influences the availability of carrion and small mammals for the wolverine to feed on; thus, wolverines remained at higher elevations, resulting in lower captures at our traplines located at a lower elevation. Despite the paucity of snow, we resumed trapping operations as usual, with Gary and Tim running traps in the Bob Marshall, Howard at the lower portions of the east and west side roads, and me at Spotted Bear. This season, I started running traps on the 3rd day of January compared to the previous winter when we started running the traplines three weeks earlier on the 11th day of December. In the last winter, our trapping efforts on all the traplines led to the capture of seven wolverines: three adult males, three adult females, and one subadult female. This winter, Howard, Gary, Tim, and I only captured two adult males and one adult female – No Nose. I captured No Nose on the 6th of January on three consecutive days during the second week of January, and again on the Friday of that week. No Nose remained the only wolverine captured in the traplines I ran out of Spotted Bear. Always the trap-prone wolverine, No Nose spent evenings in live traps along the Elam trapline on January 28th, 30th, and February 8th. At the end of January the previous year, we captured No Nose three times and captured and radio-collared two male wolverines. In mid-March, Howard located No Nose's radio collar signal near Big Prairie in the Bob Marshall Wilderness, approximately 32 air miles from Spotted Bear. Pine marten and weasels were the only mustelids I captured for the remainder of the season. Most of my journal entries chronicled my experience living and working alone in the backcountry during the winter.

Maurice's workload as Co-Op Unit leader at the university while overseeing several wildlife research projects and graduate students in Idaho kept him very busy, allowing him only two to three visits each winter season. It took a considerable amount of funds to conduct the wolverine research project, especially running 42 miles of traplines on snowmobiles and the use of an airplane for radiotracking and ferrying supplies to Spotted Bear during the winter, plus the cost of fuel for those vehicles as well as parts and maintenance. Procuring funding consumed much of Maurice's time, given the funds required to keep the research study running. Non-governmental organizations contributing to the project included National Geographic, the National Wildlife Federation, the National Audubon Society, the Boone and Crockett Club, the New York Zoological Society, the National Rifle Association, and the Wildlife Management Institute. The National Science Foundation, U.S. Fish and Wildlife Service, and U.S. Forest Service also provided funding. I looked forward to Maurice's visits, as infrequent as they were, as each added to my mental encyclopedia of lessons learned from conversations and interactions with him. Five days into January, Maurice rode up to Spotted Bear with Howard. We spent the evening talking about skiing and bird hunting, and towards the end of the discussions, my thesis. Maurice informed me that he and two of my committee members felt my thesis was ok; however, the third committee member was the lone holdout.

Almost two weeks after Maurice's visit, I observed several coyote tracks and one lynx track on Upper Bunker Creek Road. The snowmobile trail was covered with tracks as well as blood stains. Several ravens flew off upslope from the road, and upon closer look upslope, I saw a carcass approximately 50 yards from the road. I put my snowshoes on and walked up the slope to look closer. I found an elk calf carcass with only hair, the backbone, some ribs, the pelvis, and hind feet remaining. Predators and scavengers had picked it clean. I collected one of the femurs to submit to the Montana Fish and Game to analyze the marrow for fat content. The analysis indicates the elk's condition. Howard flew supplies over a day later, and I informed him about the carcass. Howard later relayed my observation to Maurice. My observation of the elk calf carcass indicated to Maurice that a cougar was hunting the Upper Bunker Creek area. He returned to Spotted Bear two weeks after my observation, hoping to track and radio-collar the cougar in order to compare its movements with radio-collared wolverines.

We skied Spotted Bear Road and took Tanner with us, as Maurice wanted to try leading the dog on a leash while on cross-country skis. Tanner would run in front of

Maurice's skis and pull the dog back and to the side. At one point, Tanner plunged to the rear, pulling Maurice down onto the snow. We both laughed about it as Maurice concluded that hunting for mountain lions on cross-country skis would not work. The next day, we snowmobiled up to Upper Bunker and examined the elk calf kill site. Maurice identified two sets of cougar tracks. I was fascinated as he interpreted the cougar's movements by looking at the tracks. Maurice was excited and enthused at finding cougar tracks. I learned quite a bit in just those 15 minutes of listening and watching Maurice reading the tracks and signs in the snow. The next morning greeted Maurice and me with a temperature of minus 2°F as we departed Bunker camp and ran the trapline on our way to Spotted Bear. As we approached the airstrip, we saw Howard waiting by his airplane waiting to fly Maurice back to Kalispell. I planned to join Maurice in Moscow, Idaho, two weeks later to complete work on my thesis and take the oral exam on my small mammal research study. I wrote the following in my journal on January 29th: "I'm going to miss this place. I am cherishing every day up here because after this season is over, I may never live like this."

In spite of the much-reduced trapping success and my frustrations with the snowmobile issues, I accepted my fate and settled into my routine. In addition to running the traplines every day, there were plenty of daily chores to keep me busy: splitting firewood, cleaning the project camps at Bunker Creek and Spotted Bear, maintaining the snowmobiles, filling out data sheets on the day's activities and providing Tanner with food and water. After dinner, I spent my evenings playing my guitar, writing letters to my family and friends, and reading paperback books. Before turning in for the evening, I would place firewood in the wood-burning stove and close the damper on the flue to keep the heat going for as long as possible, then snuggle into my sleeping bag and call it a day.

During the first Sunday of February, I ran the traplines and spent the night at the Bunker Creek Camp. Howard flew Steve Wirt up to Spotted Bear that day to become familiar with the daily routines of running the traplines. Steve volunteered to run the traplines during the time I would be in Moscow, completing my thesis and taking my oral exam. I ran the trapline back to Spotted Bear the next day and made it within five miles of Spotted Bear when the snowmobile quit running. I skied the five miles to Spotted Bear and joined Steve for lunch. Steve and I skied to the airstrip to get the other Scandic snowmobile, and then we rode from the airstrip to retrieve the malfunctioning snowmobile. Upon reaching the stranded snowmobile, we loaded it onto the aluminum sled and hauled it to Spotted Bear. We worked on the snowmobile until 7 pm, replacing a broken motor mount bolt and the electrical wires.

The next day, Steve and I ran the entire trapline, captured and released No Nose, and returned to Spotted Bear at 5 pm. That evening, I packed a few items for my trip to Hungry Horse the following morning. Steve transported me out on the east side road down to the plowed section of the road, where we met up with Howard. Howard drove me the rest of the way to Hungry Horse. It was great listening to music on my stereo once again at the house in Hungry Horse. That evening, I packed my clothes for my drive to Idaho. I phoned my parents and my older brother Ernest, and told them about my winter adventure. I spent two weeks in Moscow working on revisions to my thesis, followed by an oral exam with Maurice and my graduate committee. I prepared for the oral exam by reading my final thesis, reviewing my field notes, and attempting to predict questions the committee would ask. I answered all the questions fairly well until one committee member "got into the weeds" with questions on vegetation communities in the clearcuts and uncut forested areas I had sampled. My answers to one question were quickly followed up with more in-depth questions. My mind raced as the questions seemed to come at me rapidly, each question digging for more and more information. Throughout my school years, all of my exams were written and not oral. With written exams, I had time to think about my answers, not so with this interrogation. Finally, my stress intensified to the point where my mind went blank. I was done. Maurice spoke up and called an end to the exam. Later that afternoon, I sat alone at Maurice's home, staring at nothing in particular as the feeling of failure washed over me. Maurice walked up and asked, "What happened?" "I don't know, Maurice," I replied; "My mind went blank." Inside, I was crying, and on the outside, my eyes were on the verge of tears, and a deep feeling of humiliation washed over me. I wanted to run away and spend time alone. I believed that my goal to obtain a master's degree in wildlife science had spun out of control, nose-dived into the Earth, and gone up in flames. I later drove to Esther and Wayne's home north of Deary and walked alone through their forested 80 acres. Immersed in my failure, I wondered what I would do without a master's degree. I walked for what seemed like hours, but in reality, it wasn't. I thought of my parents and my safe place back home in South Texas. My very being longed to be there. Eventually, the peace and tranquility of the forest replaced my worry and sorrow with a commitment to face my immediate future with a positive attitude, come what may.

I met with Maurice upon my return to the university and expressed my feeling that the committee member's intense and rapid-fire interrogation was retribution for my incessant nagging him on the review of my thesis draft during the fall semester that I was on campus. Maurice reassured me and stated that the committee member had agreed to give me a written exam. I breathed a sigh of relief and thanked Maurice. I completed the written exam, and after receiving a final verdict that I had passed the exam, I drove to Hungry Horse, alone in my thoughts during the six to seven-hour drive.

After my three-week absence, I was happy to return to the solitude of the backcountry at Spotted Bear. Maurice advised me to exercise Tanner by having him run behind my snowmobile from Spotted Bear to the airstrip and back. Upon completing all of my morning chores, I loaded Tanner's portable kennel on the sled, unleashed Tanner, and had him follow my snowmobile to the airstrip for his daily exercise. I unloaded the kennel at the airstrip and placed Tanner inside. I resumed running the Elam trapline and was rewarded with the sight of a bald eagle perched on a snag. As I approached, the raptor thrust itself into the air and soared ever so freely. I reveled at the sight of this magnificent bird. Before the ban on organochlorine pesticides such as DDT in 1972, bald eagles in the lower 48 states were seriously declining due to eggshell thinning caused by these pesticides. Biologists estimated slightly less than 500 breeding pairs of bald eagles in the lower 48 states in the early 1960s. Bald eagle populations slowly increased to just below 800 nesting pairs in the mid-1970s following the DDT ban. After completing my run-up of the trapline, I returned to the airstrip, released Tanner from the kennel, and loaded it on the sled. I returned to Spotted Bear with Tanner following. The sight of the eagle soaring freely in the sky and of Tanner running untethered flooded me with a care-free sense of peace and a deep appreciation for where I was and what I was doing, especially after the stressful time during and after my oral exam at the university. I was free from the stressors of civilization and soaked up the intense elation. My reverie was short-lived when I returned to Spotted Bear after discovering I had run out of propane. Despite living alone with Gary and Tim upriver 16 to 32 miles within the Bob Marshall Wilderness Area and Hungry Horse, a 54-mile snowmobile ride down the East Side Road, I still relied on Howard and his airplane as my lifeline. Howard transported critical supplies for me to survive in the backcountry of Spotted Bear. Fortunately, I had a small propane tank to keep the refrigerator running. Having spent most of my life in South Texas, where refrigerators keep food cold, I found it amusing that this propane-powered refrigerator primarily kept my somewhat fresh vegetables and canned food from freezing. I didn't need the freezer compartment of the refrigerator as I relied on the natural freezer right outside the camp where I kept my store of beef hanging under the snowshed covering the mobile home. I hoped Howard would show up soon with a full propane bottle.

The last day of February greeted me with a hopeful sign as I walked out of the Bunker Creek tent camp and saw wolverine tracks next to the snowmobile. During the night, the wolverine ventured near the camp and took some of the bait I had stored on the sled. The following day, I encountered wolverine tracks at Upper Bunker. The wolverine tracks followed the packed snowcat track and would veer off now and then to investigate tree wells and holes in the snow underneath logs. I continued following the wolverine tracks. At one point, the tracks led away from the road onto a partial clearcuts. I stopped the snowmobile, shut the engine, and put on my cross-country skis to follow the tracks into the timber. Once in the timber, the wolverine tracks led to several tree wells. I observed blood stains in three individual tree wells with the tracks, indicating that the wolverine may have pounced on a rodent. Red squirrel tracks led to one of the tree wells, and I assumed, based on the tracks on the snow, that the squirrel was on the wolverine's menu. After following the tracks for an hour, the tracks continued across an avalanche chute and continued across a rugged, rocky area. At this point, I decided to ski back to the snowmobile as only two hours of daylight remained.

Towards the end of the first week of March, I left Spotted Bear at 9 am with Tanner following the snowmobile for his daily exercise. I encountered lynx tracks about one-quarter mile from the South Fork bridge. I encouraged Tanner to follow the tracks, and after a few sniffs of the track imprints on the snow, Tanner followed the tracks with me, trying to keep up with him. After 30 minutes and probably hiking for about one mile, I caught up with Tanner. He continued up a steep open slope as I lagged far behind. I was breathless when I reached the top of the slope, repeatedly calling Tanner. I finally caught up with him, praised him, and led him back down to the snowmobile. At the airstrip, I placed him in the portable kennel, completed running the Elam trapline, and returned to Spotted Bear with Tanner. I ran the Bunker Creek trapline, encountering wolverine tracks with the same pattern as before, tracks meandering along the road, investigating tree wells, feeding on the hanging baits next to the live traps but not entering the traps. I assumed the tracks did not belong to No Nose as she readily entered the traps for a free meal.

Rain instead of snow and temperatures in the upper 40s during the second week of March melted the snow on the South Fork bridge as well as a section of the road from the bridge to the Spotted Bear ranger station. The warmer temperatures freed the south and west-facing slopes from their snow cover. The rain and decreasing snow depth depressed me. Howard also expressed dismay over the lack of success in trapping during one of his flights into Spotted Bear. I wrote the following in my journal: "This winter has not been at all what I had hoped for. No wolverine, no marten, no fisher, and no lynx. Soon, it will be time to call it quits and the end of my primitive lifestyle at Spotted Bear. Soon, the bears will be out. Nights at Bunker camp are a little uneasy. I keep wondering if bears are out when the temperature goes up above 45°F."

With the lack of wolverine activity and captures, I welcomed the capture of weasels to break up the monotony of empty traps. While capturing one weasel in the trap near the airstrip, I readied my 35mm camera, hoping to get a picture of the small mustelid. When I opened the trap door, the weasel scurried out and hid in a burrow under a pine tree before I could take a photo. I walked towards the pine tree, hoping that the weasel would show itself so that I could get a photo. I knelt three feet away from the burrow entrance, focused the camera on the burrow, and adjusted the exposure settings. The weasel showed its head and shoulders and backed into the burrow. I took five or six photos and reached the end of my roll of film. I had a spare roll of film in the weather-proof box in the snowmobile, so I placed my camera over the burrow entrance to prevent the weasel from escaping. I heard much shrieking as I retrieved my extra roll of film and some small pieces of bait. After reloading the film in the camera, I placed two small pieces of bait near the burrow entrance and a larger piece further from the entrance. The weasel took two small pieces and ate them inside the burrow. Finally, it worked up enough courage to walk out of the burrow to snag the larger piece of bait. I succeeded in getting ten photos of the weasel before it ran off with the bait. That was my entertainment for the day.

Eleven days remained in March, with the temperatures rising and the snow pack rapidly diminishing. Howard and Steve flew over Spotted Bear camp, which was my cue to fire up the snowmobile to go pack the airstrip. As I was about to finish packing the runway, the snowmobile quit running in the middle of the runway. "Situation is normal," I said to myself. I heard Howard's airplane overhead, so I repeatedly pulled on the starter cord to start the snowmobile, but to no avail. Howard landed his airplane on one side of the runway and instructed Steve to help me drag the snowmobile off the runway. Howard informed us that he had to fly to The Bob to talk to Gary and Tim via the two-way radio. Steve and I moved the snowmobile off the runway, and Howard headed for The Bob.

I changed the coil and spark plug while releasing a plethora of invectives at the lifeless machine. After Howard returned from The Bob, we worked on the snowmobiles for the remainder of the day. It was great to have company; I'm sure I talked their ears off. I suppose Howard and Steve were more than ready for an evening of silence when they flew home at 7 pm. The following day, I ran the Elam and Bunker Creek traplines and captured two pine martens and one weasel. I encountered black bear tracks at three different sites and returned to Spotted Bear as Howard planned to return to continue our repair work on the snowmobiles.

I encountered more bear tracks when I ran the traplines during the last week of March. Maurice arrived at the end of March, and we searched for the mountain lion sign with the help of Tanner on the last day of the month. We hiked up into the elk winter range at the Upper Bunker Creek drainage, made our way halfway up the slope, and then headed down the drainage. We saw several elk and mule deer but did not see any cougar signs after hiking four miles. We resumed our search the next day at two other drainages with similar results. Even though Maurice was disappointed, we ended the evenings at Spotted Bear with thought-provoking conversations and welcomed laughter. As if to add insult to injury, I encountered fresh mountain lion tracks the next day while running the trapline. It seemed like this feline sensed that Maurice had left.

I removed all the food from Bunker Camp on the second day of April. "I'm gonna miss the winters at Spotted Bear. I'll miss the mountains, the serenity, and solitude." I wrote in my journal. High daily temperatures in the 70s the following week made quick work of snow removal on the roads. In some stretches of the trapline, a thin veneer of snow covered the road, which was barely wide enough to accommodate the snowmobile. More traps were raided by bears emerging from hibernation, so I removed live traps along Bunker Creek road since it was south-facing and received abundant sunshine and warmth to melt the snow.

On the tenth day of April, I rose at 6 am, ate breakfast, and hit the trail at 7 am. The remaining snow on the road was firm, which eased the removal and transportation of all the live traps. I removed the bunker line from Meadow Creek Gorge to Wilderness Lodge in two trips. Research staff from the University of Montana, Border Grizzly Project, volunteered their pickup truck to transport the traps across the bare road to Spotted Bear. I then removed the Elam line along the west side of the road. I left the snowmobile at the airstrip and walked to the Spotted Bear camp. As I walked back to camp, I ate my lunch under a blanket of melancholy, knowing that winter was indeed gone and my winter home would no longer be mine. I crossed the South Fork River bridge, stopped, and absorbed the sound of the rushing waters below. I reveled in the cacophony of nature's sounds, no longer drowned out by the high-pitched whine of a snowmobile engine. At the scenic pullout overlooking the South Fork of the Flathead River, I sat and soaked some of the sun's warm rays as well as the sounds of the rushing waters below. I contemplated what changes would take place along the South Fork and wondered if I would return in the future? My time at the South Fork had forever changed my life. What did not change was the strong connection to my family in South Texas, the concern with my parents' financial situation, and the possible loss of my Dad's ranch.

Additionally, in a previous phone call home, my mother informed me that my younger brother Ariel and his girlfriend, Sonia, planned to get married in June after they graduated from high school. *"They are too young to get married,"* I thought to myself. Those two issues tugged at me like a strong magnet. My only regret was not being able to say goodbye to Gary and Tim, who were still up in the Bob Marshall wilderness area.

Chapter 10: The Long Way Home

I returned to Hungry Horse, planning to drive to Moscow and complete last-minute paperwork to receive my master's degree diploma, followed by a long way home to South Texas. I had no job prospects other than an application with the U.S. Forest Service for a seasonal wilderness ranger job in southern Colorado. I planned to take the scenic routes through the mountains of Idaho, Wyoming, Colorado, and New Mexico and visit Grand Teton National Park in Wyoming, Dinosaur National Monument in Utah, Carlsbad Caverns National Park in New Mexico, and Big Bend National Park in Texas. I departed Moscow on the same route I took when I first entered Idaho in the late summer of 1974; I followed the Clearwater and Lochsa rivers back into western Montana. After driving up and over Lolo Pass, I headed south along the Bitterroot Valley to Lost Trail Pass and into eastern Idaho along the highway bordered on the east by the Beaverhead mountain range and on the west by the Lemhi range. I camped in the Bridger-Teton National Forest in Jackson Hole, Wyoming. The bed of my pickup truck had a hard-sided cover over it that served as my camper. I had all my belongings, which included my boxed-up stereo components, my sleeping bag and pad, my backpacks, and my suitcase with my clothes. I had enough room to set up my sleeping pad and bag to one side of my belongings. I spent the next day touring Grand Teton National Park and the National Elk Refuge. I drove from the Jackson Hole area to Pinedale, Wyoming, where I planned to camp at a nearby campground. At Pinedale, I purchased food for supper and drove east toward the Wind River Range. I was not familiar with the area and was hoping to camp near Squaretop Mountain and the Green River Lakes. I learned of that area from Steve Wirt and wanted to see the scenic area he had described to me.

I drove up a Forest Service Road to the Fremont Lake campground about seven miles from Pinedale. As soon as I left the grocery store and headed up the gravel road, I looked in the rearview mirror and saw a sheriff's patrol car following me. I watched my speed and assumed he was going somewhere else. As I progressed up the road, the patrol car continued to follow me until I reached the Fremont Lake campground. I drove into the campground loop road and scoped out the campsites, all of which were empty. When I reached the entrance to the loop road, the sheriff's patrol car was parked on the road leading up to the campground. I decided to explore a side road adjacent to the campground, and as I turned up the side road, I looked in my rearview mirror and saw the patrol car's roof-mounted red light flashing. I stopped my truck and made the mistake of getting out of my vehicle to ask the sheriff's deputy if there was a problem. "You drove the wrong way on a one-way road," the deputy barked. The sign designating the one-way route was a small wooden sign measuring five or six inches by 12 inches and painted brown. "I didn't see the small sign, sir," I responded. "Let me see your driver's license," he ordered. My wallet and driver's license were on the dashboard of my truck. During long drives, I would place my wallet there instead of keeping it in my pants pocket. "My driver's license is in my wallet, which is in the truck; I'll go get it," I informed him. That was my second mistake. The deputy stiffened his stance as I walked to my pickup truck. When I walked back to him with my wallet in hand, I saw his right hand was close to his gun's holster. I handed him my driver's license, and he asked me what I was doing there and where I was going. I told him I was looking for a campsite and traveling home to Texas. The deputy looked at my Idaho driver's license for what seemed like minutes and then said, "Well, Mr. Ramsey, I'm going to give you a warning this time, but if I ever see you here again…" He handed me my driver's license, and I walked back to my truck. I was furious but suppressed my anger. I returned to my truck and headed back to Pinedale, wanting nothing more than to leave Wyoming and camp somewhere else. As I drove to Pinedale, I thought of the friendship Bob and Barbara had bestowed on me when I worked in the Medicine Wheel Ranger District in the Bighorn Mountains three years prior. "This is not the Wyoming I remember," I thought and continued south toward Utah. Darkness was settling in when I departed Pinedale. I was tired of driving and hungry, fueled onward by my fury at my treatment by the deputy. I assumed he had followed my truck out of Pinedale as it had Idaho license plates.

A few years later, when I worked with the U.S. Fish and Wildlife Service in Cheyenne, Wyoming, I learned that law enforcement agents typically stopped vehicles with out-of-state license plates for exceeding the speed limit by five miles per hour. I drove south towards Rock Springs,

Wyoming, and breathed a sigh of relief when I crossed the state line into Utah. I continued driving until I reached the forested foothills of the Uinta Mountains. I spotted a side road leading into the forest and found a suitable site for camping. The next morning, I resumed my journey south toward Vernal, Utah, and into Dinosaur National Monument. I resumed my role as a tourist, and everything was right with my world.

I spent most of my time at the Dinosaur Quarry Exhibit Hall at Dinosaur National Monument. I marveled at the dinosaur fossilized bones embedded in the rock face within the exhibit hall. With many miles still ahead of me, I concluded my visit and drove west towards Steamboat Springs, Colorado. Spending two winters in the snow-covered landscape of the Flathead National Forest, I was curious to see some of the ski areas of Colorado. What little experience I had skiing was limited to cross-country skiing and one day of downhill skiing with Gary Koehler at Big Mountain near Whitefish, Montana. Suffice it to say, trying to downhill ski on cross-country skis with no ski lessons was challenging, to say the least. I'm sure the lift operators and ski patrols traded stories of the buffoon skiing downhill with skinny skis who could not compensate for the momentum of the moving chairlift and the pull of gravity at the top of the mountain demonstrating to three and four-year-old skiers how not to get off the chairlift at the top of the ski run.

At Steamboat Springs, I walked along the main street to stretch my legs and grab a bite to eat. From Steamboat Springs, I made my way along Highway 40 to Dillon, Colorado. Dillon's major landmark is Dillon Reservoir, a 3,233 acre reservoir that provides water to Denver, Colorado. The town of Dillon and the reservoir are surrounded by the Gore, Williams Fork, and Ten Mile mountain ranges with several peaks ranging in elevation from slightly over 13,000 ft to 14,278 ft, hence the name of the county, Summit. As I took in the beauty of all these snow-covered peaks, I was smitten by this country and hoped to someday live in an area like this. Seeing the towering, rocky peaks of the Tetons and Wind River Range in Wyoming, followed by the mountains in Summit County, Colorado, I thought, "The enormity of these mountains is something mankind cannot destroy." Twenty to thirty minutes later, my drive to Leadville took me past large tailings ponds and eventually past the Climax Molybdenum mine. Molybdenum mining at the foot of Bartlett Mountain began in earnest in 1914. The view of the gigantic hollowed outside of the mountain quashed my perception that mountains were invincible to the hand of man.

My route from Leadville took me to the Great Sand Dunes National Monument, the site of the tallest sand dunes in North America. According to the U.S. National Park Service, the dunes originated from a sand sheet left behind after a huge lake in the San Luis Valley receded when the lake's water pressure broke through volcanic rock and drained south into the Rio Grande. Over time, prevailing winds blew the sand up against the foot of the Sangre de Cristo mountains to the east. The sand dune area was designated as a national monument in 1932. Sixty-eight years later, Congress designated the Great Sand Dunes National Monument as a national park and preserve.

From the San Luis Valley, I drove south to New Mexico. My many discussions with Pat Aguilar at the University of Idaho piqued my curiosity about the southern extension of the Rocky Mountains in Northern New Mexico. From Taos, I took the High Road from Taos to Santa Fe. This highway winds through the foothills of the southern extension of the Sangre de Cristo mountains and passes through small farms and towns dating back to the 1700s when this area was a Spanish colony. I passed small stores with signs reading *"La Tiendita,"* (the little store). The area exuded pride in its cultural roots and history. I was enamored with the area as I flashed back to South Texas, where the Tejano and Mexican American cultures had been suppressed and oppressed for almost 150 years. From the tiny village of Vallecitos, I approached Peñasco, Pat Aguilar's hometown. After stopping and asking a local for directions to Pat's parent's house, I stopped at their house to introduce myself, but much to my dismay, they were not home. I continued driving the High Road to Santa Fe. I was enthralled with Santa Fe, its adobe houses, and its embrace of multiple cultures: Native American, Spanish, Mexican, and Anglo.

My next tourist stop was at Carlsbad Caverns National Park near Carlsbad, New Mexico. This national park has no campgrounds, so I spent two nights at a commercial campground within the city limits of Carlsbad. At the caverns, I took in the evening flight of Mexican free-tailed bats, also known as the Brazilian free-tailed bat. I joined other park visitors and sat on benches around the natural entrance to the cavern. The park guide informed the audience that one bat would initially fly out of the cavern entrance, followed by a stream of bats flying outward and upward toward the desert sky in search of food, primarily flying insects. According to the National Park Service, between 200 thousand and 500 hundred thousand bats roost in Carlsbad Caverns. The colony declined from slightly over 8 million bats in 1936 to an estimated 200,000 in 1973, with DDT and other organochlorine pesticides as the likely cause of the decline. We sat and waited as the sun set in the west. Eventually, one bat flew out of the cave's entrance. Several minutes later, a tornado-like mass of bats swirled out of the dark hole in the limestone. I explored the cave with other park visitors; we were all in awe of the eight-acre Big Room, which is the largest, readily accessible cave chamber in North America. I also visited the Living Desert Zoo and Gardens State Park in Carlsbad. The park provided exhibits of plants and wildlife native to the Chihuahuan desert. I was rewarded with the colorful blooms of several species of cacti, including strawberry cactus, claret cup cactus, and cholla.

After a week of driving and sleeping in the back of my pickup truck, I was ready to arrive home and be with my family. I decided not to continue to Big Bend National Park and headed for South Texas. I spent a month living with my parents, trying to adjust from two years of living in the backcountry of Spotted Bear and one winter of living in solitude with Tanner as my only companion, with occasional visits from Howard, Steve, and Maurice. My application for the wilderness ranger job fell through, and I worried about my job prospects. I learned more about my parents' financial dilemma and the possibility of my Dad losing his ranch.

Towards the end of the month, I received a telephone call from Dr. James Peek, a University of Idaho wildlife professor, informing me about a summer job opening at the Bitterroot National Forest in Darby, Montana. I mailed my application for the biological technician job and hoped for the best. A week or so later, I received a call from the Darby Ranger District informing me that I was accepted for the job. The first week of June, I packed my clothes, backpacking and camping gear, and my stereo for my return to Montana. Once again, I had to say goodbye to my dog Tanya as I could not take her with me, knowing that finding a place to live would be much harder with a dog.

Saying goodbye to my parents, especially my dad, was heart-wrenching, knowing what he was going through with the prospect of losing his ranch. As I drove out of their driveway and onto the highway, I glanced back towards my parents' house. I saw my Dad standing in the driveway looking at me, driving away and then bowing his head downward. During my prior departures to undergraduate school at Nacogdoches, Texas, and to Idaho and Montana, he wished me well and did not hold me back. This time, a moment that still fills my soul with tears, I saw a broken man displaying sadness that I was leaving. Tears welled up in my eyes as I drove off; the burning desire to help him pulled me back and conflicted with the push for the job, steering me northward. Leaving home for undergraduate school was hard, but this was heart-wrenching by several orders of magnitude. The thought of my father standing there with a bowed head kept playing in my head. I stopped for lunch at a rest area along Interstate 10; tears welled up in my eyes as I thought of my Dad and silently cried. I revered my Dad, whom I thought invincible, who, as a 19-year-old, survived the horrors of World War II in the Battle of the Bulge and two decades later braved the flood waters of Hurricane Beulah to rescue and deliver aid to families in the Encino area whose homes were inundated or could not leave their homes to obtain groceries or other essentials due to flooded roads. For the first time in my life, I saw my father as a broken man and vulnerable. The image of him standing with bowed head enveloped me like a pall, obliterating my desire to live and work in the mountains. My overwhelming desire to help my father and my mother compelled me to help them financially and learn more about the economic predicament they found themselves in. At the same time, I thought about my future, both personal and professional.

Chapter 11: The Mountains Are Calling

Hamilton, Montana, is approximately two thousand miles and a three-day drive from my hometown of Encino, Texas. I remember little of this road trip with one exception: it gave me lots of time to think about my immediate future after the conclusion of my upcoming temporary job with the U.S. Forest Service in the Bitterroot National Forest. My thoughts drifted to assisting my parents with their financial dilemma and the prospect of my father losing his ranch.

Instead of driving up I-25 and I-90 to Montana, I turned west onto I-70 at Denver and proceeded 157 miles to Glenwood Springs, an almost three-hour drive. From Glenwood Springs, I continued to Rifle, Colorado, as the sun settled into the western horizon. At Rifle, I turned north onto Colorado Highway 13, and on the outskirts of town, I encountered a state patrol car parked along the highway with red lights flashing and the officer stopping northbound traffic. The patrol officer asked me if I was alone, and I answered that I was, and all I had in the cargo area of my pickup truck were my personal belongings. The officer informed me that a prisoner had escaped from jail and advised me not to pick up any hitchhikers. I thanked the officer and proceeded north toward Meeker, Colorado. Years later, when I worked with the U.S. Fish and Wildlife Service (FWS), I mentioned that experience to an FWS employee who worked in the FWS Ecological Services Field Office in Grand Junction, Colorado. He looked at me and said, "That was Ted Bundy!" At the time I made the drive on June 7, 1977, I did not know that it was Bundy, the notorious serial killer convicted of kidnapping, raping, and murdering several young women and girls during the 1970s. Before his execution in 1989, Bundy confessed to 30 homicides committed in seven states between 1974 and 1978.

Upon arriving at the Darby Ranger Station, I inquired about apartments or houses for rent. The town of Darby is small, and housing was limited, so I focused my search for housing in Hamilton, 20 miles north of Darby. I found an apartment for rent in a picturesque, three-story, white Victorian house split into three apartments. The landlady named Billie lived in her half of the first floor, and the second half served as an apartment. The second floor was divided into two apartments, each with a bedroom on the third floor. Moving in did not take me that long; all I had was my stereo, a cardboard box full of my record albums, clothes, kitchen items, and backpacking-camping gear.

I reported for work at the Darby Ranger District and learned that as a biological technician, I would be conducting big game surveys in proposed timber sale units. The surveys entailed hiking transects in the timber sale units and counting and identifying groups of fecal pellets to determine elk and mule deer use. I hiked many miles every day and climbed a couple of thousand feet, if not more, in elevation. Every day, my routine began with a quick visit with my immediate supervisor, grabbing the appropriate topographic map, climbing into the Forest Service pickup truck, driving to a proposed timber sale unit, and beginning my hike up the mountain slope through the timber. Whenever I encountered a group of pellets, I would press the button on the tally counter with my thumb. After completing the survey for a timber sale unit, I would record the total number of tallies in my pocket-sized notebook. Although the work was repetitive and uneventful, I enjoyed spending my time hiking and soaking up the forested mountain landscape. At the end of each work day, I submitted my data sheets to a forester, a permanent employee of the Forest Service, who would then use the data in his preparation of an environmental assessment for proposed timber sales in the Darby Ranger District as required by the National Environmental Policy Act (NEPA). NEPA requires the federal government to "use all practicable means to create and maintain conditions under which man and nature can exist in productive harmony." As President Richard M. Nixon signed NEPA into law on January 1, 1970, he proclaimed, "I think that 1970 will be known as the year of the beginning, in which we really began to move on the problems of clean air and clean water and open spaces for the future generations of America." Section 102, Title I, of the Act requires federal agencies to incorporate environmental considerations in their planning and decision-making through a systematic interdisciplinary approach. Specifically, NEPA tasked all federal agencies to "prepare detailed statements assessing the environmental impact of and alternatives to major federal actions significantly affecting the environment. These statements are commonly referred to as Environmental Impact Statements (EIS) and Environmental Assessments (EA)."

The west side of the Bitterroot National Forest included a portion of the Selway-Bitterroot Wilderness Area. I backpacked into the wilderness area during a weekend in June with a coworker. After work, we departed for the trailhead and headed up the trail, hoping to do some fishing at some small subalpine lakes. We found a suitable campsite, and since we expected clear weather, I did not pack my tent; I set up my sleeping pad and sleeping bag under the stars. As soon as the sun dipped behind the mountains, squadrons of mosquitos descended upon us.

One slap of my hand contained a dozen or more winged casualties. I asked my coworker if he had any mosquito repellent, as I had forgotten to purchase some. He went through his backpack and came up empty-handed. We hurriedly prepared our individual meals, mostly one-handed, as our free hand was busy swatting mosquitos. After I finished my meal and cleaned up the cooking gear and mess kit, I crawled into my sleeping bag to avoid the blood-sucking marauders. I pulled the hood of my mummy bag over my head and pulled tight on the drawstring, leaving only a small opening the size of a quarter. The night sky was illuminated by a full moon, and through that small hole, I could see mosquitos circling above it, ready to enter my bag to consume some of my blood. Cold air the next morning eliminated the onslaught. Colder air causes the mosquitos to seek shelter, as temperatures of 50°F or less cause these cold-blooded invertebrates to become lethargic. When I rose to greet the day, I found dozens of squashed mosquitos peppered throughout the inside of my sleeping bag. The next evening as the sun set, my hiking partner was rifling through his backpack; he paused, turned and looked at me, and said, "Pete, you're going to kill me." "What?" I replied sardonically, expecting him to pull out his mosquito repellent. Sure enough, he slowly pulled his hand out of his backpack and revealed a small bottle of mosquito repellent. We both learned a lesson that weekend. One – always pack mosquito repellent, and two – don't backpack in early to mid-June at the peak of snowmelt as the ponded meltwater creates ample habitat for mosquitoes.

My next backpacking trip into the Selway-Bitterroot Wilderness Area later in the summer was relatively mosquito-free. One of my co-workers asked if I would like to assist Greg, the U.S. Forest Service fisheries biologist, with an alpine lake fish habitat survey in the Selway-Bitterroot Wilderness Area. The task, if I decided to take it, involved carrying the fisheries biologist's fishing float tube (aka belly boat) and float tube fins. I did not hesitate and agreed to assist with the fish surveys. The following week, I backpacked into the Selway-Bitterroot Wilderness with Greg, beginning our trek up the Tin Cup trail west of Darby and made our way seven to eight miles up the drainage and then hiked two miles up a side trail to Kerlee Lake at 7,021 feet in elevation.

After Greg completed his survey of Kerlee Lake, we hiked back to the Tin Cup Creek trail. Greg identified a lake in the Chaffin Creek drainage south of Tin Cup Creek as next on his survey. Greg had the remarkable ability to hold two identical black and white aerial photos side by side two feet or so from his eyes, and see the image in 3-D. By doing this, he was able to select an off-trail pathway up the ridge that separated the Tin Cup Creek drainage from the Chaffin Creek drainage. The Bitterroot Range extends along the Idaho-Montana border for 300 miles—Creek drainages on the Montana side flow west to east towards the Bitterroot

River. Our trek from the Tin Cup Creek trail up and over the ridge to Chaffin Creek involved hiking three miles from an elevation of 5,742 feet at Tin Cup Creek to the ridge dividing the two drainages at 9,000 ft in elevation. As we neared the ridge, we had to work our way up a boulder field. Hiking up a boulder field entails stepping from one boulder to another, with some boulders capable of shifting when walking on them. The risk of twisting an ankle or, worse, broken bones is high. The slope was steep, requiring me, at times, to hold on to large boulders with my hands to steady myself. As we inched our way up, I saw darkening clouds approaching us, signaling rain and a high possibility of lightning. I tried to hurry but realized that I had to tread carefully so as not to injure myself. As the distant rumble of thunder increased in volume, I scanned the boulder field for a gap between boulders large enough to take cover and avoid a lightning strike. I also knew I would have to remove my backpack since it had an external aluminum frame—a perfect lightning rod. After what seemed like hours, we completed the ascent of the boulder field and stood near the ridgetop, dividing the two drainages. "Wait!" Greg shouted, "I've got to take a picture." He turned around, grabbed his camera, pointed it to the dark, ominous cloud approaching from the northwest, and took a picture. A slow drumbeat of raindrops hitting the ground warned us of an impending drenching unless we quickly took shelter. We quickly walked to a rock wall with a slight angle, providing somewhat of a partial shelter. I took off my backpack and quickly pulled out my space blanket to provide Greg and me shelter from the pouring rain. Almost as quickly as the storm overcame us, it then dissipated. Clear blue skies greeted us from the gloom of the thunderstorm. We worked our way down the ridge towards Tamarack and Hart lakes within the Chaffin Creek drainage.

We set up my two-person tent on a flat-topped rock outcrop overlooking Tamarack Lake at 7,425 ft in elevation. Greg and I hiked down to the lake; he inflated the float tube and put on his chest waders and fins. I remained at the shoreline, assembled my fly rod, and proceeded to fly fish as Greg made his way across the lake. As soon as my fly settled on the lake's surface, I felt a strong tug on the fly line. As I tugged back and placed tension on the fly line, the hooked rainbow trout leaped out of the water and shook its body from side to side, trying to free itself. I carefully played the fish, and after landing it on the shore, I estimated it at

16 inches in length. I cast again and scored another 16-inch fish on the first cast. After the third cast and another large trout, Greg looked at me from the middle of the lake and shouted, "Hey, you're supposed to be working!" "I am," I shouted back, "I'm checking to see if there are any fish in this lake, and there are!" Greg finished sounding the lake to document its depth and hurriedly paddled his float tube back to shore. He assembled his fly rod and reel and joined me in fishing the lake. He, too, succeeded in catching large rainbow trout with every cast. Given the size of the fish, I kept one and released all the others I caught. Greg had the advantage of his float tube and fished more area of the lake. After Greg caught two 16-inch rainbows, he asked, "How many fish can you eat?" "As big as they are, one and a half," I replied. During the trek, we both had our fill of freeze-dried meals and looked forward to eating fish for supper. Greg packed aluminum foil and butter specifically to cook any fish we caught. "After we have three fish, we release the rest," Greg proposed. What followed was the best fly fishing I had ever experienced in my life. I lost count of how many large rainbow trout I caught and released. As much as I was enjoying the angling experience of a lifetime, pragmatic thoughts focused my attention less on

continuing to catch huge rainbow trout and paying attention to the sun working its way towards the western ridge tops and the need to start a campfire to cook the fish we kept. "I'm heading up to our campsite to get a fire started to cook our fish," I shouted to Greg. I proceeded to clean the one fish I kept as Greg continued to fish from his float tube. I climbed up to our campsite, gathered some wood, and built a small campfire. Thirty minutes or so later, Greg marches up to the campsite with a big grin on his face, holding his two 16-inch fish and a huge 21-inch rainbow. "Hey! You were supposed to keep only two and release the rest!" I admonished him. "Yeah, but I figured you would not believe me if I told you I had caught a 21-inch rainbow, so I kept it as proof. We can eat it for breakfast," Greg answered. The following week, we backpacked up another drainage in the Selway-Bitterroot wilderness. We hiked up a very steep trail to a cirque lake. As Greg floated out on the lake, I fished and caught a beautiful cutthroat trout in full display of its spawning colors. I released the fish as we still had miles to hike before setting up camp at our destination for the day.

The sun-draped Bitterroot Mountains to the west greeted my daily morning drive to work from my apartment in Hamilton to the Darby ranger station. Trapper Peak, at 10,157 feet in elevation and 12 miles south-southwest of Darby, beckoned. This peak is the highest one in the Bitterroot Mountains. I learned from my co-workers at the ranger station that a hiking trail led up to the summit, which made me determined to climb up during the weekend. In August, I did just that: I packed a lunch, drove to the trailhead south of Darby, and began my hike up to the summit. I reached the top of Trapper Peak at noon after hiking 4 miles and ascending a little over 3,700 feet in elevation.

A panoramic view of a sea of mountains north, west, south, and east filled me with a sense of wonder at the beauty of the rugged landscape. At the summit, I encountered other hikers signing their names on the summit notebook or registry. Summit registries contain a record of visitors to the summit of a mountain and are usually enclosed in a weatherproof metal container. I added my name to the registry and talked to the hikers briefly. After their departure, I ate my lunch, found a flat spot to lie down, and took a short nap. Twenty or 30 minutes later, I woke up, stood, and took in the view before hiking to the trailhead. A column of smoke pierced the clear blue sky to the northeast. I realized the fire was in the Darby Ranger District. I grabbed my pack and hiked to the trailhead as fast as possible.

As I drove into the Ranger District parking lot, I was greeted with a bustle of activity. I walked into a group of Forest Service staff and encountered an outstretched hand holding a yellow US Forest Service fire shirt. "Here, put this on," the employee barked as he handed out shirts. The US Forest Service uses yellow, 100 percent cotton shirts for wildland firefighting to protect firefighters. The color yellow is more visible in dark, smoke-filled areas. Unlike synthetic fabrics such as nylon, cotton clothing will not melt and adhere to the skin in extreme heat. I also took the required Step Test to demonstrate my physical fitness for wildland firefighting. By 5:30 pm, I was out on the perimeter of the fire digging fire line with a crew of 18 to 20 people. Fireline crews can divide into squads with four to six team members. Crews use Pulaski's, shovels, rakes, and other tools to clear a fire line. The lead person in the squad clears pine duff, twigs and branches, and each squad member that follows makes the fire line wider. Digging a fire line is hard work and is incredibly taxing after hiking a total of 4 miles up a 10,157-foot peak and back with only a sandwich for lunch and no supper. The intense roar of flames racing up the branches of a live pine tree drowned out the crackling of burning pine duff and downed branches. At times, the heat from the fire pressed on my face, and it felt like I was looking into a hot stove oven only inches away from the heating element. Our crew continued digging a fire line as darkness descended upon us, with headlamps and flames our only sources of light. As the night progressed, exhaustion crept up on me as the previous exertion of climbing up and down Trapper Peak took its toll. By three o'clock in the morning, my body just wanted to lie down and sleep. "If I sit down, I'll fall asleep. If I fall asleep, I'll die," I thought to myself. I willed myself to continue digging the fire line, shaking my head in an effort to fight the drowsy feeling and drooping eyelids. Somehow, I managed to stay awake and see daylight that morning.

Our fire line crew was replaced that morning, and we were treated to a hot breakfast at the fire camp. After gulping down my meal, I found a somewhat level spot away from the activity, lay down, and fell asleep. Later during the day, smoke-jumpers from the smoke-jumper base in Missoula descended from the sky after jumping out of their DC-3 airplane. We were informed that this fire was a training opportunity for the smoke-jumpers, who were usually deployed to fires in remote roadless areas. Our fire line crew went back into the perimeter of the fire to dig more fire lines. Someone yelled out that an airborne tanker was going to drop fire retardant near our crew, and we were instructed to lie flat on the ground. The force of the fire retardant could knock a person off their feet, resulting in serious injury. Following the aerial drop, some of the firefighters got drenched with fire retardant and used their purple-stained splotches on their hard hats as bragging rights.

After the fire line was secured and the fire contained, we began the fire mop-up phase. Mop-up is a dirty task crucial in ensuring a wildfire is out and won't flare up and reignite more of the forest. Crews walk the burned area, looking for smoldering embers and telltale wisps of smoke as they run their gloved hands through the blanket of ash covering the ground to detect hot spots. Each member of the mop-up crew carries a backpack fire pump, also referred to by fire crews as a piss bag, consisting of a bladder containing water and a small-diameter hose extending from the bladder to a hand-operated pump. The firefighter uses the backpack fire pump to extinguish hot spots during mop-up operations. Agitating several inches of a gray shroud of ash by walking, digging, or spraying water on it suspends fine particles less than 2.5 micrometers in diameter into the air and are inhaled by the firefighter. At the end of each day, I was blowing black gunk out of my nose and concluded that although I could earn quite a bit of money as a wildland firefighter, I did not want to shorten my life by jeopardizing my lungs.

Towards the end of the summer, Jeff Koloseus, one of the engineering technicians, invited several seasonal employees to his rental residence for dinner. Jeff lived in Fort Collins and was an engineering major at Colorado State University. He made and served us avocado omelets. I watched him as he prepared the omelets and took mental notes. I still make avocado omelets for breakfast on weekends to this day, 45 years later. Other memorable events from my summer job included a visit from Esther and Wayne, watching the first Star Wars movie in a theater in Missoula, learning about the death of Elvis Presley on the radio, and learning that Billie, my landlady, was a cat person. To this day, I do not know how many cats lived with her, but during hot summer days, odors, probably from several cat litter boxes, wafted up to my apartment. My summer job at the Bitterroot National Forest ended, and I started my journey back to Texas with the pall of an uncertain future for me and more so for my parents.

CHAPTER 12: SMALL TOWN NEWS

I spent nine months living with my parents in Encino, mailing job applications, and working odd jobs in the local area. I managed to earn some money cutting live oak from my father's land for firewood and selling it. During the 1970s, my only access to job openings was through the classified section of the Corpus Christi newspaper as well as through word-of-mouth from people I knew. On occasion, I would call Maurice and update him on my fruitless efforts to obtain a wildlife biology job, although all of my applications were for jobs in the Western United States. Most, if not all, of my job applications were for federal employment with the U.S. Forest Service and the U.S. Fish and Wildlife Service. I gave up on landing a wildlife job with a state wildlife management agency as most agencies at that time required that a new hire start as a game warden; I was not interested in law enforcement. My older brother, Ernesto, constantly implored me to stop being picky and just get a job. Ernesto pointed out that there were plenty of jobs in housing construction and the oil and gas industry. He received the Corpus Christi newspaper, the "Corpus Christi

Caller," and would scan the Classified Section for job announcements.

My brother informed me of a biology research assistant job at Texas A & I University, now Texas A&M University-Kingsville, in Kingsville, Texas. I applied and got selected. During my first day on the job, I learned that the work involved assisting with a research study of black drum, a game fish inhabiting Baffin Bay. Baffin Bay is a mostly hypersaline shallow inlet bay of the Laguna Madre estuarine ecosystem with an average depth of eight feet and a surface area of 100 square miles. I was conflicted after learning that the fieldwork entailed going out on a boat and sampling fish in these hypersaline waters. First, I did not know how to swim, although I'd be wearing a personal floatation device. Two, I knew absolutely nothing about operating a boat. Three, I knew nothing about fisheries biology and management. Four, the outside temperature during my first day at the university was over 95 degrees with very high humidity. My self-diagnosed affliction with PWRSS (Post Wolverine Research Study Syndrome) enveloped my mind and spirit, and I called in the next day and informed the lead research biologist that I decided not to go through with the job. Looking back years later, I wonder what direction my life would have taken had I stayed with that job. My brother was beside himself, incredulous with my decision. Eventually, I realized that I had to take a job in South Texas.

Some weeks later, my brother informed me that the local newspaper in Kingsville, the Kingsville Record and Bishop News had a job opening for a news reporter. The newspaper reported news from Kingsville as well as the nearby town of Bishop, which is located seven miles to the northeast. I had taken journalism and photography courses in high school and undergraduate school and served as the sports editor of my high school's newspaper in my journalism class. I applied for the job and was hired. Although this was not my long-term career choice, I figured the experience would help with my goal of writing articles for wildlife magazines. I worked with the newspaper for nine months and made friends with all the staff. They all were enjoyable to work with; the publisher and his wife, the copy editor, were the exceptions. I learned a lot from each of them: news reporting and writing skills, pasting up the newspaper layout, composing my news stories directly to a word processor versus writing it out on paper first and then 'typing' it onto the computer. From the publisher and the copy editor, I learned how not to treat employees. The reporters, the publisher, and two copy editors had desks in a large open newsroom. Although the publisher never gave me grief, I saw him prance around the newsroom softly clapping his hands, gleefully announcing that the news story of a barroom brawl in Bishop resulting in the death of a person meant the sale of more newspapers. Several months into the job, I became aware of the underlying drama and the animosity of the reporters toward the publisher and his wife. Upon completing a news story, reporters would have one of the two copy editors review the news story for factual content, sources, and correct typos. If I saw that the publisher's wife was busy reviewing news stories, I would give my news copy to the second copy editor to review. Some of the news reporters advised me not to give my copies to the second editor to review. I asked why, adding that she was not currently editing the copy. One of the reporters advised me to look back toward the second copy editor's desk after I placed my news story on her desk. I followed his advice, and after I sat back down at my desk, I looked back towards the second copy editor's desk and watched the publisher's wife literally take my copy from the copy editor's hands and take it to her own desk. Several minutes later, I asked the reporter why the publisher's wife had done that and was informed that she did not want the other copy editor to review the stories. "But she does not have anything to do," I replied. I shoved the drama to the back of my mind and focused on the positive aspects of my job.

I settled into my job as a cub reporter and quickly made friends with the news reporters, the editor, the advertising staff, the printers, and the front desk receptionists. When the editor and the reporters learned that I could not only take pictures but develop the film and print the photographs, I was tasked with processing the film and photos for all the reporters, a task I gladly accepted. Some days, I would spend eight hours in the dark room, stepping outside after work with dilated pupils as my retina and optic nerves would scream bloody murder, protesting the bright daylight. I was also assigned to cover local city and county governments, as well as the police and fire departments. I did write a news story involving a fish kill in Baffin Bay, a story that was right up my alley. I quoted Texas

Parks and Wildlife Department (TPWD) fisheries biologist Dick Harrington in Corpus Christi, Texas. Little did I realize then that I would work with Harrington two or three years later. I was not keen on writing 'hard news' stories but did get to write several feature stories, some of which were quite interesting for a small town.

I observed and wrote a story on a local 16-year-old girl flying a small airplane and doing three take-offs and landings at the county airport to earn her pilot's license. After the teenage girl completed her three 'touch-and-go's,' her flight instructor coaxed me to climb into the cockpit and fly with him. He initially wanted me to sit in the pilot's seat to see what it felt like to fly a small airplane. I informed him that I had ridden in a small airplane before and would ride as a passenger, and he could fly the plane. Thank you very much. The instructor hoped that by going up on the flight, he would snag me as a student pilot. I climbed onto the co-pilot seat, fastened my seatbelt, and we took off. Once the flight instructor gained his preferred altitude, he began his spiel on flying an airplane. After he described the controls, he said, "Grab the wheel so you can see what it feels like." The 'wheel' he referred to is technically the yoke, and it allows the pilot to move the airplane "up," "down," "over left," and "over right." Instead of grabbing the yoke, I gently touched it with my fingertips so as not to influence the flight instructor's ability to control the airplane. "How does it feel to be flying an airplane," he barked over the roar of the engine. I glanced to my left and saw his hands were not on the yoke. I gripped the yoke tightly. The flight instructor had me flying the airplane towards Kingsville seven or eight miles to the east. As we got closer to the city, he asked me to pull back on the yoke slightly to gain altitude. He then saw a radio tower as we neared the city, so he took over the controls, pulled back on the yoke, and increased the throttle to climb up to the required altitude. Before reaching Kingsville, he turned the airplane around, and we headed back to the airport. On the way, he demonstrated the use of the rudder pedals and the yoke. "If you pull the wheel back, you go up," he said as the airplane climbed up, "and if you push the wheel forward, you go down." He then said, "You don't want to do this," as he quickly pushed the yoke forward. We descended rapidly, and my internal organs protested. Almost as quickly as we descended, he said, "And you don't want to do this," he quickly yanked the wheel or yoke down and to the left, causing the airplane to bank sharply to the left. Again, my internal organs protested the negative g-forces. "If you don't want me to throw up in your airplane, don't do that," I yelled at him. After we landed, I thought of the times I flew with Howard in Montana and thanked my lucky stars that my first experience flying in a small private airplane was with him. I only experienced a rapid descent with him once while radio-tracking wolverines over the Bob Marshall wilderness. A cold front blew in from Canada, slapping the Cessna with a downdraft that quickly pushed the airplane downward. My 35mm camera rose from my lap upwards and level with my face, and after my internal organs ceased their protest, I looked to the left at Howard and saw him adjust the throttle, look intently at the instrument panel, and grab the yoke with both hands. "We just descended three hundred feet," Howard calmly informed me as he kept his airplane level. The cold front blanketed the Swan Range with clouds, restricting Howard's ability to fly up and over the mountain range to Kalispell.

Howard followed the South Fork of the Flathead northward as the turbulence caused the airplane to rise and fall like a yo-yo repeatedly. As we flew over a backcountry airstrip near Meadow Creek Gorge and the airstrip at Spotted Bear, I thought to myself, "I hope Howard lands here," but he kept going northward. He flew below the cloud cover and safely made our way out by flying through Bad Rock Canyon, where the confluence of the South Fork, Middle Fork, and North Fork of the Flathead River converge and flow onto the Flathead Valley. After we landed and taxied at the Kalispell Airport, I quickly got out of the airplane, looked at Howard, and said, "I'm glad you landed when you did because I was really close to throwing up." Howard calmly replied, "You should have said something earlier; I would have landed at Spotted Bear."

Other feature stories I wrote included interviews with a couple from Denmark on a bicycle tour around the world; Navy instructor pilot, Lt. Cmdr. Bill Asbell from the Kingsville Naval Air Station; a retired Border Patrol agent; a World War II veteran and survivor of the Bataan Death March in the Philippines; and a Texas A&I University professor and two graduate students. Asbell flew his own Pitts Special biplane and performed aerial aerobatics at airshows. I quoted Retired Border Patrol agent Carlos Torres stating that conservatives blamed the Immigration and Naturalization Service director Leonel Castillo as too lenient on Mexican immigrants and that Castillo "opened the border" to the immigrants. Torres declared those comments as untrue. Some things never change as immigration remains a contentious issue and political hot potato over 40 years later.

The most interesting interview was with Texas A&I University biology professor Dr. James E. Gillespie. Bob Odom, the newspaper editor, handed me a news release from TPWD on the brown recluse spider and instructed me to interview Dr. Gillespie at Texas A&I University to add local relevance to the story. The spider is so named for its shy nature as it hides during the day and is more active at night. Its venom causes necrosis of tissue surrounding the site of the bite. Dr. Gillespie exhibited no fear of the small brown spider as he removed it from a jar and let it crawl on his hand. He calmly commented, "The brown recluse will not bite unless provoked." Dr. Gillespie lifted his eyes from his hand for a few seconds, and the spider was gone. I could feel the nerves in my legs going into DefCon 2, a hypersensitive condition to detect an arachnid crawling up my leg. Several tense seconds elapsed before we saw the spider crawling on the floor. Gillespie picked up the escapee and placed it back into the jar.

After nine months with the newspaper, I applied and got accepted for a one-year temporary job with the U.S. Fish and Wildlife Service in Albuquerque, New Mexico. I announced to the newspaper staff that I had accepted a job with the U.S. Fish and Wildlife Service, and I was touched that they were sad to see me leave. I mentioned the job offer and my acceptance to my parents, and my dad expressed sorrow at my leaving for the first time. He was always supportive of all my previous moves to distant universities and summer jobs with the U.S. Forest Service, with the exception of my move to Hamilton, Montana. "Why do you have to move so far," he asked with sadness in his voice. I always looked up to my father, a role model, a community leader whom local residents respected, a man who projected self-confidence, a survivor of the horrors of World War II, and an individual with a deep religious faith that everything would work itself out. *"Si Dios quiere,"* (God willing) he would say as he dealt with his trials and tribulations. For the first time, I saw him as a vulnerable human being coping with issues weighing heavily on him. I rationalized my departure as an opportunity that could lead to a permanent job and enable me to help my parents weather this storm in their lives. I packed my few belongings and headed to New Mexico.

Chapter 13: The Land of Enchantment

I looked forward to working with the U.S. Fish and Wildlife Service (FWS), although not the prospect of living in a large city with a population of three hundred thousand approximately. After leaving home for undergraduate and graduate schools, I lived in small towns and cities with populations ranging from 2,000 to 22,000 people. I moved into a studio apartment and reported for work at the FWS Ecological Services field office located in a light industrial area near the junction of I-25 and I-40. I joined a staff of eight and two contractors, Eric and Charlie, from New Mexico State University. As a graduate student under Maurice, an employee of the FWS, I was familiar with the agency's research division, national wildlife refuges, and national fish hatcheries, but not the Ecological Services Division. The FWS Division of Ecological Services began as the Office of River Basin Studies (ORBS) in 1945 in response to massive water development plans by the U.S. Army Corps of Engineers (COE) and the Bureau of Reclamation (USBR).

The water development projects involved thousands of acres of land and hundreds of miles of streams potentially impacted by river diversions, dams, and stream channelization. ORBS staff assessed impacts on fish and wildlife resources and provided recommendations to the COE and USBR to avoid or mitigate those impacts; however, the agencies implemented the FWS recommendations at their discretion. During the late 1960s and early 1970s, environmental awareness enveloped the nation following the publication of Rachel Carson's *Silent Spring* and several catastrophic oil spills. The political climate changed, significantly changing legislation and government programs. Environmental legislation enacted during this time included the National Estuary Protection Act, amendments to the Federal Water Pollution Control Act, and the National Environmental Policy Act of 1969 (NEPA). NEPA resulted in massive changes to water development agencies and required public disclosure of the environmental effects of all Federal programs and projects. In early 1970, as a result of heightened public concerns with air pollution in metropolitan areas, roadsides, parks and natural areas littered with trash, and contamination of municipal water supplies, President Nixon sent Congress a plan to consolidate the environmental oversight and regulatory responsibilities of the federal government under one agency, the Environmental Protection Agency. In 1972, the FWS changed the name of ORBS to the Division of Ecological Services. The Division's mission initially involved continuing the work of assessing federal water development projects as well as determining the impacts of federally permitted or licensed projects impacting coastal and freshwater wetlands, as well as riparian areas.

The Albuquerque Ecological Services (ES) field office staff primarily assessed COE and USBR proposed stream impoundments and flood control projects. My first assignment entailed assisting wildlife biologist Brian Hanson with fieldwork at the Zuni Indian Reservation (the Zuni Pueblo), in western New Mexico, approximately 150 miles west of Albuquerque. The ES field office assisted the USBR Regional Office in Boulder City, Nevada, with fish and wildlife surveys within the reservation. We surveyed tributaries of the Zuni River for Zuni Mountain suckers (*Catostomus discobolus yarrow*) using electrofishing techniques. This species historically occurred in the Zuni River drainage upstream of the Arizona-New Mexico border. The removal of undesirable fish species and the introduction of non-native species to promote sport fishing reduced the population of the native Zuni Mountain suckers. The surveys led by Brian Hanson were the first systematic survey for this species in New Mexico. Brian organized a fish sampling crew that included Youth Conservation Corps staff from the Zuni Pueblo. The USBR Regional Office provided a Bell Jet Ranger helicopter and pilot to ferry electroshocking crews between sampling sites along the Rio Nutria, a tributary of the Zuni River. Merl, a Vietnam veteran and highly experienced helicopter pilot ferried us from site to site, including landing our crew in the narrow Rio Nutria box canyon. Merl found a relatively level landing site within the Box Canyon and dropped us off. He later returned to retrieve our crew after we had completed sampling the stream reach.

Brian also monitored a Gunnison's prairie dog (Cynomys gunnisoni) town in the Rio Nutria drainage for evidence of black-footed ferret (Mustela nigripes) occurrence. Although biologists at that time believed the black-footed ferret was extinct, that did not stop Brian from searching for evidence of this rare animal's existence within the Zuni reservation. Game and trail cameras were not commercially available; however, Brian secured a 35mm camera connected to a device that projected an infrared beam to a receiver. Animals breaking or interrupting the infrared beam triggered the 35mm camera to open its shutter and take a picture. A college intern spent hours reviewing rolls and rolls of film with occasional images of prairie dogs but no ferrets.

Not to be outdone, Brian resorted to spotlighting black-footed ferrets using high-powered lights to locate and identify ferrets during the night. We drove the road up the Rio Nutria to the prairie dog town as the sun was setting in the west. As darkness fell, we each aimed our spotlights out the vehicle's windows, hoping to catch the eyeshine of a ferret. I can't remember what animals we saw, but ferrets were not on the list. After the first night of spotlighting, we attempted to sleep in the vehicle and managed several cat naps but no restful sleep.

We continued spotlighting the prairie dog town the next night with negative results. The next morning, we attempted to drive back to Albuquerque, and I took the first leg of our trip behind the wheel. That was an idiotic thing to do after two consecutive nights with very little sleep. I remember dozing off behind the wheel, snapping out of it, and realizing I was driving on the left side of the highway. "Brian," I yelled, "you need to drive!" Brian woke up from his nap and asked why. "I was driving on the left side of the road," I answered. Since he was also groggy from his nap, I found a wide spot adjacent to the highway, pulled over, and we both decided to sleep before we continued our journey back to Albuquerque. We learned that there was no traffic on the two-lane highway that morning.

My next assignment involved collecting data within the Sevilleta National Wildlife Refuge, a 230,000-acre wildlife sanctuary located 50 miles south of Albuquerque and a quarter mile west of Interstate 25. The refuge was established in 1973 and was largely undeveloped by the FWS in 1978 and 1979, with only a maintenance building located on the refuge near the interstate highway. FWS biologist and project lead Jon Souder assisted with data collection when he could extricate himself from office work. The Rio Salado, an ephemeral stream and tributary of the Rio Grande, bisects the refuge unit west of the interstate. The COE office in Albuquerque provided funds for our wildlife studies on the refuge as well as along the Rio Puerco, which is also a tributary of the Rio Grande. Our field sites along the Rio Puerco were on U.S. Bureau of Land Management (BLM) lands approximately 30 miles north of the refuge. The COE would use our data for a proposed flood and sediment control reservoir project on the Rio Salado.

We characterized the various habitat types on the refuge and sampled small mammals in those habitats. We trapped small mammals in a pinyon-juniper woodland, an open grassland, a saltbush community, and a saltcedar thicket adjacent to the Rio Salado. Saltcedar, also referred to as Tamarix ramosissima, was introduced into the United States from Asia for windbreaks and erosion control and as an ornamental. Saltcedar forms dense thickets, thus displacing cottonwood trees and willows, as well as native riparian shrubs and trees. This invasive species exudes salts from its leaves, hence increasing soil salinity and preventing the growth of native grasses, forbs, and shrubs. Land managers used prescribed burning to control saltcedar; however, studies conducted a decade later showed that burning did not cause widespread mortality of saltcedar.

The saltcedar thickets along the Rio Salado were so dense that John and I had to use a portable, hand-held, gas-powered brush cutter with a ten-inch circular saw blade to cut trails for sampling transects. Since most, if not all, of our field sites were adjacent to the Rio Salado, the riverbed served as our roadway to the sampling transects. I dreaded my first drive up the dry river as I navigated the riverine sand and gravel, praying the vehicle would not get mired in loose sand. A month or so later, I managed to get all four wheels of the 4-wheel-drive government vehicle, a Chevy Blazer sport utility vehicle, stuck in loose sand. It took a student intern and me four hours to free the vehicle using a handyman jack to lift the Blazer high enough to be able to place wood branches under each tire to increase traction. The challenge was finding tree branches in this desert environment.

We collected a lot of data on small mammals inhabiting the Rio Salado floodplain in the Sevilleta Refuge and shared that information with the refuge staff and a biology professor at the University of New Mexico. The bleak and barren landscape along the Rio Puerco provided a stark contrast to the habitats within the refuge. Red clay with scant vegetation dominated the ground surface. We conducted the wildlife surveys during the winter months after completing our work on the refuge during the fall. One cold day, the student intern and I were hunched over recording data using the open tailgate of the Blazer as our desk.

The slight breeze and wind chill caused us to have our coat hoods over our heads. We were out in the middle of nowhere with only the sound of the cold wind blowing against us as we recorded data. "How goes it?" The student and I looked at each other and asked, "Did you say something?" "No," we both replied. We raised our heads and looked around and saw a buckskin-clothed person on horseback. The image startled us as we were miles from anywhere in the open country and did not expect to see any people, much less an apparition from a bygone era. The horseman asked what we were doing, and we clued him in. Just as quickly as he arrived, he continued with his horse. A man with no name and no place disappeared almost as soon as he had appeared.

Jon Souder and his significant other owned an adobe house in Albuquerque, and as was typical of most residences in the city, they had a xeriscape instead of grass in their front yard. Native cactus, rabbitbrush, and a couple of bleached deer skulls adorned their yard. During one field sampling trip, Eric and I spied a bleached cow skeleton. Eric and I looked at the skeleton completely from skull to hooves and then looked at each other with a broad smile. "We should take this and place it in Jon's front yard," one of us said. The skeleton remained intact, and we were able to lift it onto the vehicle and transport it to Albuquerque. Later that evening, Eric and I waited until almost midnight and transported the bovine skeleton to Jon's front yard. We stealthily unloaded the skeleton from Eric's pickup truck and placed it in Jon's front yard next to one of the deer skulls. The next day, Eric and I anxiously waited for Jon to arrive at the office, hoping for his reaction. There was none. Silence! Nada! Nothing. Much to our dismay, Jon kept his cool and denied Eric and me a good belly laugh. At the end of the day, he calmly congratulated us for a well-executed gag.

Eric's parents lived in Anthony, New Mexico, located on the New Mexico-Texas state line 18 miles north of El Paso. His father, Gus, worked as an engineer at the White

Sands Missile Range, 41 miles north-northeast of Anthony, and his mother, Helen, was a stay-at-home mom and raptor rehabilitator. I kept asking Eric about her work with raptors, which led to him inviting me to travel to his hometown to meet his mother. I informed Eric that I was interested in writing an article on his mother's raptor rehab work and submit it to a magazine. I rode to Eric's hometown in his multi-colored GMC pickup truck with a black front wheel fender.

I spent the weekend following Helen as she cared for a variety of raptors and peppered her with questions for my magazine article. A Swainson's hawk under her care was crippled by a rifle shot and would never fly again. Most of Helen's patients were victims of "thoughtlessness and uncaring persons armed with rifles and out for some fun." Injured hawks and owls were brought to her by New Mexico Game and Fish Department personnel and private citizens who happened to find the wounded birds along roads. She rehabilitated barn owls, burrowing owls, a long-eared owl, Swainson's hawks, red-tailed hawks, kestrels, golden eagles, and northern harriers (previously known as marsh hawks).

I thoroughly enjoyed meeting Helen and Gus. In addition to working as an engineer at White Sands, Gus served on the local school board. My evenings with them were filled with thought-provoking and interesting discussions. I kept in touch with them for years. On the drive back to Albuquerque, Eric stopped at the U.S. Border Patrol checkpoint north of Las Cruces. I was familiar with Border Patrol checkpoints as one was located ten miles north of my hometown in South Texas. The agents knew us, and after we stopped, they waved us through. "Are you U.S. citizens?" the agent asked. "Yes, sir," Eric answered. I sat silently on the passenger side, and Eric gave me a quizzical look as the agent looked at me. I gazed at Eric, and after a few seconds, it dawned on me that I had to answer the agent. "Yes, sir," I replied, almost yelling. The agent waved us through. "You jerk! You did that on purpose!" Eric shouted. I explained that I was used to the Border Patrol agents near my hometown waving us through without questioning our citizenship. "I thought you answered for the both of us," I added. "No! He wanted you to talk so that he could confirm that you are a U.S. citizen," Erik replied. A few weeks later, I submitted the manuscript on Helen's work with raptors to New Mexico Magazine. The magazine published the story in its January 1981 issue.

I made life-long friends during the 14 months I lived and worked in Albuquerque. FWS Fisheries Biologist Carl Couret transferred from the Honolulu, Hawaii, ES field office and joined our team. I did not work on any of Carl's New Mexico projects; however, we shared an interest in fishing and hiking. Through Carl and his significant other, Sui, I met Dan and Susan Kutvirt. Dan and Susan worked at the New Mexico Tumor Registry at the University of New Mexico, and they, too, shared an interest in hiking and cross-country skiing. My initial concerns about living in a large city quickly faded as I immersed myself in fieldwork and weekend fishing, hiking, and backpacking with Carl. During the winter, Dan and Susan organized a cross-country skiing weekend with lodging at the University of New Mexico's D.H. Lawrence Ranch, located 18 miles north of Taos. Unfortunately, the ranch did not have enough snow to ski on, so we drove west to the Carson National Forest and west of Tres Piedras to cross-country ski. All seven in our party brought enough food to feed an army, so much so that we named our gathering the "DH Lawrence Ski Bloat."

The week after Mount St. Helens erupted, covering most of Washington state and Northern Idaho with a blanket of ash, Jon Souder and I drove to Moscow, Idaho; Jon was visiting his brother who lived in Moscow, and I, Esther and Wayne. I purchased an extra air filter for my car as recommended to drivers traveling to Idaho due to the amount of volcanic ash in the area. Upon reaching Moscow, Jon and I saw several persons on the rooftops of buildings along the main street sweeping ash off the roofs. I reconnected with Esther and Wayne at their place near Deary; the conifers on their land remained covered with a thin layer of gray ash. They relayed their experience during the eruption of Mount St. Helens and recalled hearing what sounded like the rumble of thunder. Ash fell soon, followed by darkness as the cloud of ash blotted out the sun. Jon, Esther, Wayne, and I drove to Electric City, Washington, to visit with Kemper McMaster. Gary Koehler joined us during that visit for a memorable reunion.

As my year-long term drew to a close, Assistant Field Supervisor Joel Medlin had my back and kept me informed on potential job openings with the FWS. During the spring, ES field supervisors from throughout the country met in

Albuquerque. Joel invited field supervisors Roger Banks from Charleston, South Carolina, and Roy Perez from Corpus Christi, Texas, both of whom had upcoming permanent job openings. Both of them interviewed me during their brief visit. In late May, I flew to Corpus Christi to be with my parents during the conclusion of the civil suit trial involving the fate of my Dad's ranch. Since my dad could not afford a lawyer, he consulted with several attorneys during the previous three years and finally obtained a lawyer who agreed to take his case on a contingency fee basis. At the conclusion of arguments presented by the plaintiff and defense attorneys, 12 jurors had to decide on each of the twelve issues presented to them, and all were written in legalese. When they reached their decision and the presiding judge announced the verdicts on all 12, the plaintiff and defense attorneys were at a loss on whether my Dad retained ownership of his ranch. Weeks later, I learned that my Dad no longer owned the farm. My dad and his attorney considered appealing the decision.

The next month, I packed my few belongings into my car and moved to Corpus Christi, leaving my cross-country skis at Carl's house. The Sparkling City by the Sea welcomed me with high humidity and equally high temperatures. Although I was glad I had a permanent job with the FWS, I did not enjoy the oppressive subtropical heat. I stayed with my brother and his wife and daughter while I looked for an apartment. My overall goal was to find my way back to live and work at the Land of Enchantment and spend more time with the friends I made there.

CHAPTER 14: SAVE THE DIRT, SAVE THE BAY

The Corpus Christi ES Field Office (CCESFO) was located in a one-story commercial office building near South Padre Island Drive, one of the busiest highways in the city. The field office staff included the field supervisor, an assistant field supervisor, a secretary-cum-administrative officer, and three biologists, with me as a fourth. The field supervisor and his assistant each had their own separate offices. The two offices occupied by the biologists were so small that the two desks for the occupants were butted up against each other. I shared an office with a co-worker who smoked a pipe and cigarettes. Being a non-smoker, I endured second-hand smoke at my desk as the federal government did not prohibit smoking in federal office buildings until 17 years later. When I could, I would go outside for short walks when the biologist would light up a cigarette. FWS funds covered staff salaries and the cost of office space; however, the field office was dependent on transfer funds from the COE and the USBR for purchasing field equipment, travel, and other expenses related to assessing proposed water development projects. The amount of transfer funding depended heavily on the negotiation skills of the field supervisor in procuring money from the COE and the USBR. The COE Galveston District and the USBR Regional Office in Amarillo were extremely frugal in doling out money to the Corpus Christi ES field office. Field equipment was limited to a 14-foot flat-bottomed aluminum boat, one Danforth anchor, and a larger 18-foot fiberglass boat that had not floated the area's bay waters in quite some time. The bulk of the work done by the office involved reviewing COE wetland permits issued under Section 404 of the Clean Water Act and Section 10 of the Rivers and Harbors Act. Most of the fieldwork, if not all, was limited to what the staff termed 'windshield surveys.' A windshield survey involved driving to a site proposed for either industrial/commercial or residential development on wetlands. Real estate developers kept our office staff busy reviewing wetland permits and conducting windshield surveys of proposed canal housing developments along the coast between Rockport, Texas and North Padre Island, as well as rapid development in South Padre Island in the Lower Rio Grande Valley.

My first assignment entailed acquiring technical information on fish and wildlife and their habitats within the Nueces River watershed for the U.S. Bureau of Reclamation office in Amarillo, Texas. The dam-building era began in 1936 with the construction of Hoover Dam on the Lower Colorado River and ramped up after World War II. The 1970s ushered in the National Environmental Policy Act of 1970 and the Endangered Species Act of 1973, legislation that provided powerful legal tools to environmental lobbies to oppose new dam projects. Political leaders of both parties also frowned on spending taxpayer's dollars on new dam projects lacking financial justification and ideal building sites. The bureaucratic inertia of the federal dam-building agencies lagged behind the political reality and the public's environmental awareness as engineers continued to plan and assess suitable sites for water development projects at the behest of state water development agencies, municipalities, and lobbyists. The planning aid report identified problems and needs regarding fish and wildlife resources of the Nueces River Basin. Two of the major problems I identified included the need to document habitat loss within the river basin and the need for adequate river flows to sustain the Nueces and Corpus

Christi Bay estuarine ecosystem. I completed the draft planning aid report in four or five months and submitted it to the Texas Parks and Wildlife Department and the National Marine Fisheries Service for review.

Following completion of the planning aid report, the supervisor assigned various small projects for review. Deskbound with tasks I found unchallenging, I became depressed to the extent that, for the first time in my life, I dreaded getting up in the morning. I missed the fieldwork that I did in Montana and New Mexico. My weekends were relegated to watching professional football games at my brother Ernest's house and spending time with my niece and nephew. In retrospect, I had the opportunity to reconnect with my parents and my two brothers and their families. I missed the mountains, I missed my friends, and missed hiking and camping. I'd temporarily fill my yearning by visiting my friends in Albuquerque in the fall for some trout fishing and backpacking in the mountains, cross-country, and downhill skiing during the winter. Either the field supervisor, his assistant, or the administrative officer, Ethel, probably noticed my demeanor, which led to my field supervisor assigning me to assist biologist Johnny French with the assessment of a COE project to increase the depth of the Corpus Christi Inner Harbor from its current depth of 40-feet to 45-feet. Deepening the 9-mile-long harbor and maintaining the 45-foot depth over a period of 50 years would result in the removal of almost 60 million cubic yards of silt and sediment. The enactment of several environmental laws in the 1970s constrained the COE's past practices of dumping material dredged from navigation channels and ports into bay bottoms. In 1975, the COE proposed to create a leveed containment area in Nueces Bay to confine the sediment removed during the deepening of the Inner Harbor. The FWS somehow succeeded in forcing the COE to abandon that plan. The COE proposed to dispose of the dredged material into a constructed containment area within Nueces Bay. The COE regrouped and developed an alternative disposal plan using upland farmland north of the bay to locate the dredged material containment areas. When the farmland location became public, over two hundred citizens protested that alternative. The COE backtracked and resurrected the 1975 plan to site the containment areas in Nueces Bay. The bay proposal involved constructing levees eight feet above mean low tide (MLT) and raised at a future date to 17 feet

MLT to contain the dredged material. The dredged material containment would eliminate two thousand acres of Nueces Bay, an estuary providing an important nursery habitat for shrimp and fish.

Commercial and sport fishermen as well as several local environmental organizations, opposed filling in two-thousand acres of Nueces Bay with mud. 'Save the Dirt,' a euphemism for saving habitat, is the mantra of the FWS ES Division, which made the mission of Ecological Services quite apparent to me. I was no longer 'pushing paper'; I had a clear purpose, doing my part to help save two thousand acres of an estuary from becoming an industrial waste disposal site. Fortunately, Johnny's photographic memory and knowledge of environmental regulations served as a great starting point as I dove head-first into the challenge and learned as much as possible about the 45-foot project and its impact on Nueces Bay. I poured through numerous COE technical reports in our field office library on dredging and dredged material disposal. The COE reports ranged in length from less than 100 to over 400 pages and covered everything related to dredging and dredged material disposal: types of dredging equipment, calculating the size of dredged material containment areas and levee heights, beneficial uses of dredged material, management of containment areas, as well as the environmental impacts of dredged material disposal. This plethora of engineering and environmental information provided me with information to assess a 45-foot project adequately. I also read the COE draft environmental impact statement on the project proposal. Working with Johnny, I learned the importance of researching regulations and the missions of regulatory agencies such as the COE to understand the limitations on their actions.

The COE initially proposed constructing the dredged material containment areas on 1,450 acres of farmland north of Nueces Bay. That proposal created a publicity firestorm as farmers, the Farm Bureau, a plethora of local businesses with ties to the agricultural economy, and the public took pen to paper and flooded the COE as well as the local airwaves with their cries to save prime farmland. The COE quickly reverted to dumping 50 years' worth of muck from the bottom of the harbor onto Nueces Bay. An anti-environmental political climate in the early 1980s paved the way for such an egregious proposal with James Watt as

Secretary of the Department of the Interior and Anne Gorsuch as the Administrator of the U.S. Environmental Protection Agency. The environmental activism of the 1970s, as well as the enactment of regulatory protections for our air, water, wetlands, forests, fish, and wildlife, led to a political backlash resulting in the organization of movements such as the Sagebrush Rebellion, a group advocating the privatization of public lands such as our national forests as well as lands managed by the U.S. Bureau of Land Management. The Nueces Bay alternative rallied several environmental groups and public sentiment against destroying such a large bay area. The Corpus Christi Port Authority inflamed local and regional environmental sentiment with the jobs versus environment argument, stating that filling in 2,000 acres of the bay would create prime industrial real estate in the harbor and create jobs. The COE now had commercial and sports fishing groups, the Sierra Club, the Audubon Society, the Texas affiliate of the National Wildlife Federation, and local and regional residents, letting them know that the bay should not be used as a dump site.

Nueces Bay is a 27-square-mile secondary bay of Corpus Christi Bay and receives water from the Nueces River. The average depth of the bay is 2.3 feet, with a maximum depth of six feet. Nueces Bay provides a nursery habitat for three species of shrimp, blue crabs, and several species of commercial and sport fish species. The bay also provides feeding and resting habitat for waterfowl and other aquatic birds. Johnny and I compiled information from the Texas Department of Water Resources (TDWR) on contaminants present in the bottom sediment from the Inner Harbor and fish species in Nueces Bay from the Texas Parks and Wildlife Department for incorporation into the FWCA report that FWS would submit to the COE. A year into the project, FWS ES Division staff from our regional office in Albuquerque, New Mexico, visited our office, and we provided them with an update on our progress with the FWCA report. As we went over the TDWR sediment quality data emphasizing high concentrations of arsenic, cadmium, chromium, copper, lead, nickel, and zinc, Charlie Sanchez, regional environmental contaminants coordinator, advised us to collect sediment from the Inner Harbor and submit it for chemical analysis. "We need our own data to verify this, Pedro," Sanchez said, "let's get some sample jars, get the field office boat ready, and go collect sediment samples from the harbor tomorrow." I spent the rest of the afternoon getting the 14-foot Jon boat, Ekman dredge, life jackets, and sample jars ready for the next day's fieldwork.

Charlie and I launched the Jon boat into Corpus Christi Bay at a boat ramp near the entrance to the Inner Harbor. Once in the water, I started the small outboard motor, twisted the throttle on the tiller, and pointed the boat into the harbor. The eight-and-a-half-mile-long Inner Harbor is separated from Nueces Bay by a narrow strip of land approximately one-third of a mile wide, created by the disposal of bottom material excavated during the construction and subsequent maintenance dredging of the Port of Corpus Christi. Several dredged material containment areas, railyards, and industrial facilities are located on this man-made narrow peninsula. The port channel is 300 feet wide, with five turning basins approximately 800 feet wide to allow ships to turn and exit the harbor. As we entered the first turning basin, we suggested we collect a sediment sample at this location. "Go to the middle of the channel," Charlie instructed. I glanced eastward beyond the port entrance toward Corpus

Christi Bay. "There's a ship coming in, Charlie," I cautioned him after seeing a large oil tanker approaching the port about two miles from us. "That's okay; it's far away," Charlie replied. I steered the Jon boat to the middle of the turning basin and was greeted with a loud blast of the ship's horn. I quickly pointed the boat to shore, where we watched the steel behemoth enter the harbor. After the tanker passed us, we waited a few minutes and continued with our sediment sampling task. We navigated past oil storage tanks and refineries along the south side of the harbor. The north side of the harbor was quite narrow and relegated to smaller industrial sites and bulk materials such as petroleum coke.

As we navigated past a mountainous stockpile of petroleum coke, Charlie looked at the black pile of material and asked me what that was. "Petroleum coke," I answered. "Let's sample here," Charlie replied. I turned off the outboard motor, and as we prepared to lower the Ekman dredge, we drifted into an airborne plume of petroleum coke dust. "Charlie, we have to move out of here," I said as I yanked on the starter cord of the outboard. With each frantic yank of the starter cord, the outboard motor only coughed and sputtered. The black dust stung my eyes as we continued to drift. Finally, the outboard motor, which had not seen action since who knows when, let out a meek reply, letting me know to increase the throttle. We had power! I steered us away from the coke plume, and we resumed our sampling. "Charlie, drop the anchor so we don't drift back into the coke dust," I instructed him. Charlie grabbed the Danforth anchor and heaved it over the side. Keep in mind my previous discussion of the paucity of field equipment at the field office. The Jon boat only had one line used for the anchor ride, for tying the boat next to a dock, and for pulling the boat onto shore.

Occupants on the boat had to remember to tie the rope to the anchor before heaving it over the side. Did I mention that our office was in the poor house in terms of funds available for the procurement as well as operation and maintenance of field equipment? "Pedro! I lost the anchor," Charlie exclaimed with a worried tone. *"What?!?"* I answered. I had not informed Charlie that the one line on the boat had not been fastened to the anchor, now resting in the bottom muck of the Corpus Christi Inner Harbor.

Charlie's emphasis on obtaining our own data also led to the collection of fish in the Nueces Bay area proposed for dredged material disposal. CCESFO biologist Don Meineke and I procured an otter trawl net for the sampling effort. The otter trawl net is designed for catching bottom-dwelling fish. The net, made of twine webbing, is shaped like a funnel. The mouth of the funnel-shaped net is held open by two wooden panels or 'doors' when the net is pulled by a boat. Prior to working at the CCESFO, Don was a fisheries biologist with the U.S. National Marine Fisheries Service and could identify the fish species caught in the otter trawl net. I, on the other hand, had no experience identifying marine fish species and would have spent hours going through taxonomy keys to identify them. My tasks were to operate the 14-foot Jon boat and help Don haul the otter trawl net onto the boat after each trawling run.

Networking with the public, especially environmental organizations, was one of many lessons I brought from my work at the Albuquerque ES field office. The field supervisor at that time told me of his experience working at a national wildlife refuge along the East Coast and providing information to environmental organizations concerned over proposed activities or projects threatening the refuge. I reached out to several individuals, including the local chapters and regional offices of the Audubon Society, Sierra Club, the Wildlife Management Institute, and several sport fishing organizations. Ted Jones, president of the Coastal Bend Audubon Society, was media savvy and kept the project proponents on the defensive. He would feed the local press information on the project impacts on a weekly basis rather than providing them with all the information at once. This kept the media and the public engaged on the issue. One week, Ted would contact the three television stations for interviews and talk about the proposal to dispose of 50 years of dredged material into Nueces Bay, converting 2,000 acres of the bay into industrial real estate. He concluded the interviews with a teaser, "Next week, I will discuss pollutants present in the bottom sediment in the harbor and their threat to marine and bird life." Week after week, the public learned of threats to water quality, commercial and sport fishing, bird life, and recreation. I learned the value of public outreach from Ted by watching him interact with the media and listening to his discussions on outreach strategy.

Opponents to the bay disposal site latched on to an alternative site, the McGregor Ranch, not considered by the COE, a 1,500-acre site located on the Nueces River delta upstream of the bay. The landowner was willing to sell his ranch for dredged material disposal. Uplands comprised slightly over one-third of the McGregor Ranch site, with the remainder classified as temporarily or seasonally flooded areas and 64 acres of freshwater wetlands. The alternative site proposed by the environmental groups squashed the argument of saving prime farmland versus saving the bay, as both could be saved. The Audubon and Sierra Club chapters collaborated with other local environmental groups and sport and commercial fisheries organizations and formed the Nueces Bay Conservation Coalition to save Nueces Bay. A public opinion poll conducted by political scientist Dr. Robert Bezdek of Corpus Christi showed that 54 percent of a randomly selected list of 362 registered voters opposed the Nueces Bay disposal site, and 20 percent supported dumping the dredged material in Nueces Bay.

The Corps published its draft supplement environmental impact statement in August 1981 and held a public hearing on the 45-Foot project a month later. Eight hundred people attended the public hearing. The COE allotted five minutes to each person providing oral comments on the dredging project. The hearing lasted late into the evening. Opponents to the Nueces Bay disposal alternative dominated the hearing. Kay McCracken, author of a weekly bird-watching column in the Corpus Christi Caller, stepped up to the podium to air her grievance on the bay proposal. She focused on the threat to herons, egrets, and other colonial-nesting fish-eating birds nesting on small islands in Nueces Bay. The District Engineer, Col. James Sigler, announced that her five minutes were up. McCracken continued with her comments as Sigler raised his voice, admonishing the elderly presenter to step away from the podium. His stern command was greeted with a chorus of 'boos' from the audience. The COE reinforced their villainous image, which was prevalent among the hundreds of people in the Bayfront Auditorium that evening.

A plethora of newspaper editorials, news stories, and letters to the editor followed. The Nueces Bay Coalition drafted an alternate environmental assessment of the proposed deepening of the Inner Harbor with the McGregor

Ranch site as the preferred alternative. The Coalition divided the task among the members according to their expertise: aquatic ecology, geology, engineering, avian ecology, etc. The Coalition submitted the completed document to the COE District Engineer in Galveston. Several weeks later, Coalition members repeated hearsay that the COE held a mock trial in their Galveston District office comparing the Coalition's alternate assessment with the McGregor Ranch site to the COE's preferred alternative of Nueces Bay, the McGregor Ranch site prevailed. A year later, a COE spokesman acknowledged greater long-term damage to shrimp, fish, and the estuarine environment if the dredged material was dumped into the bay. "The Corps now agrees with what the Coalition has said all along. We would have killed them in court," said Ted Jones to the Corpus Christi Caller. The Corps revised its disposal plan from 50 years to 25 years using portside upland disposal sites.

Additionally, the COE proposed raising the levee heights at existing dredged material containment areas along the Inner Harbor. The Corpus Christi Caller quoted COE Major General Hugh G. Robinson as saying, "The (old) plan had enough unknowns to make us nervous. Our engineering studies showed us clearly that we could cause more damage than we initially had thought." The determined efforts of the Coalition and the public outcry spared Nueces Bay from an irreparable wound.

During my quest to obtain pertinent information related to the assessment of the 45-foot project, I visited the local U.S. Geological Survey (USGS) office at Corpus Christi State University (now known as Texas A&M University, Corpus Christi. The agency occupied a two-story building that once housed the university's science department. I asked a few of the USGS staff how they were able to acquire office and laboratory space on campus, and they succinctly responded that they had merely asked. I was aware of the General Services Administration's (GSA's) efforts to move all federal agencies to a multi-story office building in downtown Corpus Christi. None of the field office staff, including yours truly did not want to work in downtown Corpus Christi. It's not that the downtown area was a poster child for urban blight; conversely, it was the crown jewel of Corpus Christi that made it the "sparkling city by the sea." The location had a plethora of negatives:

limited parking, traffic congestion, crowded, lack of storage for field equipment, and commuting to the central business district. GSA's policy required federal agencies to locate their office space in the central business district. This policy probably resulted from the need to revitalize downtown business districts. I visited with the university's marine biology professor, Dr. Wes Tunnel, and asked him if the university was interested in providing office space on campus for the FWS. "We'd love to have the FWS on our campus," Dr. Tunnel enthusiastically replied. I mentioned the idea of moving onto the CCSU campus to our field supervisor, and he conveyed to me that it was not a good idea. I gathered additional information to convince him of the benefits of such a move onto the university campus. I learned that another ES field office in the country was located on a university campus. I telephoned a biologist at that office and wrote down the benefits he mentioned: access to the university library and scientific journals, access to professors with expertise in marine ecosystems, and a pleasant environment to work in as compared to working in the concrete and asphalt jungle in a downtown area. I asked my supervisor to at least visit the campus and talk to Dr. Tunnel. After much persuasion, he relented. He obtained approval from the FWS regional office in Albuquerque, and we moved into a portion of the first floor of the Old Science Hall. Our office space consisted of two classrooms and three small offices: one for the administrative officer (aka secretary), Ethel McGuire; a second for the field supervisor; and the third for the field supervisor. One of the large classrooms provided the space for our office library, a large conference table for meetings, and space for two biologists, Johnny French and Paul Lazarine. The second classroom provided space for Don Meineke and me—battleship grey metal bookcases and filing cabinets served as partitions for our office spaces in the large classrooms. At the time, our office could not afford partitions to set up office cubicles.

As work on the 45-Foot Project wound down, the regional office delegated consultations under Section 7 of the Endangered Species Act to the ES field offices. Section 7 requires Federal agencies to consult with the FWS "to ensure that actions they fund, authorize, permit, or otherwise carry out will not jeopardize the continued existence of any listed species or adversely modify designated critical habitats." I worked with staff from the

Aransas, LRGV, and Santa Ana national wildlife refuges on proposed projects that could affect the endangered whooping crane at Aransas NWR and the ocelot and jaguarundi at the LRGV and Santa Ana NWRs. Charlie Sanchez knew of my interest in environmental contaminants (EC) work after our bottom sediment sampling adventure in the Corpus Christi Inner Harbor. This led him to ask me to draft an EC sampling plan for the Lower Rio Grande Valley area.

I dove into the task and contacted the refuge managers, Nita Fuller at Santa Ana and Robert 'Bob' Shoemaker at LRGV, and requested their input on contaminant sources that could impact the refuges. The Lower Rio Grande Valley's (Valley) fertile alluvial soils make it one of the most productive truck farming areas in the country. Since the early 1900s, the thorny brush was cleared, and the land plowed to grow a plethora of vegetables, citrus, sorghum, and cotton. The Rio Grande provided water for irrigating these crops in the semi-arid climate of the valley. Farmers applied DDT, toxaphene, and other organochlorine pesticides to protect their crops from insects, a variety of herbicides to keep weeds at bay, and defoliants on cotton to facilitate harvesting the cotton bolls by mechanical cotton pickers. I submitted a sampling plan targeting the Rio Grande reaches adjacent to refuge units as well as drainage ditches and Delta Lake, an off-storage reservoir holding water for irrigation from the Rio Grande. The Valley is not technically a valley but a delta. Prior to the impoundment of the Rio Grande by Falcon Dam in the 1950s, flood waters from the river deposited silt onto its delta, creating what became one of our country's most productive agricultural areas. A string of small cities sprung up like beads on a necklace within the delta two to ten miles from the river. The sampling plan was shelved, but my interest in contaminants fieldwork grew.

In 1983, the FWS began staffing ES field offices with environmental contaminants (EC) specialists. Previously, the FWS research division investigated how contaminant impacts primarily on migratory birds and fish and ES headquarters and regional staff assessed federally-funded or permitted projects for contaminant impacts to fish and wildlife resources. Brian Cain transferred from the research division to the ES field office in Galveston. Brian was tasked with providing EC support to the Galveston and Corpus

Christi ES field offices. A year later, Gerry Jackson transferred from a fisheries research facility in Yankton, South Dakota, to the Corpus Christi ES field office and began the task as an EC specialist of procuring equipment for conducting contaminant field investigations.

His first task included assessing national wildlife refuges (NWRs) in South Texas for known or suspected contaminant issues. Gerry visited refuges in the Lower Rio Grande Valley and the Aransas NWR to inventory paints, solvents, petroleum products, and pesticides stored in warehouses and workshops. Gerry inventoried items no longer used for proper disposal at a permitted chemical disposal facility. He also requested and received approval to hire a biologist to assist him with fieldwork. Tom Maurer transferred from an FWS fisheries research field station in Lakewood, Colorado, and joined the staff at our field office. After work on the 45-foot Inner Harbor Project lessened, my job reverted to desktop fish and wildlife conservation, so I volunteered to accompany Gerry and Tom on fieldwork as often as I could when the custom-built work boat arrived from KANN Commercial Workboats from a mid-western state located along the Mississippi River. Gerry decided to test the boat at Mesquite Bay off of Aransas NWR. Tom, assistant field supervisor Tom Grahl, and I joined Gerry on the field trip. Gerry named the flat-bottomed work boat 'KANN Do,' initially a dig at the field supervisor's responses of "can't do" to ideas presented to him by staff.

Gerry navigated the KANN Do from the boat ramp at Aransas NWR to a shallow bay southeast of the refuge. Gerry navigated around small islands created from material dredged from the Gulf Intracoastal Waterway. At mid-day, we dropped anchor and ate lunch while enjoying a slight breeze from the gulf. Tom Grahl grabbed his fishing rod and reel and repeatedly cast and retrieved his fishing lure, a gold-colored spoon. After several unsuccessful casts, an explosion of water several feet from the boat startled all of us as a four-foot tarpon leaped out of the shallow waters— a small gold spoon hung from the fish's bony mouth. The tarpon seemed to hang above the water's surface, but it writhed in seconds; its large body moved right, and the gold spoon went left. We were all stunned and speechless for a few seconds. To this day, the image of the leaping tarpon is burned into my memory. I continued assisting Gerry and Tom with collecting bottom sediment for contaminant analysis from San Antonio Bay adjacent to the Aransas National Wildlife Refuge and Corpus Christi Bay.

There never was a dull moment with contaminants field work as it mitigated my work as a "desk-jockey" with most of the other tasks I performed at the field office. During one sampling trip at San Antonio Bay with Tom Maurer, the crew of a bay shrimp trawler waved at us, so we approached their boat. A crew member informed Tom and me that the trawler's rudder was broken and asked if we could tow their trawler to the dock at Hopper's Landing, a family-owned and operated marina two-and-a-half miles north of the refuge. Tom and I wondered if the 'KANN Do' could tow the much larger trawler, but the crew member told us the boat still had power but no steering. We towed the trawler to the marina, and the crew thanked us and gave us a burlap sack filled with oysters they had harvested from the bay. We refused, but the crew insisted, so we returned to Corpus Christi with the sack full of live oysters. We spent the remainder of the day shucking oysters at Gerry's house and enjoying a great feast of fried oysters.

One field trip to San Antonio Bay led me to get three t-shirts made with a colorful map of Shoalwater Bay with the caption "I walked Shoalwater Bay." Shoalwater Bay is located approximately 11 miles east of the refuge and across San Antonio Bay. Shoalwater Bay extends 4-and-a-half miles from the southwest to the northeast. The shallow bay is separated on its northwest side from the Gulf Intracoastal Waterway by a dredged spoil island and separated from Espiritu Santo Bay by Long Island on the southeast side. Shoalwater Bay is appropriately named as it is one-and-a-quarter mile wide. It is approached from San Antonio Bay and 350 yards at its narrowest point, giving the bay a somewhat triangular shape. While sampling sediment near Shoalwater Bay, we noticed a line of blue crab trap floats extending at intervals toward the narrow end of the bay. Gerry's curiosity about the bay and its potential for sediment sampling led to exploring Shoalwater Bay. Gerry managed to navigate the 'KANN Do' approximately two-and-a-half miles into the bay. At that point, the water became too shallow, so Gerry raised the outboard motor, and we climbed off the boat. We grabbed the line off the bow and waded through the less than two-foot-deep water. We towed the 'KANN Do' one to one-and-a-half miles, hoping there was a pass with water deep enough to pull the boat into the deeper Espiritu Santo Bay. The prevailing southeast breeze from the gulf lessened the sun's oven-like heat as I forced each foot forward through the shallow waters. The weight of the water sapped my energy. We reached the end of the bay and were thankful there was a shallow-water passage into Espiritu Santo Bay, so we were able to return to the boat ramp and Corpus Christi.

Assessing federally permitted or licensed projects for impacts to species protected by the Endangered Species Act (ESA) occasionally involved fieldwork. This also provided me with the task of problem-solving and searching for information in scientific journals that would support project alternatives to avoid or minimize impacts on listed species. Since our field office was located at the CCSU campus, we had access to the university library and scientific journals. Our office received a request from the COE for ESA-listed species in the lower Laguna Madre between Port Isabel and South Padre Island. The regional utility company, Central Power and Light (CPL), planned to install an electric power transmission line extending approximately 12 miles across the Laguna Madre between Port Isabel and South Padre Island. South Padre Island became a destination spot during spring break for college students in the mid- to late 1960s and rapidly sprouted condominiums, hotels, vacation homes, and a plethora of businesses serving permanent residents and tourists. Since the transmission line involved setting power poles across the Laguna Madre, CPL submitted an application for a permit from the COE to comply with Section 10 of the Rivers and Harbors Act of 1899. This Act requires authorization from the Secretary of the Army, acting through the Corps of Engineers, for constructing any structure in or over any navigable water of the United States.

Section 7 of the ESA requires federal agencies to "consult with the Service to ensure that actions they fund, authorize, permit, or otherwise carry out will not jeopardize the continued existence of any listed species or adversely modify designated critical habitats." Biologists estimated the Texas population of brown pelicans in 1921 to be approximately 5,000 birds. Brown pelicans suffered a significant decline in the 1930s because commercial fishermen believed that the fish-eating birds were causing a decline in commercial fish species. This myth justified the slaughtering of thousands of this species, and by 1939, the brown pelican population in Texas plummeted to an estimated 500 individuals. The increased use of organochlorine pesticides such as DDT in the late 1940s and continuing into the 1970s further reduced the pelican population to the extent that no brown pelicans were sighted in Texas in the 1976 Audubon Christmas Bird Count[3].

I obtained recent brown pelican population data from Kirke King, FWS research biologist at the Patuxent Wildlife Research Center's field station in Victoria, Texas, and author of several scientific papers on the brown pelican in the Texas Gulf Coast. I made use of the CCSU library and searched wildlife and ornithology scientific journals for publications on bird collisions with powerlines. With Kirke's guidance, I created a spreadsheet on our office's brand-new desktop computer to estimate trends in the brown pelican population in Texas based on various mortality rates caused by the proposed power line. The population model accounted for the hatching rate, fledging rate, and mortality rate. I ran several mortality rates and determined that the likeliest scenario would threaten the continued

---

[3] Source: Christmas Bird Counts, American Birds, Vol 28-48, Nat. Audubon Society, NY, NY, 1974-1994.

existence of the subpopulation of brown pelicans in the mid and lower Gulf Coast of Texas. After Kirke reviewed the population model and the mortality estimates, I forwarded my assessment to the endangered species staff at the regional office. The regional office endangered species office changed my recommendation to deny the permit and, instead, install an underwater transmission line along the bottom of the Laguna Madre to serve South Padre Island. The regional endangered species office provided an "incidental take" statement requiring monitoring the powerline for pelican mortality and reinitiating a Section 7 consultation when a specified number of pelican mortality occurred. "How are they going to effectively monitor pelican mortality along 12 miles of powerline over open water in all kinds of weather?" I wondered aloud. I was furious, especially after having done all the background research and consulting with Kirke, who had conducted several studies on brown pelicans on the lower Texas Gulf Coast. The COE biologist who received the FWS biological opinion was at a loss as to why we had not issued a jeopardy opinion. I did a lot of soul-searching regarding my work with the FWS and seriously thought about whether I should continue working with the agency.

As I mulled over my career options, I received a letter from Gary Koehler, who was working on his PhD under Maurice and studying bobcats in the Frank Church River of No Return Wilderness Area in central Idaho. He was in his last year of fieldwork and invited me to visit him at the University of Idaho's Taylor Wilderness Research Station in the heart of the wilderness area, where he was conducting his bobcat study. His letter could not have been timelier. I did not hesitate to take him up on the invitation, reasoning that I could also benefit from time in the wilderness and contemplate returning to graduate school for a PhD. I told my supervisor I was taking three weeks of annual leave to clear my head. I assumed he understood from the tone of my voice that I was going to take that much time off, come hell or high water. Fortunately, he did approve my leave.

CHAPTER 15: INTO THE WILDERNESS

The University of Idaho Taylor Wilderness Research Station (aka Taylor Ranch) is located in the heart of the Frank Church River of No Return Wilderness in central Idaho. It is a roadless area of over 2.3 million acres with steep canyons, rugged mountains, and whitewater rivers. I first learned of the Taylor Ranch in Maurice's article on his mountain lion research published in the 1969 issue of National Geographic magazine. Gary conducted a research study on bobcats in this wilderness area from 1982 to 1985 for his PhD under the guidance of Maurice. Gary lived in the Taylor Ranch with his wife, Mona, and his brother, Tim, who assisted him with fieldwork. Gary asked me to book a flight to Boise where his father-in-law, Bert, would meet me and drive us up to Arnold Aviation at the Cascade, Idaho airport, 78 miles to the north. Bert and I would fly into the Taylor Ranch with backcountry pilot Ray Arnold. Ray flew mail, groceries, propane, and other supplies to privately owned inholdings in the wilderness area patented decades earlier as homesteads or mining claims. We traveled up Idaho Highway 55, which paralleled the Payette River. Seeing the cascading waters of the Payette tumbling over rocks, the tall Ponderosa and lodgepole pines, the smell of the mountains, and the warmth of the sun rekindled memories of my time in the South Fork of the Flathead River in Montana. It stoked the fire in my soul and my love for the mountains. I wrote the following in my journal: "I now know that the restlessness in my soul was a longing to return to the mountains. I must fit my career goals around this desire. When I'm in the mountains, my soul is at peace." Bert and I spent the night in Cascade and drove to the Cascade Airport the next morning after we had breakfast. We helped Ray load his airplane with boxes of groceries and our gear. Included in the freight was a cake for Mona that Gary had ordered in appreciation for her help with Gary's bobcat study. Mona would be flying out of the Taylor Ranch a week later as this was Gary's last season with fieldwork.

Bert volunteered to take the back seat, having flown into the Taylor Ranch before visiting Gary and Mona. The cargo compartment behind Bert and the space to the right of Bert's seat was filled with boxes containing groceries and other supplies destined for the Taylor Ranch. I climbed onto the co-pilot's seat and fastened my seatbelt. Ray performed all the pre-flight checks, started the engine, and taxied to the runway. Ray increased the throttle, and we quickly gained altitude. As we became airborne, I looked over my shoulder at Bert and smiled with a look that said, "Well, Bert, we are on our way." I looked down out the window and watched the runway become a blur and the view of the airport grow smaller. My adrenaline rush took me back to my flights with Howard over the Flathead National Forest and the Bob Marshall Wilderness eight years earlier. I was filled with excitement and anticipation of reuniting with Gary and Tim and meeting Mona. During the flight to Taylor Ranch, 71 miles to the northeast of Cascade, Ray handed me three cardboard boxes with yellow and blue surveyor tape streamers wrapped around them. Ray informed me that he was delivering the packages to a mine eight miles east of Yellow Pine, Idaho. "Open your window," Ray instructed. I opened the window on the passenger door, and the roar of the Cessna's engine filled the cockpit. "When I say 'Now,' push the boxes out and downward immediately," Ray barked over the din of the engine and the propeller slicing through the air. I readied the boxes in position inches from the open window.

"Now! Now! Now!" Ray shouted. I hurriedly pushed the boxes one after another out of the window and tried watching them as they fell. All I saw was the white snow-covered landscape below as I closed the window. "I hope they find them," I said.

As we continued to our destination, I watched the sea of mountains below us extending to the horizon in all directions. The drainages were narrow, unlike the wide drainage valleys in the South Fork of the Flathead. As we neared the Taylor Ranch, I could see the cabins and the airstrip adjacent to Big Creek. At this lower elevation, snow hung onto north-facing slopes and tree-shaded areas. Ray circled the area and checked the wind sock next to the grass-covered airstrip. Big Creek paralleled the airstrip on the north side and the base of a steep slope on the south. As the Cessna descended, I saw scattered trees on the slopes reaching upwards towards the wings. Ray circled again and descended downstream from the airstrip. As the Cessna circled and descended, the stall warning blared its ear-splitting alarm twice. Ray methodically increased the power as it did so. I looked out at the narrow landing area and the towering slopes on each side and silently said a prayer. Ray successfully guided the aircraft downward and touched down on the narrow grassy strip. The end of the runway and Big Creek rapidly zoomed in before us, and just as I thought we would run out of airstrip, Ray quickly turned the airplane around, and we headed back towards the opposite end of the airstrip. Mona and the Taylor Ranch caretakers, Jim and Holly Akenson, met us at the end of the airstrip. Mona smiled, hugged her father and then me, and introduced me to Jim and Holly. Everyone pitched in to transfer the cargo from the airplane into two carts. After all the supplies were unloaded, Ray climbed back into his airplane and headed for Cascade. Mona, Bert, and I pulled the carts to the cabin and spent the next hour transferring the supplies to the cabins. Gary and Tim were upstream running the trapline and would return to the Taylor Ranch the next day. I took my gear into Tim's cabin and rejoined Bert and Mona at the main cabin that served as Gary and Mona's wilderness home. Bert and I sat at the kitchen table and enjoyed the view of the open meadow sloping down to the north bank of Big Creek. We noticed a herd of bighorn sheep making their way down towards the creek as Mona was about to feed us a lunch of cheese and crackers. The three of us grabbed our jackets and hiked across the pack bridge spanning Big Creek. We slowly climbed up the slope so as not to disturb the herd. Mona and Bert sat near a large Douglas fir as I inched my way towards the herd. I took several photos of the sheep and rejoined Mona and Bert. As I sat there, I absorbed the place and time and felt my soul at peace. Later that evening, I wrote the following in my journal. "My mind feels rested and relaxed. This is going to be excellent therapy."

I walked over to the horse corral and saw Tobie and Topper, the two mules we used to pack live traps, food, and gear into the Bob Marshall during the Wolverine study. I stroked their necks and softly told them it was good to see them again. I also met Kahmir, Gary and Mona's bobcat. Maurice made arrangements to obtain Kahmir as a kitten from a zoo so that Gary could observe and learn bobcat behavior up close. Maurice had done the same with mountain lion cubs during his mountain lion study at Big Creek in the 1960s. Mona and Gary named the feline Kahmir since they initially would call him "come 'ere," so the name stuck. After breakfast the next morning, Bert, Mona, and I, with Kahmir following us, took a short half-mile hike to Rush Creek, a tributary of Big Creek. After observing a herd of elk and some mule deer, we hiked back to Taylor Ranch. As we approached the ranch, I saw Tim walking toward one of the cabins. I quickened my pace down the slope toward Gary and Mona's cabin and saw Gary lying on the grass, enjoying the sun. I was elated to see them and hugged them both. After some conversation we enjoyed a lunch of cake, Cheetos, and Tillamook cheese. Our evening was filled with laughter and conversation with nuggets of flashbacks to Tim, Gary, and my days at Spotted Bear.

The next two days, I joined Gary and Tim as they hiked up the Big Creek drainage to check their traps. We hiked two or three miles and observed a herd of about 14 bighorn sheep, 12 of which were impressive rams. We stopped and had lunch near Cabin Creek, five miles from the Taylor Ranch. After we ate lunch, we lay back and soaked up the mountain air and sun for several minutes. As I lay there, my mind was clear; my soul was at peace with life, and the world and felt truly free. It was a wonderful feeling. Gary and Tim set a trap to capture a coyote, one of the targeted species for Gary's research study, to study interactions and movements between bobcats and coyotes.

We hiked one-and-a-half miles up Cabin Creek to an outfitters camp that had several log cabins. According to Gary, the U.S. Forest Service purchased the camp and planned to remove the cabins to preserve the wilderness character of the area. We continued our hike back down Cabin Creek and one mile upstream along Big Creek to Cave Creek, the site of Gary and Tim's camp. A large wall tent provided shelter at Cave Creek camp with a small wood-burning stove to cook meals and provide warmth during the cool nights. The next morning, after breakfast, Gary and I hiked up a slope to check some traps. On the way up, I observed eight ravens flying to the east of Cabin Creek. I grabbed binoculars out of my pack and saw a fresh carcass on the slope. We hiked towards it and found that it was a mule deer. Only a skeleton with bits of flesh and legs remained. We assumed that coyotes had killed the animal. We also observed a golden eagle feather approximately five yards down the slope from the carcass.

We returned to the Taylor Ranch and celebrated Easter on Saturday evening with a delicious dinner of baked ham, salad, and sourdough biscuits. Jim and Holly joined us for dinner, and Kahmir entertained us by rolling and nuzzling someone's sweaty t-shirt. On Easter Sunday morning, the 'Easter bunny,' Bert, left us all boxes filled with chocolate Easter eggs and marshmallow bunnies. After breakfast, I accompanied Gary to Rush Creek to check traps at that site. I assisted Gary with the live-trapped 40-pound coyote after he immobilized it with ketamine.

I filled out the data sheet while Gary weighed the canid and placed small, numbered ear tags and a radio collar on the coyote. I measured the coyote's total body length, the width of the paws, shoulder length, tail, and head size. Since Rush Creek was close to the Taylor Ranch, Gary hiked back to the cabin to place the blood sample in the freezer. I remained with the coyote, carried it up the slope, and laid the animal under some shade to recover from the ketamine. Gary returned, and we both hiked to Cave Creek Camp, where we spent the night. When Gary and I arrived at the Taylor Ranch the next day, Bert walked over to meet us. "Mona has a surprise for you," he said. Gary and I entered the cabin, and our eyes locked on the blueberry tarts on the kitchen table. Gary brewed some coffee to go with the baked goods. Food, coffee, laughter, and conversation were never lacking during the evenings at

Taylor Ranch. Most memorable were the dinners we ate as we sat around the fire pit near the cabins. Gary and Tim would grill elk steaks and chicken. During one after-dinner conversation, the topic of the Middle Fork of the Salmon River topic came up. Mona or Gary encouraged me to hike down Big Creek to see the Middle Fork, a distance of almost seven miles.

I began my hike to the confluence of Big Creek and the Middle Fork of the Salmon at 9 am the next morning. Several miles down the trail, I saw pictographs on a rock face 15 to 20 feet above me. I stopped and photographed the artwork done by native Americans centuries ago. I reached the Middle Fork in two hours. I sat on a large boulder adjacent to the 'river of no return,' listening to the whooshing of the water flowing through the canyon. The seven-mile hike gave me plenty of time to contemplate my immediate future. After spending a few days with Gary and Tim on the bobcat study, I decided to apply for a PhD. Upon my return to the Taylor Ranch, I realized I had left my camera's detachable automatic film advance on the large boulder at the Middle Fork gorge. I hiked back to recover it the next day and completed the hike in four hours. That afternoon, I said goodbye to Bert and Mona, who were flying back to civilization. Mona cried as she said goodbye to Kahmir, saying she had not returned to the Taylor Ranch since Gary had finished his fieldwork. He would be returning soon to the university to analyze the data and complete his dissertation. As I said goodbye and hugged Mona, I, too, realized that soon I would be leaving the Taylor Ranch and coping with civilization.

After 12 days at the Taylor Ranch, I reluctantly said farewell to Gary, Tim, and Kahmir. Mike Dorris, a backcountry pilot from McCall Aviation, landed at the Taylor Ranch airstrip. Tim grabbed his pack; I hugged him goodbye, and he boarded the airplane bound for the Acorn Creek airstrip, where Tim would check traps as he hiked back to the Taylor Ranch. Mike returned to pick up Gary and me. I walked over to Kahmir's pen to say goodbye. I petted the bobcat, and he rubbed his head against my leg. I crouched down, and Kahmir stood on his hind legs, placed his front paws on my shoulders, and rubbed his head against mine. I left Kahmir as tears welled in my eyes, heavyhearted at the thought of leaving. I returned to the airstrip, boarded the airplane, and flew for about an hour and a half as Gary radio-tracked bobcats. We returned to the Taylor Ranch airstrip, and after removing the radio-tracking antennas from the wing struts, Gary and I loaded two kennels (pet taxis) for the three cougar hounds that Gary and Tim used to tree mountain lions to immobilize and attach radio collars to them.

I kept recalling Tim yelling at the dogs at 5 am in the morning as they howled, "Rip! Shut up! Box, Rip, Polly!" As we led the hounds from their pens near the cabin to the airplane, the dogs strained to run ahead, probably anticipating that we were taking them out to hunt for mountain lions. After everything was loaded, I said goodbye to Jim and Holly. Mike taxied onto the airstrip and quickly did the preflight checks. We took off, and I took one last look at Taylor Ranch and the airstrip until the mountains pulled the curtain and obstructed my view. It was a short flight to the Cabin Creek airstrip, Gary's destination. He planned to hike upstream along Big Creek to meet up with Tim. I only had time to say a quick goodbye to Gary, who I loved like my own brother. I did not talk very much on the flight to McCall as I was drowning in melancholy.

Prior to my departure from the Taylor Ranch, Gary instructed me to drive his 1964 red Datsun pickup truck, 'Ole Red,' to Moscow, Idaho. We landed at McCall at noon, and Mike unloaded the dogs, kennels, and my gear. I walked to Gary's pickup truck, found the key, and started the truck. The starter kept turning and turning, but the engine would not fire up, an omen of what lay ahead on my journey to Moscow, Idaho, 190 miles to the north and a four-hour drive. My frustration reached a critical threshold. "Damit Koehler! This truck should be put out to pasture!" I yelled inside, 'Ole Red.' A pitiful castigation heard only by the hounds tied up near the hanger. "I wonder what else will go wrong with this truck?" I asked myself. I walked to the hangar and asked Mike if he had any starting ether to help fire up the recalcitrant 21-year-old truck. I dare call it a rust bucket, but I can't because it showed no rust. "I don't have to start ether, but I can pour some gasoline in the carburetor to help start it," he replied. I opened Datsun's hood and removed the cover of the air filter holder thingy to expose the throat of the carburetor. Mike poured a smidge of gasoline; I turned the ignition key. The engine sputtered, so we tried again. The truck woke up from its long coma as there was no telling when Koehler was last out of the Taylor Ranch and drove his ancient chariot. I drove the truck, parked it near Mike's airplane, and left the engine running, fearing that if I turned it off, it would return to its comatose state. I loaded my duffle bag into the cab and placed the kennels, snowshoes, and dog food in the back of the pickup. Gary's truck had a wooden canopy cover over the cargo area, resembling a *ginormous* doghouse. I gave the hounds some water prior to loading them into the kennels. Rip went in first, then Spike. I only had two kennels, so Polly was out of luck. I moved the two kennels to the middle of the pickup bed and left space for Polly between the kennels and the cab. I tied her up with two leashes, one fastened to one side of the pickup bed and the other to the opposite side so that she could not jump off the truck. Once the canine trio was secured, I drove away from the airport, drove a mile or so, pulled over at a convenience store, left the truck engine running for fear it would not start if I didn't, walked into the store, and purchased two sodas and a sandwich to eat on the road.

I climbed back into 'Ole Red' and drove. As I neared Cascade Lake, the road made a 90-degree left turn. I thought of the hounds in the back of the truck, so I pumped the brakes, took the turn at 15 miles an hour, and heard a metallic pinging sound coming off the pavement. I looked back and saw the gas cap skidding across the street. "Oh swell," I thought, "now all I need is a car to run over it." I pulled off to the nearest parallel parking space and parked the truck. I followed SOTOP (Standard Old Truck Operating Procedure) and left the engine running. "I wonder what else will go wrong," I thought to myself as I got out of the truck and ran across the street to retrieve the gas cap. I laughed out loud as I thought of the sound the gas cap made as it skipped across the asphalt.

I quickly grabbed the metal escapee, walked back to the truck, and secured it in place. I heard a click as it locked in place and wondered if the key to the locking gas cap was in the truck. "Has to be," I said to myself. I resumed my journey northward. I made a pit stop at Riggins, 57 miles north of McCall, to provide water to the three hounds, then continued to White Bird, Idaho.

I passed through the small town of White Bird and started the climb up the White Bird grade. Gary had described White Bird grade to me as a climb up and over a mountain dividing the Salmon River drainage and the

Camas Prairie to the north with an uphill grade of seven percent. Although Gary did not mention the slope percentage and probably said it was "steeper than a cow's face." Any ordinary vehicle would have no problem making it up and over the pass; that being said, the 21-year-old 'Red' was no ordinary vehicle. Ole Red strained up the grade in third gear, sputtering a painful and mournful cry as if in its death throes.

I depressed the clutch and repeatedly depressed the gas pedal, which only slowed our speed up the mountain further. I downshifted to second gear, and Ole Red screamed as I slowly let out the clutch, and we inched our way up the hill. "Come on, Red, come on," I pleaded as if the pickup truck could hear me. I shifted to third gear, and the sputtering and coughing resumed, followed by a quick downshift to second gear. Depress the clutch shift, pump the gas pedal, shift, repeat. I repeated this process until, midway up the grade, I pulled off at a scenic overlook to let the engine cool off. The sun's heat beat down on the asphalt, truck, dogs, and me. After 30 minutes, I climbed back into Ole Red and proceeded up the grade. I even had to downshift to first gear a few times. Finally, I saw the top of the pass.

"Only a few more curves, and we'll make it Red," I said. This was like a near-death experience where time supposedly slows down. After what seemed like hours, Ole Red made it to the summit, a climb of 2,664 feet, but I was not counting at the time. It was all downhill to Grangeville. "Thank God! I yelled in excitement, followed up with a few 'yee haws' and 'yays.'

I stopped at a convenience store in Grangeville to give the dogs water and buy myself a soft drink. Two hours later, I pulled into a gas station at Lewiston and looked for the key to the gas cap. I opened the glove box, but there was nothing; under the seat, zilch; behind the seat, nada. I asked the service station attendant for the distance to Moscow, "30 miles," he replied. "I can probably make it," I thought to myself. The stress of barely making it up the White Bird summit and staring up the I Lewiston grade, an uphill climb of 2 thousand feet, I never thought of looking for the key to the gas cap above the visor on the driver's side. Ole Red slowly inched us up the highway at 30 miles per hour as I held my breath and kept my fingers crossed. I did not continuously hold my breath as the lack of oxygen would have obviously caused me to pass out. Rather, it is an expression alluding to a state of anxiousness or nervousness. "I made it," I yelled with excitement upon reaching the top of the escarpment. I continued north on Highway 95 to Moscow, and soon Murphy's Law, "Anything that can go wrong will go wrong, and at the worst possible time," descended on me like a sledgehammer on a ten-penny nail. Nine to 10 miles south of Moscow, Ole Red began to sputter. Since Ole Red was on a short downhill grade, I quickly concluded the inevitable: the truck had run out of fuel. I shifted Ole Red to neutral and coasted. There was little to no space to park on the right side of the highway, so I coasted left onto a driveway leading to a farmhouse about 500 yards away.

"Great, just great," I muttered to myself. "I knew disaster would strike before this trip was over." I walked to the farmhouse, hoping that someone was there and I could call Maurice to rescue me and the dogs. I knocked on the door several times; no one was home. Perfect! I fished my address book out and a piece of paper from my duffel bag and wrote down Maurice's name and phone number. I tried unsuccessfully to flag down cars speeding toward Moscow. When all seemed hopeless, a pickup truck pulled over. The driver, a young man named Zane, offered to telephone Maurice and relay my predicament to him. Maurice soon drove up with fuel for Ole Red. After refueling the pickup truck, I climbed into the cab, lowered the visor, and there was the key to the gas cap. I refueled Ole Red, and Maurice transferred the hounds and two kennels to his truck. I started Ole Red and followed him to Moscow.

While in Moscow, I reunited with Maurice and his family, as well as Esther, Wayne, and their toddler Nick. I spent a week in Moscow and Deary. While there, I prepared a Mexican dinner for his family and his graduate students at Maurice's house. During that week, I visited with one of Maurice's former PhD graduate students working on a post-doctoral project. I learned of his unsuccessful attempts to secure a permanent job in spite of his credentials, so I dropped my idea of returning to graduate school. I decided to continue working for the FWS and hope for the best. During my flight home from Idaho to Corpus Christi, my hopes to live and work in the mountains faded as the airliner climbed above the clouds, obscuring my view of the rugged landscape below. I had plenty of time to contemplate my life and career during the long flight and resolved to make lemonade out of lemons; in other words, focus on the positive aspects of my life. I returned to Corpus Christi with the thought that everything happens for a reason. I was not wrong. Living and working in Corpus Christi allowed me to reconnect with my parents, my two brothers and their families, and my life-long friends at Encino.

Chapter 16: Whooping Cranes and Civil Engineers

During my flight from Idaho to Corpus Christi, I resolved to make lemonade out of lemons – in other words, to focus on the positive aspects of my life. Gerry became more and more of a mentor, listening, offering words of encouragement, and asking thought-provoking questions. He motivated me and the rest of the staff. Gerry's leadership and interpersonal communication skills helped our office grow and succeed to the point where the regional director awarded our office a plaque designating our office as "office of the year." For all intents and purposes, Gerry became the *de facto* leader of our field office. He coordinated with our field supervisor, whose leadership and motivational skills paled in comparison to Gerry's. During my tenure with Ecological Services, I felt that our field office was the proverbial "red-headed stepchild" of the FWS, neglected for the most part and severely underfunded and understaffed. Since most ES field office work entailed reviewing federal water development permits and permits to dredge and fill wetlands, and federally permitted or licensed projects, division policy dictated that only field supervisors could sign outgoing correspondence, no matter how trivial. I found the field supervisor's reviews and edits of my draft letters and reports extremely frustrating as my writing was grammatically correct. Many of his revisions were changes that were trivial and a matter of personal preference. The field supervisor justified his revisions, saying his signature was on the outgoing correspondence. For me, it meant additional time and effort to deal with an already heavy workload. Staff frustrations with the field supervisor led to a first-ever retreat off-site to discuss strategies for addressing various water development projects as well as endangered species conservation. During side conversations with Gerry and late-night conversations out of earshot of the field supervisor, the staff and I unloaded our grievances regarding the field supervisor's deficient leadership skills. Gerry, in essence, became our de facto intermediary when communicating with the field supervisor.

Ideas flowed from Gerry like a stream flowing down a steep mountainside during late spring and early summer runoff. His input and efforts led our office to obtain funds to pay CCSU graduate students to conduct research studies related to our work. One study evaluated the success of mitigation measures our office recommended on wetland dredge and fill permits issued on the Upper Laguna Madre. That student later joined the field office as a permanent FWS employee. Our office became a human dynamo, achieving conservation results on the ground and out in the bays. Gerry's mentoring and leadership, as well as the camaraderie in the field office, motivated me to tackle three environmental issues: the loss of thorny brush habitat in the Lower Rio Grande Valley in South Texas, the loss of whooping crane habitat due to maintenance dredging of the Gulf Intracoastal Waterway (GIWW) at the Aransas NWR; and impacts to the Laguna Madre from maintenance dredging of the GIWW. Throughout the history of the Lower Rio Valley (Valley) in Texas, natural ecosystems and humans have coped with the feast-or-famine nature of water quantity in the river and from rainfall. According to the International Boundary and Water Commission's Texas Clean Rivers Program, Water diversions and heavy water consumption left about 20 percent of the river water to flow into the Gulf of Mexico.

The insatiable thirst for water and the continued increase in the human population led the Rio Grande Municipal Water Authority to propose the construction of two dams within the channel of the Rio Grande downstream from the existing Falcon Dam. The dams would store precipitation runoff flowing into the river downstream from Falcon Dam as well as allow the diversion of additional water from the Rio Grande. The field office received some funding from the Santa Ana and LRGV NWRs to assess the proposed channel dam project and its potential impacts on river flows, riparian habitat, and the refuge units along the river. I tackled that project, researched the history of water development in the Valley, its effects on the ecology and wildlife of the lower Rio Grande, and the potential impacts of the proposed channel dams on the riparian corridor and wildlife inhabiting the remaining small, isolated tracts of thorny brush habitat that once covered 90 percent of the Valley. I completed a 32-page report concluding that the proposed channel dams could remove vital links in the riparian corridors, which necessitated a more thorough understanding of the corridor's role in the survival of the ocelot and jaguarundi in the Valley.

The increase in population resulted in a concurrent increase in demands for municipal, industrial, and rural water supplies. In 1982, the Port of Brownsville's Navigation District, several cities in Cameron County, and a municipal water district formed a regional water authority and proposed the construction of a channel water storage dam downstream of Brownsville to address projected water demands resulting from anticipated industrial growth along the Port of Brownsville and the Brownsville Ship Channel. The water storage proposal would create impoundments 30 miles long within the river channel. The channel dam concept never passed the proposal stage despite an intensive lack of effort by its promoters. Approximately 17 years later, the proposal was resurrected from the dustbin of history, lending credence to conservationists' adage that "proposed water projects never die," they returned to threaten our natural environment.

Through my involvement with the Coastal Bend chapter of the Audubon Society, I helped conduct surveys of colonial nesting waterbirds on small rookery islands in Nueces and Corpus Christi bays as well as on the Upper Laguna Madre. Gene Blacklock, a member of the Coastal

Bend chapter of the Audubon Society, conducted surveys of rookery islands on Nueces Bay and instructed me on the survey protocols. Gene worked at the Welder Wildlife Refuge (rewrite the description of his position at Welder - environmental education). As we approached a rookery island, the herons, egrets, terns, and gulls would take flight, filling the air with their raucous calls. I would maneuver the 14-foot Jon boat toward an island and increase the throttle to get the bow of the boat onto the oyster shell beach. Once the boat was partially on the island's shore, Gene would grab the line or rope attached to the bow of the boat, jump off, and quickly pull the boat further onto the island. Time was of the essence as the eggs were exposed to the sun, so we had to estimate quickly the number of birds circling overhead and those remaining on their nests guarding their eggs. I wore a hat during all of my fieldwork outings to protect me from the sun as well as defensive cover during rookery island bird surveys from aerial bombardment of excrement, either oral or otherwise, from the swirling mass of gulls and terns.

The experience I gained in assisting with those surveys led to additional colonial waterbird surveys in the

Upper Laguna Madre with Dr. Alan Chaney. Dr. Chaney was a biology professor at Texas A&I University, now Texas A&M University-Kingsville. Dr. Chaney coordinated the surveys at the Upper Laguna Madre. Never passing up an opportunity for fieldwork, I somehow connected with Dr. Chaney and offered to assist with the surveys on the Upper Laguna Madre. The KANN Do served as the proper transportation vessel to conduct the surveys, given the distances involved.

The initial dredging of the Gulf Intracoastal Waterway through the Upper Laguna Madre and the subsequent periodic removal of sediment to maintain its authorized depth left a string of small islands along the sides of the 12-foot-deep channel created by the disposal of the dredged material. Some of the spoil islands created nesting habitats for colonial nesting waterbirds such as herons, egrets, terns, and gulls. Gene Blacklock and Dr. Alan Chaney pointed out that fishermen would sometimes pull up to rookery islands during the nesting season, get off their boats to fish from the island, stretch their legs, or empty their bladders. This causes the nesting birds to immediately take flight, inadvertently breaking some of their eggs as they hurriedly push off their nests to become airborne. This also exposes the eggs to the sun, causing the developing embryos and chicks to die from the heat or from predation by gulls and grackles swooping into the exposed nests for an easy meal. Colonial nesting waterbirds in the Texas Gulf Coast typically nest from late February through August when recreational use by coastal anglers and boaters is highest, putting them at greater risk of coming into contact with people. According to the Texas Parks and Wildlife Department, disturbance by humans can often lead to nest failure and, in some cases, complete abandonment of an island.

With repeated disturbances, an entire colony of nesting waterbirds may abandon an island and give up on breeding for the year. Over time, this can potentially lead to significant population declines. I contacted Lee Sausley, a news reporter from a Corpus Christi TV station, and asked him if he would be interested in doing a story urging boaters and anglers to keep their distance from rookery islands during the nesting season. Sausley jumped on the idea and the opportunity to go out on the Laguna Madre with us. His story aired on the 6 pm and 10 pm news.

The State of Texas General Land Office (GLO) manages the state-owned dredged spoil islands and permits the construction of small fishing cabins on some of the islands. Prior to 1973 trappers, commercial fishermen, and others built shacks or cabins throughout the bays and estuaries along the Texas Gulf Coast. The Texas legislature authorized the continued use of these cabins for recreational purposes only through the issuance of a permit or contract by the GLO and payment of fees to that state agency. State law considers the cabins to be state-owned structures, and the contract authorizes the use of the site, not ownership of the structure, for a term of five years. Recipients of cabin permits are required to adhere to all terms and conditions of the permit.

Ken Collins and I hauled the KANN Do to the Bird Island Basin boat ramp at Padre Island National Seashore Bird Island Basin, loaded a cooler containing our lunches and drinking water into the boat, and then backed the boat and trailer down the ramp. Once the boat was in the water, we drove the vehicle and trailer off the ramp, parked it, and climbed aboard the KANN Do. Dr. Chaney guided us to each bird rookery island. U.S. Geological Survey biologist Chris

Onuf joined us on the surveys, so our crew of four quickly surveyed each island to minimize disturbance of the breeding birds. After surveying several rookery islands and in the midst of surveying another, a cold blast of wind enveloped us as if Mother Nature had suddenly turned on a giant fan.

"Temperature feels like it dropped 20 degrees," I yelled out. "A cold front just roared in," replied Dr. Chaney. We made our way back to the boat, hoping that the adult birds would return and sit on their eggs to keep them warm and viable. As soon as we climbed aboard the KANN Do, we were pelted with cold drops of rain. We pulled the boat away from the island, and the rain intensified. "I know a cabin nearby that is not locked where we can get in out of the rain," Dr. Chaney shouted above the roar of the Mercury outboard motor. We quickly made our way to the cabin, secured the KANN Do to the dock, and went inside. We sat around a small kitchen table as the rain pelted the cabin roof and windows. Someone found a deck of cards, grabbed the deck, shuffled the cards, and remarked, "Looks like we're going to be in here for a while; everyone here knows how to play hearts?" The wind and rain continued with relentless fury for what seemed like hours. After waiting and playing hearts for two or three hours, we all agreed to wait for a decrease in the intensity of the wind and rain and return to Bird Island Basin.

The rain gods must have heard us, and the rain's intensity lessened. We returned to the KANN Do amidst the light rain and proceeded to Bird Island Basin. Mother Nature let us know that she was not done with us yet as the wind and rain intensified. The rain quickly pooled up on KANN Do's deck such that when Ken or I increased the throttle, the bow of the boat would angle slightly upward, forcing the water on the deck to flow towards the stern. Chris advised us to decrease the speed to avoid flooding the battery, providing power to the outboard motor. That led us to drain the pooled-up rainwater on the deck by increasing the throttle to the point just below the battery level, allowing Chris to remove the drain plug on the stern and drain the water out. The procedure was repeated several times as we made our way to Bird Island Basin. As we neared Bird Island Basin, the rain stopped. We reduced speed entering the basin and saw a National Park Service (NPS) boat and crew about to leave the basin. The NPS crew told us they were about to search for us as our office had called and informed them that we were out and unaccounted for. "You should get a marine two-way radio for your boat," one of the NPS employees told us. We returned to our office and made that requisition request to our field supervisor. From then on, the KANN Do crews could communicate when necessary.

Although the initial dredging and subsequent maintenance of the Intracoastal waterway created small islands that served as rookeries for colonial nesting waterbirds, periodic dredging as well as barge and large boat traffic resulted in habitat loss for the endangered whooping crane at the Aransas National Wildlife Refuge 25 miles up the coast from Corpus Christi Bay. I made several trips to the refuge to assess maintenance dredging of the GIWW section on the refuge and impacts on the whooping crane habitat. On each trip, Tom Stehn, refuge wildlife biologist, and David Blankenship, National Audubon Society biologist, would comment on marsh erosion due to boat and barge traffic along the GIWW. After hearing them voice the same comment during several of my visits, I proposed placing wooden stakes at several locations where Tom and

David had noticed the loss of marsh habitat. Tom and I made a follow-up trip along the GIWW and marked each site previously identified by Tom and David with two wooden stakes 48 inches long and one by two inches wide.

We placed one stake at the edge of the marsh vegetation adjacent to the canal, the second one several feet away from the canal, and the first stake. Since GPS units were not commercially available until a few years later, we resorted to using a handheld compass and a tape measure. We took compass bearings from the second stake to the first one at the edge of the marsh and recorded the distance. "If the difference a year later is a few inches, the rate of erosion will be difficult, if not impossible, to quantify," I commented to Tom after we hammered one stake into the ground. We returned to each site a year later and found the edge of marsh vegetation had retreated two to three feet! We were both shocked but not surprised. Tom later found historical aerial photographs of the refuge taken before the excavation of the GIWW through the refuge in the 1940s. He used a planimeter, a measuring instrument used to measure areas in two-dimensional maps, to measure the number of acres of marsh shown in historical aerial photographs taken prior to the construction of the GIWW and compared that value to the footprint of the canal and open water habitat adjacent to the canal. His analysis showed approximately # acres of whooping crane habitat lost due to the construction and maintenance of the GIWW as well as to erosion caused by boat and barge traffic along the canal.

To document the impact of water displacement by barges as well as wakes caused by boats traveling along the GIWW, Ken and I later video-recorded barges and large commercial boats plying through the canal and the water displacement and wakes eroding the shoreline. We shared the video with our colleagues from the local offices of Texas Parks and Wildlife and the Texas General Land office, which also dealt with the environmental impacts of maintenance dredging. A few years after I transferred to the ES office in Cheyenne, Wyoming, Tom Maurer and Ken Collins informed me that the Corpus Christi ES field office purchased several 80-pound sacks of premixed concrete, sand, and gravel, wrangled up volunteers from a local scout troop, and armored the marsh sites identified by Tom Stehn and I several years earlier to protect them from wave action created by boat and barge traffic. They also managed to get a local TV station to cover the story on-site. According to Tom and Ken, the U.S. Army Corps of Engineers went into damage control as they probably had 'egg on their face,' especially with the TV news report showing Boy Scouts doing the work that the COE should have done. The Corps later armored eroded marsh areas with riprap.

Conflict with the COE did not end there. Maintenance dredging of navigation channels such as the GIWW is accomplished with a hydraulic dredge, a floating vessel that works like a giant vacuum cleaner by sucking a mixture of bottom material and water from the channel bottom. The dredge lowers a pipe with a cutter head that loosens the bottom material, which is then pumped up the pipe through the dredge pump and out through the discharge pipe. The discharge pipe varies in length depending on the location of the disposal area. Past dredged material disposal practices by the COE consisted of placing the end of the discharge pipe a distance away from the GIWW and disposing of the dredged material into the bays smothering seagrass and oyster beds that provided habitat for countless species of invertebrates and fishes.

After several dredging cycles, the material consolidated, piled up, and emerged to form islands along the GIWW. Congress amended the Clean Water Act (Federal Water Pollution Control Act) in 1972, placing additional restrictions on the dredging and filling of wetlands, including bays and estuaries. When practicable, the COE discharged dredged material into a leveed containment area adjacent to the GIWW. The COE designed the containment areas to allow the dredged sediment to settle to the bottom, and the water to decant back into the bay.

The engineers factored in two to three feet of freeboard when designing the levees. During one dredging cycle, a containment area levee breached, allowing water and silt to spill into the bay, which is a critical habitat for endangered whooping cranes and covering seagrass and oyster reefs.

Communicating and negotiating with civil engineers presented a challenge; it seemed like they spoke a different language. I took it upon myself to learn negotiating techniques. I took a negotiating class at Corpus Christi State University and purchased two books, *"Getting to Yes"* and *"Getting Past No,"* to increase my chances of convincing the engineers to design their projects to avoid or minimize impacts on fish and wildlife habitat. The techniques I learned paid off when I first used them when accompanying Tom Stehn and two engineers with the COE to identify dredged material disposal options within the whooping crane critical habitat. Tom, the two engineers, and I scoped out an island with remnants of a leveed containment area of the refuge but within whooping crane critical habitat. Tom and I stood on the partially eroded levee as the engineering party walked down the levee onto the flats covered with sea oxeye daisies and other ground-covering vegetation. "Let's wait here," I advised Tom, "if we go with them, we will have to negotiate our way back here." The engineering party stopped a considerable distance from us, and after realizing that we were not with them, they looked back at us. "What are you doing way out there?" I shouted, "The levee is over here." The men trudged back to our location. We succeeded in getting the engineers to restore the existing levees rather than enlarging the containment area and chewing up the whooping crane habitat.

Maintenance dredging impacts were not limited to whooping crane habitat. Disposal of the dredged slurry in other estuaries, such as the Upper and Lower Laguna Madre, also smothered seagrass beds in those estuaries. Two lessons from Gerry Jackson came to the forefront, 'don't settle for the way things have always been done' and 'think outside the box.' The Fish and Wildlife Coordination Act of 1934 and subsequent amendments to the act authorize the FWS to evaluate impacts to fish and wildlife from federally-funded or licensed/permitted projects in coordination with state fish and wildlife agencies to protect fish and wildlife when federal actions result in the control or modification of a natural stream or body of water. The CCESFO assessed the environmental impacts of dredge and fill projects, including the maintenance dredging of the GIWW, and met with local and regional staff from the National Marine Fisheries Service (NMFS), the Texas Parks and Wildlife Department (TPWD), and the Texas General Land Office(TGLO) to coordinate agency responses to the permitting agency, typically the COE.

The idea of reevaluating the environmental impacts of maintenance dredging the GIWW was brought up during one of the interagency coordination meetings. The discussion led the group to propose reviewing the final environmental impact statement (FEIS) produced by the COE a decade earlier and identifying deficiencies in the report. Each agency staff member at the interagency meeting volunteered to review specific chapters of the FEIS. The interagency group identified several shortcomings in the FEIS, and I volunteered to draft a report to submit to the COE. I drafted a cover letter for my field supervisor's signature and presented it to him along with the report. "What's this?" he responded as I handed the report and cover letter to him. In retrospect, I should have given the field supervisor a heads-up on the team's effort and the report. The tone of his response prompted me to intensify my efforts to apply for FWS jobs at other FWS locations.

Chapter 17: Things Happen For A Reason

The year I moved from New Mexico to Corpus Christi, a large oil company leased the mineral rights for oil and gas exploration and development on my late grandmother's ranch. My mother, aunts, and uncles inherited the ranch, subdivided the surface land between them, and shared ownership of the mineral rights. The oil company eventually drilled several gas wells, providing my mother and her siblings with royalty payments and a much-needed financial life ring for my parents. After a few years, my mother complained that her royalty checks were much reduced, yet her siblings did not have any significant reductions in the royalties they received. Her consistent monthly complaints led me to review legal documents pertaining to her mineral rights.

I learned that since my parents did not have the money to cover the attorney fees for appealing the civil case on my Dad's ranch, my parents resorted to using my mother's mineral rights as collateral prior to the oil company drilling wells on what used to be my grandmother's ranch (Longoria Ranch). According to my parents, their attorney summoned them to his law office to sign a legal document sometime after the wells were completed and producing natural gas. My parents recalled going into a room with only the attorney and my parents present with their attorney instructing them to sign a document. I asked them if their lawyer had informed them of the purpose of the legal documents they were signing, and they replied that he had not. "Did he tell you to read the document?" I asked them. "Sign here," according to my parents, was all he said. I only had to read a few lines of the legal document to learn that the document conveyed a large portion of my mother's mineral rights in perpetuity. Given the amount of royalties from the wells, the financial benefit to the lawyer more than paid for the costs of appealing the civil case on my dad's ranch.

I researched the Texas State Bar Rules at the Corpus Christi State University library and learned that by not explaining the purpose of the legal document that the attorney instructed my parents to sign or by not allowing my parents to review the document, the attorney was at odds with the State Bar's rules of conduct. I wrote and mailed a lengthy letter to the State Bar of Texas and cited the specific rules I believed the attorney did not follow. The State Bar contacted me and informed me they were investigating several other cases involving my parents' attorney. A civil trial ensued; however, 'the glass was half full' in terms of justice for my parents. The State Bar attorneys informed me and my parents that the chances were high that my parents' attorney would file for bankruptcy and my mother would not receive monetary compensation from the defendant. My parents faced two options: settling out of court or continuing with the trial. I explained the options to my mother and father.

The settlement resulted in the attorney retaining one-quarter of the mineral interest and paying my parents for a portion of the amount of royalty money he received. Sometimes justice is not impartial and quite often history repeats itself, especially in South Texas; two more landowners, i.e., my parents in South Texas, were scammed out of their property, as countless others lost their land grants and mineral rights to unscrupulous, highly educated individuals. Before 1900, Mexican American landowners facing drought and financial problems sold their ranches for as little as 50 cents per acre. Others had their lands confiscated for delinquent taxes. Legal battles over lands and minerals continue to plague landowners in the Wild Horse Desert to this day.

The legacy of intra-family property disputes plagued my parents throughout the years, as she owned 89 acres of surface land and mineral rights she inherited from her mother. My mother sold the surface rights of the 89-acre tract and one-quarter of the mineral rights. Having suffered through almost a decade of financial hardship after my father lost his ranch, my mother started receiving a substantial amount of oil and gas royalties in the 1980s. They placed a portion of their royalty money in savings and used their windfall to realize their dreams—my father's plan was to have enough land to raise a few cattle, and my mother's to build her dream house large enough to accommodate her three sons and grandchildren when they came to visit. After natural gas was discovered in the Longoria Ranch, the owner of the 89-acre tract filed a lawsuit claiming that my mother had intended to sell him a larger share of the mineral rights. The lawsuit forced the oil company to place the oil and gas royalties my mother received in escrow. My parents had to subsist on the royalty money they had saved; they were now at risk of depleting their savings, which they eventually did. My father had to take out loans for subsistence and pay the mortgage on the house. Several of the loans were from a savings and loan association embroiled in the national savings and loan crisis in the early 1990s. Eventually, the money ran out, and my father ran out of options. To make matters worse, my parents were still obligated to pay off the loans to the Federal Deposit Insurance Corporation (FDIC). The FDIC contacted my father requesting payment on the loans or losing their home; however, my father was destitute. The intense stress suffered from the possible loss of his home possibly contributed to a ruptured cerebral aneurysm. My father, whom I looked up to, loved, and was my role model, passed away on April 23, 1993, at the age of 67.

Hardly a workday went by in the Corpus Christi field office, and I didn't keep my eyes and ears open for job vacancies in FWS offices west of the Mississippi River, specifically in states with mountains and public lands. To quote John Muir, the mountains kept calling me, and I had to go. Living in Corpus Christi limited me to traveling once or twice a year to hike, backpack, and camp in national forests in northern New Mexico and southern Colorado. I also missed doing fieldwork, collecting and analyzing data, and interpreting the results in a technical report. I kept trying for jobs with the FWS Division of Research, but that proved fruitless. That yearning subsided for the most part in 1986 when a cute young lady named Julie approached my desk. I learned that she worked with Minerals Management Service (MMS), a federal agency with a field office located on the Corpus Christi State University campus. I don't remember the details of the conversation, but I do vividly recall Julie saying that she played racquetball. I asked her what else she liked to do. "I like to camp," she replied. That's all I needed to hear. A wonderful friendship transpired after sharing a conversation and a meal at a local pizza restaurant. I was transformed from a wilderness backpacking snob, 'no car camping for me,' to car camping in several state parks in the Texas Hill Country and a 550-mile drive to Big Bend National Park. I, in turn, introduced her to backpacking at Lost Maples State Park, 100 miles northwest of San Antonio.

As my relationship with Julie continued to grow, she informed me that MMS was downsizing its Corpus Christi office. Her choices were limited, as were the locations of MMS offices. Julie did not want to return to New Orleans, Louisiana, where she started her career with MMS. "Where else does MMS have offices? I asked her. She listed Anchorage, Alaska; Los Angeles, California; the Washington, DC area, and Denver, Colorado. I perked up at the mention of Denver and told her about Colorado, the Rocky Mountains, public lands, and many camping opportunities. She applied for a transfer to the MMS office in Denver and was soon on her way to the mile-high city. After succeeding in helping my parents achieve financial security, I resumed my quest for a job in or near Denver. I landed a job as an environmental contaminants specialist with the FWS Ecological Services field office in Cheyenne, Wyoming, in 1988. I moved to Fort Collins, Colorado, and carpooled 60 miles to work. A year later, Julie and I exchanged wedding vows in Corpus Christi in the presence of family and friends. We purchased our first house in Fort Collins. She carpooled to Denver, and I continued carpooling to Cheyenne.

Sometimes justice is not objective and history repeats itself, especially in South Texas; two more landowners, i.e. my parents, in South Texas were scammed out of their property as had countless others that lost their land grants and mineral rights to unscrupulous, highly educated individuals. Prior to 1900, Mexican-American landowners facing drought and financial problems sold their ranches for as little as 50-cents per acre. Others had their lands confiscated for delinquent taxes. Legal battles over lands and minerals continue to plague landowners in the Wild Horse Desert to this day.

The legacy of intra-family property disputes plagued my parents throughout the years that she owned 89 acres of surface land and mineral rights she inherited from her mother. Having suffered through almost a decade of financial hardship after my father lost his ranch, my mother started receiving a substantial amount of oil and gas royalties in the 1980's. They placed a portion of their royalty money in savings, and used their windfall to realize their dreams; my father's to have enough land to raise a few cattle and my mother's to build her dream house large enough to accommodate her three sons and grandchildren when they came to visit. After natural gas was discovered in the Longoria Ranch, her cousin filed a law suit claiming that my mother had intended to sell him a larger share of the mineral rights. The law suit forced the oil company to place the oil and gas royalties that my mother received in escrow. My parents had to subsist on the royalty money they had saved; they were now at risk of depleting their savings which they eventually did. My father had to take out loans to for subsistence and to pay the mortgage on the house. Several of the loans were from a savings and loan association that became embroiled in the national savings and loan crisis in the early 1990s. Eventually, the money ran out and my father ran out of options. To make matters worse, my parents were still obligated to pay off the loans to the Federal Deposit Insurance Corporation (FDIC). The FDIC contacted my father requesting payment on the loans or risk losing their home; however, my father was destitute. The intense stress suffered from the possible loss of his home quite possibly contributed to a ruptured cerebral aneurysm. My father, whom I looked up to, loved, and was my role model, passed away on April 23, 1993 at the age of 67. To this day, 30 years later, tears well up in my eyes when I think about the loss of my father and his undying love and compassion.

CHAPTER 18: SELENIUM, WETLANDS, OIL PITS, AND BIRDS

A month prior to transferring to my new job in Cheyenne, WY, I was advised to attend a national meeting of FWS Environmental Contaminants Specialists (EC Specialists), most of whom had PhDs with academic and career expertise in wildlife toxicology. As I mingled with the group, I felt my self-confidence taking a nose dive; my ears were bombarded with a cacophony of toxicological terms. I felt out of place that I didn't belong with this group. I had the same feeling in graduate school at the University of Idaho in the Big Game Management class, attended by students who had worked on student projects on wildlife management and taken courses on the subject. My experience with contaminants work was limited to writing a paper in graduate school on biomagnification of the pesticide DDT in peregrine falcons and bald eagles, drafting a proposal for collecting water and sediments in the Lower Rio Grande Valley for pesticide analysis and assisting Gerry Jackson and Tom Maurer with collecting sediment samples in Corpus Christi Bay and the bays adjacent to the Aransas

National Wildlife Refuge. I returned to Corpus Christi and kept telling myself, "I can do this; I can do this." I opted to live in Fort Collins, a university town of 100,000 diverse amenities and a commute of 50 to 60 miles to the ES field office in Cheyenne.

I hit the ground running on my second day working in Wyoming, attending an interagency meeting on contaminant investigations of Department of Interior (DOI) irrigation projects to assess irrigation-related contamination of national wildlife refuges, migratory birds, and endangered species; there was no time for self-doubt, only time to quickly learn as much as I could to get the job done. My anxiety over not having a college degree in toxicology and being limited to assisting, I was generally familiar with the issue of selenium contamination caused by irrigation following the discovery by FWS biologist Felix Smith and research biologist Harry Ohlendorf in 1983 of deformed grebes, coots, and other aquatic birds at the Kesterson National Wildlife Refuge in California. Their research findings were aired on the CBS news show "60 Minutes" and made newspaper headlines nationally, raising a fire-storm of public inquiries asking members of Congress and Interior Secretary Donald Hodel if other wildlife refuges were contaminated. The media firestorm and the nationwide public outcry forced Hodel to initiate interagency contaminants investigations of other federal irrigation projects and impacts on migratory birds and endangered species. I learned that I would be conducting contaminants investigations on two irrigation projects in WY: the Kendrick Irrigation Project (Kendrick Project) immediately upstream from Casper and the Riverton Irrigation Project (Riverton Project) approximately 10 to 15 miles north of Riverton. I met Dr. George T. Allen, FWS biological technician from the Billings, Montana ES Field Office, who would be assisting me with the Kendrick Project selenium investigation. Irrigation runoff, as well as subsurface drain water from the Kendrick Project, created four major wetlands in the semi-arid landscape: Rasmus Lee Lake (120 acres); Goose Lake (100 acres); Illco Pond (2 acres); and 33-Mile Reservoir (10 acres). Since these wetlands were located on private property, we obtained permission from the landowners and would notify them prior to entering their land so they would know who was on their land. During one such visit to advise a landowner of our presence, I saw two ranch hands standing next to the barn and corral. We stopped close to them, and I saw a look of fear on their faces. Having grown up in South Texas, I immediately sensed why they reacted the way they did.

"No somos la migra," ("We are not Immigration," the Border Patrol agents), I informed them as they saw the federal government license plates on our truck and assumed we were with the Border Patrol or federal law enforcement.

We also conducted contaminants investigations in Fremont County at the Riverton Irrigation Project located near Riverton, Wyoming. Irrigation runoff and drain water flowed into a natural depression in the landscape and created Ocean Lake. The 11,505 acre lake and smaller ponds in the project area created a habitat for Canadian geese, ducks, eared grebes, American avocets, black-necked stilts, and other aquatic birds. I looked forward to the fieldwork. Little did I know that I would spend my entire workdays during the summer and fall working and living in Casper and Riverton. George drove from Billings to Casper every Monday during that first summer and assisted me with fieldwork each week. I viewed George as my mentor as he guided me with sampling protocols, sample preservation, bird surveys, and much more; his patience, compassion, and love for critters, large and small, led to a life-long friendship. When other work tasks kept George in Montana, John Malloy, a temporary employee, would drive to Casper to assist me with fieldwork. Each Monday morning, I would load the government vehicle with sampling gear, data sheets, coolers, waders, and my luggage and make the two-and-a-half-hour drive to Casper. The fieldwork was intensive during my first two years working in Wyoming. I spent more time living in Casper than Fort Collins from June through October. It's not that I complained, as I was doing fieldwork studying and observing wildlife, which is why I chose a career in wildlife biology to begin with.

Fieldwork consisted of collecting biological samples from the study area and from a reference area to determine selenium concentrations in the food chain. We collected aquatic vegetation and aquatic insects from ponds receiving irrigation runoff and subsurface irrigation drain water; addled aquatic bird and waterfowl eggs from nests on or near the four major wetlands; fish from two of the ponds that received irrigation drain water and from the North

Platte River reach adjacent to and downstream of the Kendrick Project. Biological samples were also collected from reference sites located beyond the Kendrick Irrigation Project that were not irrigated and did not receive any drain water. We monitored the nests of Canada geese, American avocets, eared grebes, and puddle ducks, such as mallards and teals, to determine nesting success and conducted weekly bird surveys to record the number and species of aquatic birds using the four main wetlands within the Kendrick Project. We documented 42 species of birds using the four prominent wetlands in the irrigation project study area. We followed strict protocols for collecting biological samples for selenium and other trace element analysis.

Processing aquatic bird eggs, especially addled Canada goose eggs, felt like disarming a small bomb as bacteria in addled eggs exposed to the hot sun turned the contents into a foul-smelling liquid. The decay of globulin and keratin, two proteins in eggs, releases hydrogen sulfide, which has a very potent sulfurous smell. We quickly learned to drill a small pinhole in the shell to release the gas in the egg, but not before we had one or two potent goose eggs explode. Fortunately, we were dissecting those eggs outside, not in the motel room. Immediately after processing addled eggs, I would head for the bathroom and take a shower to mentally and physically rid myself of the odor. Other hazards included stepping into seemingly bottomless muck that behaved like quicksand in the lake bottom and white patches of alkali on the ground surface that could conceal soft mud under the surface. At times, we had to drive across the alkali mudflats to reach nests that were too far to carry all the sampling gear on foot. I'd drive fast across those mudflats to maintain momentum lest the truck sinks into the soft ground. Getting mired in the mud meant walking one-and-a-half to two miles to the paved highway, trying our luck to get a ride to Casper, calling the ES office at Cheyenne, informing them of our dilemma, and figuring out whether to get a tow truck or just having someone come and help us free the truck. At the end of the day, we'd stop at a car wash in Casper to rinse the grayish-black muck from our wading boots, sampling equipment, and the truck.

We conducted fieldwork regardless of the weather: cold temperatures in late spring and early summer, rain, hot days in July and August, and the relentless WY winds. We set light traps an hour before sunset and checked them the next morning, placing the aquatic insects into small glass vials. Waterboatmen are quite small, measuring less than one-quarter inch or 13 mm long, with copepods even smaller at one to two millimeters. At times, transferring them from the light trap into glass vials became a laborious, time-intensive effort. Biota collections continued through September, followed by continued bird surveys in the four major wetlands in the study area during October.

Each week, we would meet in Casper or Riverton on a Monday afternoon, conduct fieldwork late into the afternoon or early evening, continue the fieldwork each day through Friday morning, return to our offices and homes that afternoon, spend the weekend at our homes (Fort Collins for me and Billings for George and John), and then repeat the process the following week. I gained a few pounds from eating two meals in restaurants each weekday during those two years. George and I were compatible in terms of where we chose to go for dinner; breakfast was typically at the motel or hotel if they had a restaurant or one within walking distance. John, on the other hand, was very frugal. Even though we were on *per diem* and were reimbursed for our meals and lodging, John preferred to take advantage of special deals at Taco Johns, a fast-food Mexican restaurant, as well as other fast-food restaurants. After two or three weeks of working with John and eating fast food, I put my foot down and told him, "John, I will buy you supper. Let's go," and drove both of us to a full-service restaurant with tables and wait staff.

I spent November through March working on data analysis and writing progress reports at the field office in Cheyenne as well briefing DOI and agency managers from Washington, DC as well as presenting a summary of the Kendrick irrigation project selenium study as well as data from the first year of fieldwork to a subcommittee of the National Academy of Sciences. I approached data analysis and interpretation like a suspense or detective novel, turning the page to find the protagonists and their actions leading to the death of the victims, in this case, aquatic birds. I also did not mind my role as a 'desk jockey' as winters can be brutal in Wyoming. Occasional blizzards and black ice transformed my one-hour drive to or from work into a nerve-wracking two-hour white-knuckle grip on the steering wheel reinforced with views of cars, trucks, and sometimes semis sideways or wheels up and roof down off the highway. March spring snow storms sometimes roared like a lion zeroing in on its prey. One spring storm reduced visibility to 10 feet and my vehicle's speed to 10 miles per hour, extending our commute to three hours; I learned that a 40-car chain-reaction pile-up occurred behind us on the interstate. Sometimes, I had to attend meetings in Casper or other cities in WY even though I preferred not to drive WY highways during the winter. In January 1991, FWS Special Agent Jim Klett requested my assistance at a meeting in Rock Springs with a corporate employee of an energy company to discuss the mortality of waterfowl at a 250-acre hypersaline evaporation pond at a coal-fired power plant.

Below-freezing temperatures and a slight breeze made the early morning four-hour drive to Rock Springs uneventful; however, as the day progressed, the temperature remained below freezing, but the wind ramped up, blowing snow across the highway, creating intermittent patches of glare ice on the pavement. Dry pavement meant driving the speed limit and looking far enough ahead to detect the patches of ice, thus giving me time to slow my speed to avoid skidding on the glare ice. My return to Cheyenne became a five-hour trip filled with a tsunami of adrenaline, a death grip on my vehicle's steering wheel, repeated prayers, and numerous cars, as well as pickup trucks sliding off the interstate. The culmination of my trip experience added one more surge of adrenaline with dense fog and the sight of a semi-tractor trailer with all 18 wheels up in the air on the interstate median. As I drove past that massive vehicle, I thought of Dorothy in the movie *"The Wizard of Oz"* as I kept saying to myself 'there's no place like home, there's no place like home, there's no place like home,' though I did not click my heels together since I was driving.

Although the return trip was nerve-wracking, the meeting that morning opened the door to providing technical assistance to FWS law enforcement (LE) agents on migratory bird mortality incidents in industrial wastewater ponds caused by contact with hypersaline water, surfactants, and oilfield-produced water. At the Rock Springs meeting, we discussed options to prevent or reduce the mortality of waterfowl in a hypersaline evaporation pond. Water used in the power plant scrubbers to reduce sulfur emissions was discharged into a large evaporation pond that attracted waterfowl and other aquatic birds, such as grebes, seeking a rest stop during migration. My first approach involved seeking information on effective bird deterrents to prevent birds from landing on the evaporation pond and having their feathers coated with the hypersaline water, resulting in salt crystallization on their feathers. Birds remove the salt crystals off their plumage by preening their feathers, thus ingesting some of the salt as they draw their individual feathers through their bill. Ingestion of salt crystals by grebes causes impairment of their nervous system, which alters their ability to hold their head in an upright position; thus, drooping their heads into the hypersaline water and drowning. The typical average concentration of sodium in seawater is 10.5 parts per million of sodium in one liter of water. Another way to visualize this amount is one drop of ink from an eyedropper in 10 gallons of water. I collected samples of water from the evaporation pond. I submitted them for selenium, arsenic, and trace element analysis at a laboratory under contract with the FWS and to the Wyoming Department of Agriculture Analytical Service Laboratory to determine the amount of sodium and chloride in the samples. Sodium concentrations were 62 to 63 percent higher than concentrations of this element in seawater.

Throughout my career, I investigated other bird mortalities in industrial wastewater ponds, including oil refinery wastewater ponds in Casper and trona mine tailings ponds near Green River. Trona [4]is a naturally occurring mineral mined underground, brought to the surface, and processed into soda ash used to make glass, paper products, laundry detergents, and many other products such as baking soda and detergents. Each mine had one or more hypersaline ponds ranging in size from approximately 225 to 1,100 acres to contain mine tailings and process wastewater. At cooler temperatures – typically < 40°F – a sodium salt compound precipitates out of the water and crystallizes on solid objects, including birds, in the ponds or on the water's surface. I searched for scientific publications on the effectiveness of a variety of bird deterrents that could be used at the trona mines to minimize bird mortality. One of the mines resorted to using an airboat and a crew of two mine employees to haze birds

---

[4] Trona is a sodium carbonate compound that is processed into soda ash or bicarbonate of soda, or baking soda, as it is commonly known.

off the ponds and recover debilitated birds as well as bird carcasses from the tailings ponds. Rather than fly off the ponds, the grebes would dive underneath the water, resulting in more exposure to the mine tailings wastewater. The airboat crews transported the salt-encrusted victims to a building dedicated to bird rehabilitation; there, the two-person crew washed the salt off the birds, gave them time to recover, and then released them back into the wild. I delved more into this issue by interviewing the trona mine staff tasked with managing and operating wastewater disposal. One mine shared data of live birds and bird carcasses recovered from their trona evaporation ponds during the 1999 fall season and included 622 eared grebes recovered, habilitated, and released to a freshwater pond near Rock Springs, Wyoming, and 12 mortalities. Other birds recovered comprised less than one percent of the total number (146 birds) and included western grebes, pied-billed grebes, ruddy ducks, a common loon, American coots, mergansers, northern shovelers, and puddle ducks such as teal and gadwalls. All of those 146 birds, except two birds, were successfully released to nearby freshwater ponds or the Green River 15 to 20 miles southeast of the mines.

Jim Klett also sought my help with bird mortalities in oilfield production skim pits and open-topped tanks. Skim pits are earthen pits at an oil well site designed to collect formation water produced along with the oil. The industry refers to the pits as 'skim' as oil typically remains on the water surface and is periodically skimmed off into tanker trucks, also called vacuum or vac trucks, that transport the oil to an oil recycling facility. Some oil companies dispose of the oilfield wastewater in open-topped tanks if the volume of wastewater is low enough for containment in storage tanks. The frequency of oil removal depends on economic and logistical factors such as the price of crude oil, the amount of oil in the skim pit, distance of the pit from the nearest vac truck facility, and the number of vac trucks and drivers available at the facility. Oil can remain in a skim pit for weeks and possibly months. Production skim pits are typically less than one acre in size, with one or more skim pits at a well site. Depending on the volume of oilfield wastewater produced, several pits in a series are used to contain the produced water. In WY, oil companies could discharge the produced water into ephemeral drainages if the discharged water met the state's water quality standards or transport the produced water to a commercial oilfield wastewater disposal facility (COWDF) for disposal. Numerous upsets and faulty or leaking equipment resulted in oil and oily sheens being discharged into drainages and ponds.

Standard oil industry practice consisted of suspending several strings of multi-colored plastic pennants or flagging over the oil pits to deter aquatic birds such as grebes and ducks from landing on the pit fluid. Each year, migrating aquatic birds navigate the gauntlet of shimmering oil-covered pits and ponds, which appear to be suitable places to stop and rest during their lengthy journey. Insects entrapped along the shore attract songbirds looking for an easy meal. Raptors and scavengers such as raccoons and coyotes feed on partially oiled carcasses located along the pond edges. Birds contacting the oily sheens and crude oil will preen their feathers to remove the offending material, thus ingesting some of the oil, which could result in chronic or acute effects. Birds that manage to extricate themselves from an oil pit and are unable to fly will seek shelter under small shrubs such as sagebrush, probably to hide from predators and shade them from the sun. A coating of black oil will cause birds to overheat and die from heat stress. The risk to birds is not limited to contact with oil. An LE agent collected 116 dead rosy finches in November 2010 from a reserve pit at a well site in western Wyoming and submitted 16 of the birds to the FWS National Fish and Wildlife Forensics Laboratory at Ashland, Oregon, to determine the cause of death. A reserve pit is an earthen pit excavated adjacent to a drilling rig to contain drill cuttings, drilling mud, and other waste fluids generated or used in the drilling process. According to the necropsy report from the lab, the rosy finches died from inhaling the vapors or gases emanating from the reserve pit containing oilfield waste.

At the behest of Jim Klett, I organized a seminar on bird mortalities associated with oilfield wastewater pits and hypersaline industrial wastewater ponds. Approximately 200 persons representing the oil industry and the trona mines, as well as staff from state and federal agencies that regulated the oil industry and the trona mines, attended the seminar. Presentations included topics on the physical and toxicological effects of oil on birds by a veterinarian from the FWS National Wildlife Health Laboratory in Madison, Wisconsin, and presentations on the liabilities to oil companies under the Migratory Bird Treaty Act (MBTA) and the Endangered Species Act (ESA) by an Assistant U.S. Attorney and Terry Grosz, FWS Assistant Regional Director for Law Enforcement. Shortly after that seminar, I drafted a letter informing oil operators of the bird mortality problem at oil pits and recommendations to prevent or minimize the risk. The WY ES Field Office routinely sent a letter to oil operators applying to the Wyoming Department of Environmental Quality (WDEQ) for a wastewater discharge permit, apprising them of the mortality problem, solutions to the problem, and potential liability under the MBTA for the mortality of migratory birds in oil pits.

The technical assistance I provided to law enforcement and the trona mines led to requests I received from other FWS law enforcement agents, the U.S. Environmental Protection Agency (EPA) and Department of Justice (DOJ), the WDEQ, and the Wyoming Oil and Gas Conservation Commission (WOGCC). It all began with an invitation from the EPA Regional Office in Denver to join their enforcement staff and attorneys from the U.S. Department of Justice in a field inspection of an abandoned oil recycling facility located five or six miles west of Glenrock, Wyoming. The EPA Regional Office in Denver was in the process of issuing an administrative order requiring the operator of the abandoned oil recycling facility to remove all oil and oily fluids from earthen pits and storage tanks as well as remove infrastructure from the site. Participants at the site visit include EPA staff from their Denver Regional Office as well as their headquarters in Washington, DC, a wildlife toxicologist from Clemson University in South Carolina, attorneys representing the oil company responsible for the abandoned facility, FWS Special Agent Bob Prieksat, and me. A chain link fence surrounded the facility, and the ground inside and outside the enclosure was covered with weathered oil.

Bob and I walked slowly, head bowed downward, scanning the ground for bird carcasses. A stream of partially weathered oil softened by the heat of the sun flowed under the fence, threading its way through scant vegetation down a slight incline. An attorney representing one of the facility operators crowed as we surveyed the site, "What's the big deal? My son's room is dirtier than this site." I used a stick to pry several lumps in the weathered oil, some of which were oil-covered dirt clods, and others, unfortunately, were oil-covered songbird carcasses. I pried the carcasses loose and motioned Bob to come take a look. We placed the bird carcasses into plastic bags and labeled the bags with the time, date, and location as the industry attorneys looked on and became deathly quiet. At the end of the day, I joined the EPA and DOJ staff at dinner that evening in Casper and learned about Section 7003 of the Resource Conservation and Recovery Act (RCRA), the regulation that led them to the abandoned oil recycling facility. Section 7003 gives the EPA the ability to enforce the cleanup of sites that may present an imminent and substantial endangerment to health or the environment. Several court cases and the EPA interpreted that an endangerment is imminent "if the present conditions indicate that there may be a future risk to health or the environment even though the harm may not be realized for years." If an EPA RCRA officer investigated an oil pit or evaporation pond with oil on the water surface, the EPA could order an oil company or COWDF owner/operator to take corrective action, such as preventing oil discharges into open pits, immediately removing exposed oil from pits, or closing pits to eliminate the risk to migratory birds and other wildlife, even in the absence of any bird or other wildlife mortality. The oil company or COWDF owner/operator had to submit a work plan to EPA for approval describing how and when they planned to clean up or close the facility. The facility owner/operator faced fines amounting to several thousand dollars for each day of noncompliance with the cleanup completion time frame specified in the RCRA 7003 order.

Several years later, FWS Special Agent Gary Mowad in Lakewood, Colorado, asked me for information on oil pits and migratory bird mortality in Wyoming. Mowad, a pilot, planned to conduct aerial surveys of skim pits in Colorado and Wyoming oilfields along with Brad Miller, EPA RCRA Enforcement. I provided Mowad with the locations of several oil and gas fields in Wyoming. The following year, the EPA initiated a Problem Oil Pits (POPs) Team tasked with conducting aerial surveys of oilfields in Colorado and Wyoming to identify oil pits that could pose a threat to wildlife.

Mowad, Miller, and EPA attorneys met with state oil and gas regulatory agencies, state environmental agencies, tribal energy and environmental agencies, the Bureau of Land Management (BLM), and the Bureau of Indian Affairs (BIA). Mowad explained the nature and extent of threats to wildlife, and EPA explained the survey process. Mowad and the EPA staff invited co-regulators to participate in the surveys. After their presentation, a Wyoming Oil and Gas Conservation Commission (WOGCC) employee stood up, voice filled with indignation, and asked, "Why are you trying to do our job?" Years later, that employee became a strong advocate for preventing the mortality of birds and other wildlife in oil and gas production facilities after visiting well sites with open wastewater pits.

The POPs Team surveyed oilfields in Wyoming, Montana, and Colorado during the first year (1997), North and South Dakota in the second year (1998), and Utah in the third (1999). I assisted EPA RCRA enforcement staff with follow-up inspections of commercial oilfield wastewater disposal facilities (COWDFs) in Wyoming in March 1998. COWDFs accepted oilfield wastewater from oil companies for a fee. The COWDFs usually had one or more containment ponds. The effort earned the POPs Team an award from the EPA Region 8 Administrator in Denver in 1998. The intensive investigations and outreach conducted by the POPs Team raised my hopes that these efforts would change the waste treatment and disposal practices of the oil industry. Although the effort did reduce the use of open-topped tanks and earthen pits for wastewater disposal, bird mortality continued to occur. Two years after the POPs Team completed their investigations, a game warden with the Wyoming Game and Fish Department (WGFD) received a report of two mule deer fawns covered with oil next to abandoned or orphaned oil pits on Bureau of Land Management (BLM) land west-northwest of Casper. The warden had to euthanize the fawns and, upon further inspection of the oil pit, observed oiled bird carcasses in or near the pits. Seventy-five bird carcasses were recovered from the oil pits. Since the oil pits were orphaned, the EPA Regional Administrator in Denver ordered the BLM to take immediate measures to eliminate threats to the environment from the two oil pits, produce plans for the cleanup and closure of the pits, and immediately begin daily inspections of the site and keep birds and wildlife away from the pits.

RCRA 7003 became a useful tool in compelling oil companies and operators of commercial oilfield wastewater disposal facility operators to clean and remove or minimize the risk to migratory birds and other wildlife.

Prior to that precedent-setting action by EPA, FWS enforcement of the Migratory Bird Treaty Act (MBTA) was the only regulatory tool available to compel the oil industry to prevent or reduce the number of bird mortalities at oil and gas production facilities. The paltry fines levied under the MBTA ($200 per bird killed) amounted to pocket change for the oil companies as they readily paid the fines, but many took no action to close the oil-filled death traps for birds, prevent the discharge of oil into skim pits, or immediately remove the oil from the pits. Additionally, FWS law enforcement agents could only enforce the MBTA if they recovered bird carcasses from the pits as evidence. When LE agents investigated oil-covered skim pits, they informed the oil companies of the consequences of bird mortality occurring in the pits and recommended options to prevent or reduce mortality. Some of the larger companies enclosed their skim pits with netting to exclude birds; others stuck to 'business as usual,' resulting in continual bird mortality in oil production skim pits.

Four years after aerial surveys and follow-up site inspections were completed, the EPA Denver Regional Office released the results and recommendations in a 71-

page report. The EPA recommended more frequent no-notice inspections by state and federal oil and gas regulatory agencies, providing compliance assistance to oil companies and their staff, conducting outreach and education to ensure compliance, and initiating formal enforcement actions "when recalcitrance is suspected based on an operator's past behavior." The outreach paid off as environmental and state oil and gas regulatory agencies in Colorado, Montana, Utah, and Wyoming strengthened their regulations pertaining to the containment, discharge, and disposal of oilfield wastewater. Shortly thereafter, other oil-producing states followed suit. Although oil companies took measures to prevent or reduce the risk to migratory birds and other wildlife in production skim pits, risks remained at COWDFs as these facilities used larger evaporation ponds for the disposal and treatment of oilfield exploration and production wastes. The EPA found that "problems at COWDFs were the same as those found at production facilities (exposed oil on pits, bird and wildlife mortality, improper or non-existent secondary containment for storage tanks, oil spills and leaks, discharges of oil to surface waters, violations of permitted discharge limits, and groundwater contamination), although often of greater magnitude." During the spring and fall of 1998, I assisted the EPA in the inspection of 12 COWDFs. Non-compliance at most of these facilities remained a recurring problem as birds fell victim to exposed oil in the evaporation ponds.

Most of the COWDF operators complied with WDEQ regulations requiring them to remove oil from the skim ponds; however, some did not, thus compelling the state regulatory agency staff to conduct frequent inspections of those facilities. Most COWDFs were located in remote locations and on private property away from public view, limiting the potential of WDEQ receiving reports of non-compliance from the public. Two years later, WDEQ staff contacted me for assistance following their repeated efforts to achieve compliance from a recalcitrant COWDF owner-operator. I conducted a field inspection of the COWDF with Randy Lamdin, RCRA Enforcement, from the EPA's Denver Regional Office, along with an employee of the COWDF facility. Randy and I continued to receive requests to conduct field inspections of COWDFs from WDEQ and occasionally from the WOGCC on oil and gas production facilities. From the year 2000 to 2011, we conducted follow-up inspections on 26 COWDFs; of those, three were owned and managed by one owner/operator and had the highest frequency of exposed oil in the evaporation ponds and the highest number of bird carcasses we recovered. All of the evaporation ponds at these COWDFs ranged from a one-quarter acre in size (approximately 100 ft by 250 ft) to 15 acres in size.

We conducted 20 and 21 inspections from 1998 until 2011 in two COWDFs and recovered a total of 56 bird carcasses, 10 in one COWDF and 46 in the other. The third COWDF remained problematic, with 37 inspections and 58 bird carcasses retrieved from the oil-covered ponds. Most of Randy's and my travels inspecting oil pits in Wyoming followed a set routine; however, unexpected events sometimes made our trips quite memorable. In April 2001, a spring snowstorm roared through Eastern Wyoming as Randy and I were driving from Gillette, Wyoming, to Cheyenne, forcing us to stop at Wheatland to assess the road conditions. Strong winds and over a foot of snow between Chugwater and Cheyenne resulted in the closure of Interstate 25. We decided to get two rooms at a Wheatland hotel and continue our journey home the next morning. As we completed our room registrations and received our individual room keys, an elderly couple from Minnesota walked into the hotel office and requested a room. The registration desk attendant informed them that the last room had just been taken. Randy and I looked at each other and offered one of our rooms to the elderly couple. "Randy and I will share a room," we told the registration desk attendant. The elderly couple was very appreciative.

On Monday, September 10, 2001, Randy and I drove to Casper, Wyoming, to conduct a follow-up inspection of the closure and remediation of oil pits at the Poison Spider oilfield on BLM land, 18 miles west of Casper. Tuesday morning, September 11, I turned on the TV set in my hotel room in Casper and tuned in to the CNN news channel. I looked at the TV screen and saw black smoke coming out of a black hole in a glass facade; there was no commentary from the news anchors. The silence was deafening. I dialed Randy's room number and told him to turn his TV set on. I watched for a few minutes until I walked to the hotel's restaurant to eat breakfast and start our trip to the oilfield. Over breakfast, we did not know the details of smoke billowing out of the building and assumed the pilot of a private airplane had crashed into the World Trade Center in New York City;   however, as we discussed this, we concluded that the skies were clear so visibility was probably not the cause. We finished our breakfast, drove to the oilfield, and listened to the news on the Wyoming Public Radio station. We could not believe what we were hearing. The somber voices of the news reporters described an airliner had flown into the North Tower of the World Trade Center and a second airliner had crashed into the South Tower 17 minutes after the first one. After we arrived at the remediation site, we focused on our work. After our inspection was completed, we climbed into our vehicle and resumed listening to NPR. A third airliner crashed into the Pentagon in Washington, DC, approximately 30 minutes after the attacks at the WTC. Almost 30 minutes later, United Airlines Flight 93 crashed near Shanksville, Pennsylvania, after passengers and crew stormed the cockpit. We were stunned. It was surreal. On the drive up to Casper the afternoon before, the skies were clear except for the contrails of commercial airlines flying over Wyoming. During our drive back to Cheyenne, there were no contrails in the clear blue Wyoming sky, and the Federal

Aviation Administration had grounded all flights. I called our office, and a voicemail instructed all staff to return home as our office was closed until further notice. I felt anger and rage at the thought that madmen would take thousands of innocent lives in the name of God. I returned home and hugged my wife, my 6-year-old son, and my 5-year-old daughter.

The next several weeks were a blur filled with news stories of the 9/11 attacks. That evening, after my son and daughter were in bed and asleep, I walked into their rooms and gently touched their heads as I prayed for their safety; my mind flooded with anxiety over their future.

Randy and I accompanied BLM or Wyoming Oil and Gas Conservation Commission (WOGCC) staff during most of the oil pit and oil and gas production site inspections; however, there were instances when we would have to inspect sites without them. This usually occurred during follow-up visits to sites we had previously visited a few months before. Going solo was not an issue on BLM public land; however, we relied on WOGCC to accompany us in inspecting well sites located on private lands. Most landowners granted us access, requesting that gates be shut after we opened them to pass through. Some well sites were located on "split-estate," where the surface rights are in private ownership, and the rights to development of the mineral resources are publicly held and managed by the Federal Government. The "split-estate" originated in the Homestead Act of 1916, where the Federal Government granted the surface rights to a homesteader but retained the mineral rights. We inspected wells located in split-estates with a BLM Petroleum Technician (BLM PT) without any protest from the surface owners; however, one surface owner did make things difficult for us in northeastern Wyoming as we followed the BLM PT to a Federal well site located on privately-owned land. Accessing the well site involved driving over a cattle guard, also known as a cattle grid. Cattle guards are structures placed over a depression in the ground to prevent livestock from crossing an enclosed piece of land to another area. Cattle guards are typically placed between private and public lands or on private lands where gates are not appropriate; in this case, oil and gas well sites requiring access by state or federal oil and gas regulatory agencies, oil company staff or contractors, and tanker trucks hauling oil, condensate, or produced water from the well site. The evenly spaced bars or pipes are close enough together that a car or even a person can walk across them but wide enough apart that they prevent livestock from crossing. As the BLM PT approached the cattle guard, a ranch truck drove up and parked on the cattle guard blocking access to the well site. Randy and I stopped our truck a short distance from the cattle guard and waited for the BLM PT to find out why the truck was blocking our progress. The driver of the ranch truck, an elderly lady, informed the BLM PT that it was private property and we were trespassing. After a few minutes, I walked up to the cattle guard, approached the ranch truck, and calmly told the lady that if she let us go through, we would be on our way and leave her property. The BLM PT, Randy and I talked among ourselves as we sat in our vehicles and agreed that the better course of action was to leave the area even though we had the right to visit the well site.

 "You're on private property and you're trespassing," the lady said. I apologized and added that if she let us through, we would continue on the road and not stop until we left her property. "You're on private property, and you're trespassing," she replied with an angry tone. This back-and-forth dialogue with her continued for several minutes repeatedly warning us "you're on private property and you're trespassing," never deviating from her response. We waited in our vehicle unable to go anywhere as she had parked her truck blocking our ability to go anywhere. She finally relented after 30 or 40 minutes and moved her truck to let us proceed. I assume she disliked the federal government and employees and relished the chance to make their lives difficult when the opportunity presented itself.

In addition to the one or two irate landowners, we also encountered a few hazards inspecting oil pits: hydrogen sulfide gas, rattlesnakes, ticks, quicksand, and exploding rotten goose eggs, with hydrogen sulfide as the deadliest. Hydrogen sulfide gas in oil and gas fields is produced by the microbial breakdown of organic materials in the absence of oxygen. Hydrogen sulfide (H_2S) is extremely hazardous, smells like rotten eggs, and is colorless, flammable, and soluble in water. It is heavier than air and can collect in low-lying areas such as oil pits, emergency spill pits, natural depressions, and ephemeral draws. At low levels, we could detect H_2S by smell.

However, the odor cannot be detected at concentrations above 100 parts per million. Continuous low-level exposure can also cause a person to lose the ability to smell the gas even though it is still present. At high concentrations, the ability to smell the gas can be lost instantly. I carried an H_2S gas detector to alert me if the concentration was in the air and would emit a loud beeping sound if the gas approached chronic concentrations.

Five days after the news of the Deepwater Horizon oil spill in the Gulf of Mexico on April 20, 2010, an employee of an environmental consulting firm left a message on my voice mail asking for the phone number of bird rehabilitators in the Rawlins, WY area. I called an engineer at the Sinclair Refinery to get more information on the oil spill. A malfunction of the refinery's wastewater system resulted in an oil release into a ditch, leading to a process water evaporation pond approximately 230 acres in size. The engineer reported 12 oiled grebes (1 dead and 11 live birds), adding that refinery employees recovered and transferred oiled live grebes to a Wyoming Game & Fish Department (WGFD) biologist in Sinclair for cleaning. I drove to Sinclair and conducted a site assessment of the spill. Refinery staff and contractors surveyed the pond shoreline for oiled birds and removed oil from the pond perimeter. Kim and I made another site visit four days later, accompanied by FWS Special Agent Scott Darrah, and we recovered additional bird carcasses, primarily western grebes and eared grebes, that succumbed to hypothermia due to cold temperatures and light snowfall. Most of the bird carcasses were coated with light oil instead of a thick, heavy oil; had the ambient temperature been warmer, crews could have recovered the live birds and washed the oil off their feathers. I bagged and tagged bird carcasses recovered from the main pond as Kim and Scott surveyed the East Pond, immediately adjacent to the main pond. The East Pond did not receive direct wastewater discharge from the process water evaporation pond; however, subsurface seepage probably contributed water to the East Pond, which varied in size from 55 to approximately 100 acres. The white salt-covered emergent vegetation, soil, and shoreline of the East Pond contrasted sharply with the bright green, eutrophic pond water. I submitted the carcasses recovered from the East Pond to the USGS National Wildlife Health Lab for necropsy and sent algae samples to the University of Wyoming to identify the algae species, specifically to determine if the algae included the type that produces cyanotoxins, known to cause bird mortality via ingestion. A University of Wyoming botanist determined that the algae did not produce cyanotoxins.

I reviewed scientific journals online for information on cyanotoxins and bird mortality; I came across a scientific publication on surfactants produced by marine algae that caused a large red tide in Monterey Bay, California, resulting in the mortality of seabirds. I searched online for scientific publications on how feathers repel water and learned that water repellency in feathers depends on the structure of the feathers as well as the surface tension of water. I continued my search and came across a study on the effect of water surface tension on feather wettability in aquatic birds published in the Canadian Journal of Zoology that provided a water surface tension value, resulting in water wetting potentially leading to hypothermia. I collected and submitted water samples to the engineering department at the University of Wyoming for surface tension analysis. The surface tension on the water was below the threshold for feather wettability. The USGS National Wildlife Health Lab diagnosed the probable cause of death as salt toxicosis due to the ingestion of salt, as well as hypothermia due to the encrustation of salt crystals on the feathers. I learned that if the volume of salt ingested exceeded the amount removed from the blood by the kidneys, the excess sodium in the blood would eventually be circulated into the brain. Salt applied on roads during the winter to lower the freezing point of water and prevent ice from forming can be consumed by birds mistaking it as grit. Wildlife forensic pathologists have documented cases where bird mortality resulted from the ingestion of road salt.

Salt toxicosis occurs when birds ingest lethal amounts of salt crystals while preening their salt-encrusted feathers. When the amount of salt ingested exceeds what a bird's kidneys can remove, the sodium collects in the bloodstream and is transported to the brain, resulting in a condition known as hypernatremia. Birds can typically tolerate high concentrations of salt or sodium in their diet if they can access fresh water. Access to freshwater can be compromised if a bird cannot fly due to salt encrustation on its feathers. I continued searching the scientific literature for answers on what other factors could cause feathers to lose their ability to repel water and retain their ability to insulate birds. I stumbled upon two scientific journal articles on bird mortality incidents that occurred in Monterey Bay, California, associated with an extensive red tide caused by dinoflagellates, one-celled organisms that produce toxins. The article described the affected birds as "coated with a slimy yellow-green material on their feathers, which were saturated with water, and were severely hypothermic." The authors determined that the foam contained "surfactant-like proteins, derived from the organic matter of the red tide," which coated their feathers and compromised their natural water repellency and insulation. I found additional scientific publications of similar incidents in the Salton Sea and Tulare Lake Basin in California, where a change in water surface tension caused grebes to become waterlogged, "engaged in heavy preening, and eventually came onto shore" during the die-off events. I submitted water samples for surface tension analysis to the engineering department at the University of Wyoming, and two of the samples were below the threshold for feather wettability. Unfortunately, I was not able to collect additional water samples to increase the sample size because the refinery staff pumped

water out of the pond to reduce its depth and eliminate the
attraction for grebes.

CHAPTER 19: ONCE-IN-A-LIFETIME FWS DETAIL

During my stint as a newspaper reporter-photographer with the *Kingsville Record* and *Bishop News*, the editor advised me to "shoot, shoot, shoot" with my camera to increase my chances of getting a good photo. I went through many rolls of 35-mm film to capture the perfect images. This lesson paid off years later, in January 1996, when I received a 'once-in-a-lifetime' FWS assignment from Sharon Rose at the FWS Public Affairs office at the Denver Regional Office. She asked if I was available to travel to Canada to photograph the capture and processing of wolves at Fort St. John, British Columbia, Canada, for reintroduction into Yellowstone National Park and the Frank-Church-River-of-No-Return wilderness area, a 2.4-million-acre wilderness area in central Idaho. The FWS reintroduced wolves from Alberta, Canada, into Yellowstone the previous year and planned to transport and release wolves from an area north of Ft. St. John, with one group released into Yellowstone and the other at the Frank Church River of No Return Wilderness.

Wolves were extirpated from the park by trappers and hunters from the U.S. Biological Survey's Animal Damage Control (ADC) program by the 1930s and elsewhere in the Lower 48 States, culminating in an intensive effort to eliminate these predators to protect livestock. ADC eliminated an estimated 1,800 wolves and 23,000 coyotes in 39 U.S. National Forests in the year 1907 alone. According to an ADC poster from the 1940s, more than 3,849 wolves were killed by the predatory animal control agency's work and its cooperators since the agency was organized in 1915. In 1924, the last known wolves in Yellowstone, two pups discovered near Soda Butte, were officially killed by park rangers fearing that if wolves remained, they would eventually increase and prey on livestock outside the park boundary. The initial capture of wolves from Canada for reintroduction into Yellowstone in 1996 was contentious in Canada and the United States. The American Farm Bureau and the individual farm bureaus for the states of Idaho, Montana, and Wyoming filed a lawsuit in 1994 to prevent the FWS from transporting wolves from Canada into Yellowstone and Idaho. Judge William Downes of the Federal District Court in Cheyenne, Wyoming, denied the request for an injunction and allowed the transportation of wolves captured in Canada to Yellowstone. In Canada, a wildlife conservation group from Vancouver, British Columbia, protested that Canada was not doing enough to protect wolves and offered a $5,000 reward to anyone who freed the wolves captured in British Columbia. The FWS instructed everyone at the Fort St. John work center not to divulge their location to anyone outside the group for fear that the protestors would travel to Fort St. John and disrupt their work.

Sharon instructed me to call Nan Rollison, Public Affairs Specialist at the FWS Headquarters (HQ) office in Washington, DC, for details and travel arrangements. I called Nan and received instructions on making travel arrangements to Canada. She ended the call imploring me to "make sure you get a patch shot," which meant getting a photograph of a person wearing an FWS shirt or jacket with the agency's logo. Sharon Rose and Nan advised me to prepare for subzero temperatures as low as 40 degrees below zero. I packed my winter clothes and gear, purchased several rolls of 35mm color slide film, and booked a flight from Denver to Fort St. John, BC. After the last leg of my flight landed at Fort St. John, I stepped out to the tarmac as the subzero air at 15 degrees below zero enveloped my face like a thousand pinpricks. A volunteer with the wolf capture crew transported me from the airport to the motel at Fort St John. After arriving at the two-story motel, I grabbed my gear, and after registering at the front desk, I made my way to my room. The stairs and entrances to all the rooms were located outside, with only the walls and a wooden door 2-and-a-half inches thick keeping the subzero air out. I entered the room, closed the door, and noticed the interior side of the door was covered with frost.

Colder subzero temperatures dominated the remainder of the week I spent there, with the mercury descending to 40 degrees below zero. The winter days are very short at 56 degrees latitude, with only 714 miles between Fort St. John and the Arctic Circle. Morning light at 9 am pierced the morning fog created by the condensation of water vapor emanating from vehicle exhausts as well as the furnace vents on building rooftops. The impenetrable fog made driving a vehicle through an intersection a challenging and high-risk endeavor whenever I drove into Ft. St. John to purchase film or run other errands. Fort St. John is 279 ft lower in elevation downstream from the

Provincial Park work center where volunteers and FWS staff processed the captured wolves; thus, the topography down the river valley contained the colder, denser air. Visibility at the Work Center site usually remained adequate compared to Fort St. John, where thick ice fog impaired the visibility. As the day progressed, the Earth's tilt kept the sun low on the horizon and dimmed to an orange orb fading at mid-afternoon towards darkness.

Although I was no stranger to subzero and single-digit temperatures, having experienced them in Idaho, Montana, Colorado, and Wyoming, taking photographs at 40 degrees below zero the next day pushed the envelope as the coldest temperature I worked in at Spotted Bear was 23 degrees below zero. At Fort St. John, I wore thick, wool convertible mittens that allowed me to flip the fingertip cover back to expose my fingertips so that I could adjust the f-stop, shutter speed, and press the shutter on my 35mm SLR camera. I kept my camera at the ready close to my face and my right index finger on my camera's shutter as the flight crews rolled the helicopters out of the hanger, fueled their aircraft, loaded gear in the cargo compartments, and conducted their pre-flight checks. I kept my right index finger exposed to press the camera shutter at a moment's notice as I did not want to miss any good photo opportunities. Soon, my fingertips were frostbitten and felt like rocks at the end of my fingers. I walked fast to the parked and idling pickup truck, opened the passenger-side door, climbed in, and drummed my fingers on the dashboard; the tips were rock-hard. I held the fingers of my right hand over the heater ducts at the bottom of the windshield and increased the flow of the warm air to thaw my fingertips.

The two helicopters and the fixed-wing Cessna airplane took off in search of wolves in the Canadian Rockies approximately 150 miles to the north and west of Fort St. John. Two wolf trackers, experts at identifying wolf tracks and trails from the air over the snow-covered landscape, searched for wolf packs from the Cessna airplane. Each helicopter crew included the pilot, a dart gunner from the Alaska Dept of Fish and Game, and Carter Niemeyer from the U.S. Dept of Agriculture's Animal Damage Control. Once the wolf tracking experts located a pack, they radioed the helicopter pilots with the location; the pilots would fly the helicopter to a suitable landing spot, usually on a frozen river channel or relatively flat terrain with no trees. Carter and the dart gunner would climb out of the aircraft and remove the door on the side of the dart gunner. The pilot would then transport the dart gunner to the location of the wolf pack and fly low enough for the dart gunner to aim the dart gun at a wolf's upper hind leg to immobilize the animal. It would take three to eight minutes for a wolf to fall after it had been darted. Once the wolf was down and unable to move, the helicopter pilot would hover over the wolf's location to obtain a fix on the location and return to the clearing and land where Carter waited. Carter and the dart gunner would reattach the door to the helicopter and return with the pilot to the wolf's location. Wading in thigh-deep snow, they would carry the wolf to the helicopter that would fly the crew and wolf to the airport at Fort St. John. At Fort St. John, the wolf was taken to the provincial park work center, where each individual wolf was placed in a large, chain-link kennel. The kennels were covered with large tarps to lessen a wolf's ability to see wolves in adjacent kennels, and volunteers were walking near the kennels. Each wolf remained in the kennel until the volunteer staff was ready to work on it in the work center building. Each wolf was immobilized and transported into the building on a stretcher, where it was photographed, marked with a tattooed number, and fitted with small ear tags and a radio collar. Volunteers also took and recorded several body measurements of each wolf.

With the light fading, I returned to the motel, a two-story building with all exterior doors located via an outdoor walkway. I opened the door to my room, entered, and closed the door behind me; I noticed frost coating the interior side of the door. I took my mittens off, looked at my right-hand frostbitten fingertips, and was flooded with a wave of foolishness at not protecting my fingers from the subzero cold. I mentally kicked myself as I lay in bed for being so thoughtless. I joined the crew at dinner and tried to hide my right-hand fingers, which had turned dark brown from the frostbite. I waited for an opportune time to approach one of the volunteers, who was a physician, and addressed him as quietly as I could, "Doc, I did something stupid this morning when I was taking photos and got frostbite on my fingers." The doctor took my right hand, examined my fingers, and said, "Looks like only the outer layer of skin was damaged. You'll lose the upper layer of skin, but otherwise, you'll be okay." I breathed a sigh of relief and learned a valuable lesson. I thought I should have known better, having worked in subzero temperatures during the wolverine study at Spotted Bear; however, the subzero temperature here was twenty degrees colder at 40 degrees below zero. Subzero temperatures persisted throughout the time I spent there. One morning, a staff member walked out from his second-floor room onto the balcony holding a cup full of hot water, held the cup out beyond the balcony railing, and tossed the boiling water into the air, which quickly froze into small crystals - instant snow.

Dave Walsh, videographer from the U.S. Bureau of Reclamation office at Boise, Idaho, and I spent most of the week at the Provincial Park work center where volunteers and FWS staff processed the captured wolves. Throughout the week, the flight crews took off from the airport during the morning to locate and capture wolves and returned to the airport during the afternoon, where they were met by FWS staff and volunteers to transport the wolves to the Work Center for processing. Dave and I anxiously awaited an opportunity to join the helicopter crews to take action photos of the dart gunners, the pilots, and the recovery of immobilized wolves. The pilots' first priority was meeting the quota of wolves captured for the Yellowstone reintroduction effort, which meant minimizing weight and passengers on the helicopters. I took photos of staff assembling large, chain link kennels approximately 16 ft. long, 6 ft. wide, and 6 ft. high to hold each individual wolf after processing. I had more than enough photos of FWS staff and volunteers assisting the veterinarians in withdrawing blood samples from the wolves, checking their pulse with a stethoscope, and recording body measurements from each wolf.

After spending three days at the Work Center observing and doing the same thing day after day, I volunteered to drive Dave to Pink Mountain, 86 miles up the Alaska Highway, to retrieve his rental vehicle. We both grabbed sleeping bags from the Work Center for survival in the event that we encountered vehicle mechanical problems or struck a moose on the highway and had to spend the night in the vehicle. Driving up the Alaska Highway, I saw that the landscape was mostly black spruce trees, snow, and a few moose, a welcome change from being cooped up at the Work Center. After we arrived, we tried to start the parked pickup truck without success. Dave walked into the service station next to Mae's Kitchen and obtained a battery charger, so we promptly hooked it up to the truck's battery and plugged it into an outlet. Dave entered the restaurant and ordered hot tea as Ken Taylor, one of the dart gunners, walked in. Dave asked him if he could ride along in the helicopter to shoot video; he received a thumbs up, grabbed his video gear, and took off with the helicopter crew. I stayed in the restaurant and ordered lunch. After Dave returned, we attempted to start the truck to no avail, so we decided to leave it and headed back to Ft. St. John at 3:30 pm as the sun was beginning to set. Back at the Work Center, we learned that the wolf crews captured three wolves and had to trudge through deep powder snow up to their armpits to retrieve the immobilized canines.

After almost a week confined to the Work Center, I finally got the opportunity to fly with one of the helicopter crews to photograph the capture of wolves in the Canadian Rockies. We took off from the airstrip between 10:30 am and 11 am with clear, blue skies granting us incredible views of the Canadian Rockies, moose, and bison as we flew north to the Besa River, a tributary of the Prophet River within the Mackenzie River Drainage that flows northward into the Arctic Ocean. I viewed the sea of rugged snow-capped peaks that extended to the horizon as I listened to radio chatter between the helicopter pilot and the fixed-wing aircraft searching for wolf packs. The pilot, Clay Scott, landed on a rounded mountaintop that presented a suitable landing area for the helicopter. Ken and I climbed out to stretch our legs; I walked a short distance from the helicopter and took several photos of the aircraft and the views from our summit before the pilot summoned us back after receiving a message from the fixed-wing crew that they spotted a wolf pack. Clay landed the helicopter at the confluence of two rivers covered with a thick layer of ice. Ken and I got out and removed the doors on the passenger side of the helicopter to allow Clay better visibility. Ken took a clear shot with a tranquilizer dart gun and laid the doors on the frozen river. Chasing a wolf from a helicopter requires deft maneuvering at high speeds and low elevations, usually at a level just above the height of the tree canopy. A harness attached to the aircraft kept Ken from falling out as he leaned out to get a shot with the dart gun while trying to get a clear shot at the wolf's hindquarter. It probably took the ketamine three to five minutes to immobilize a wolf, so the pilot continued to follow the wolf, desperately trying to run away from the helicopter overhead. Once the wolf lay down, the pilot had to find a clearing wide enough to land the helicopter to retrieve the wolf. At times, Carter Niemeyer and the dart gunner walked through chest-deep snow to recover a wolf. While Clay and Ken took off to locate the wolf pack, I stood next to the door on the frozen river and waited for about 30 to 40 minutes. Clay and Ken landed; we attached the doors to the helicopter, boarded, and flew over the site where the wolf lay in a stand of timber next to the Bessa River. Its black coat made it easy to spot on the white snow. Clay landed on the ice-covered river. Ken and I climbed out and made our way to retrieve the wolf. We waded through waist-deep snow that made me sweat from forcing my feet and legs through the deep snow. Ken spotted the wolf and shouted out his find. He picked up the wolf and carried it out of the timber towards the waiting helicopter. I boarded the helicopter, and Ken loaded the wolf into the back seat, its hind legs on the floor and its head and front legs on the seat. The wolf was blindfolded with a mask that covered its muzzle as well as its eyes to protect the handler as well as calm the animal. We flew east-northeast to a fuel cache along the Alaska Highway. When the wolf began to stir as the effects of the ketamine wore off, Ken would administer an additional dose to the animal. Clay refueled the helicopter and then headed south to Mae's Kitchen, where we landed at a nearby airstrip. From Mae's Kitchen, we flew down to Fort St. John in the late afternoon and were graced with a beautiful sunset and the sight of moose and coyotes in the snow-covered landscape.

Once the requisite number of wolves were captured and processed, the next step involved two Work Center volunteers entering a large, chain link kennel containing a captive wolf and restraining the wolf with a pole snare, a long hollow pipe with a rope or cable-threaded through the pipe and forming a loop or snare at the end. Once the volunteer restrained the wolf with the pole snare, the second person would immobilize the canid using a pole syringe or jab stick, a syringe with ketamine mounted on the end of an extendable pole. I grabbed my FWS windbreaker and offered it to Alice Whitelaw as she and Val Asher got ready to retrieve each penned-up wolf. "Here! Wear this," I said. "Why?" Alice asked.

"I need a photo of someone wearing the FWS logo," and added that Nan Rollison had instructed me to get "a patch shot." Alice prepared a pole syringe or jab stick mounted on the end of an extendable pole. As Alice and Val entered a kennel, the captive wolf would move toward the back corner of the enclosure, raise its hind legs, and rake its paws on the kennel wall, trying in vain to avoid them. Val placed the snare over the wolf's head, and Alice immobilized the wolf with ketamine using a jab stick. Alice wrapped her arms around the wolf's chest, and Val carried the wolf by the hindquarters. After the wolf was immobilized, they placed it on a stretcher and carried it into the work center, where volunteer veterinarians took blood samples and weighed each wolf then placed the immobilized animal in an aluminum crate. The crates were loaded into a large U-Haul van and transported to the airport, where the crates were loaded into a DC-3 cargo airplane. Dave and I documented the entire operation on video and photos, capping the long day with a celebratory dinner at a local pizza restaurant at 10 p.m. Since I had shipped the exposed rolls of film to Nan Rollison at HQ, I did not get to see the results until several weeks later when she sent me duplicate slides of some of the photos I took at Fort

St. John. I called Nan when I returned home and asked if she had received the film and had it developed. "Pete, you got the shot! You Got the shot!" Nan exclaimed with excitement in her voice. I breathed a sigh of relief, knowing I had succeeded and had not let her down. My best photo was displayed at the Service's National Conservation Training Center at Shepherdstown, West Virginia, along with other photos taken by FWS staff.

Chapter 20: Collaboration and Sharing Expertise

EC Specialists from most states attended the EC national meetings on inter-agency symposiums and gave presentations on their EC investigations. The Division of EC at headquarters organized these biennial meetings and rotated each location at one of the FWS regions. The EC national meetings served to forge professional relationships between attendees. By meeting other EC Specialists face-to-face and learning what contaminant issues they worked on, I knew who to contact for technical assistance on EC problems I dealt with. The presentations covered a myriad of environmental contaminant issues: selenium, mercury, lead, lead shot in wetlands and risks to waterfowl, oil spills, legacy contamination from the use of organochlorine pesticides such as DDT and toxaphene, PCBs, and the improper disposal of solid and hazardous waste. Many EC investigations were conceived at these biennial meetings, especially during the social gatherings following the technical presentations, with many leading to the cleanup and restoration of environments damaged by the release or improper disposal of solid and hazardous waste. I always had a camera with me during field investigations to document what I was observing, such as oil-contaminated soil, water, and vegetation; bird and other wildlife carcasses; corroded pipes and tanks at oil production sites; and oil leaking from pipes, tanks, and wellheads. I used the photos during my presentations to oil company staff and in symposia.

The EC biennial meetings were held in hotel conference centers, usually scheduled during less busy seasons when occupancy rates were lower. EC Specialists throughout the 50 states gave technical presentations of their EC investigations. Attendees lodged at the same hotel, which facilitated daily after-hours social gatherings as libations flowed to celebrate our group's successes in saving the planet, or at least our collective portion of it, from the perils of pollution. During the mid-week of the EC meetings, various awards were presented during dinner to EC Specialists who were lauded by their peers for their accomplishments in contaminants work. At the first EC biennial meeting I attended, three EC Specialists obtained a toilet seat with the lid attached and conspired to create an award, initially reviled by some attendees who associated the award with the worst presentation given during the week. After several meetings, some EC Specialists coveted the award. The honoree of the 'Toilet Seat Award' then joined the 'selection committee' that determined the worthy recipient at the next biennial EC meeting. Several biennial meetings later, Dan Audet, one of the EC Specialists, put together a slide presentation roasting one of his EC colleagues who was about to transfer from the FWS to the private sector. The slide presentation was synchronized to music and included images of the subject conducting fieldwork. Hysterical laughter filled the meeting room while the subject of the roast took it in good stride. The presentation became a tradition during the biennial meetings, and I dare say many looked forward to it. I took on the role of creating the slide presentations after Dan transferred to the National Park Service. I obtained digital images from willing collaborators, setting the images to music. I added text bubbles on the images of EC Specialists to 'tell' a story. One such slide story involved Dr. Selenide, intent on poisoning the world with selenium, and the hero "Bruce Almighty," an EC Specialist, intent on stopping the evil villain, Doctor Selenide. I used slides of EC Specialist

Bruce Waddell doing EC field work as the protagonist and a cartoon of the evil Dr. Selenide contaminating the environment with selenium. Laughter and humor were pervasive at these gatherings and not limited to the meetings.

After an EC meeting in Apalachicola Falls State Park and Lodge in Georgia, I and three other EC Specialists loaded our bags into a rental car and proceeded to drive 85 miles south to the airport in Atlanta. EC Specialist Rick drove the car while some of us either caught up on our sleep or watched silently as stands of pine trees whizzed by. After about an hour, the other passengers and I realized we had been traveling for almost an hour and had not reached our destination. I implored Rick to stop at the next store to ask for directions. After driving a few miles, we spotted a general store, and Rick pulled up to the front of the weathered, wooden building. I walked up to the store's screen door, which displayed a metal NEHI Soda sign. I asked the proprietor for directions to Atlanta, and years later, I still laugh at his response, "Atlanta?!? This road goes to Chattanooga!" I thanked the gentleman, sauntered up to the car, and instructed Rick to turn around and head back as the road we were on led to Tennessee. We made sure not to let Rick drive to and from future biennial EC meetings.

In 2001, Linda Lyon, an EC Specialist with the NWRS in HQ, asked me to participate in the development of a training course for refuge staff in oil and gas exploration and production. I assisted as a co-instructor in the three-day class that later led to a week-long course held annually from 2005 to 2013. Following the inauguration of Barack Obama as the 44th President of the United States in 2009, conservatives launched the Tea Party movement promoting lower taxes and a reduction of the national debt as well as the federal budget deficit through decreased government spending that ultimately resulted in significant budget cuts in the Department of the Interior and the U.S. Fish and Wildlife Service.

The last EC biennial meeting was held in 2010. Obtaining funding for contaminant studies became increasingly difficult, so I focused my efforts on conducting investigations of oil pits and COWDFs with the EPA. Eventually, I saw the writing on the wall as funds declined not only for the FWS but also for the EPA, thus reducing the number of field inspections that we could conduct. In November 2012, I received a call from NWRS staff at our headquarters office offering me a transfer to the National Wildlife Refuge System's (NWRS) Branch of Wildlife Resources based in Arlington, Virginia, but allowing me to work remotely from an NWRS office located at Fort Collins. After commuting to Cheyenne from Fort Collins for a little over two decades, I was ecstatic and accepted their timely offer as two to three years later, the FWS directorate reorganized the HQ office and downsized the Division of EC to a Branch office. The EC budget was significantly reduced, resulting in EC Specialists either retiring, being assigned to work on endangered species or other FWS issues, or transferring to other federal agencies. My transfer to NWRS was a perfect capstone to my career.

Chapter 21: 'Flying' With The Blue Goose

The iconic image of a blue goose in flight on refuge entrance and boundary signs, as well as FWS brochures and exhibits, was created in the 1930s by J.N. "Ding" Darling, Chief of the U.S. Biological Survey, a precursor of the U.S. Fish and Wildlife Service.

The creation of national wildlife refuges in the United States dates back to the year 1902 when members of the Boone and Crockett Club proposed to create a system of wildlife refuges across the United States and solicited the support of fellow member President Theodore Roosevelt. President Roosevelt issued an Executive Order on March 14, 1903, establishing Pelican Island National Wildlife Refuge along Florida's central Atlantic coast. One hundred and twenty years later, as I write this, there are 588 NWRs in the United States, collectively totaling 850 million acres of land and water set aside for the conservation and protection of fish and wildlife. The FWS obtains lands for inclusion in the NWRS through fee-title and easements from willing sellers or donations from landowners. NWRs are located in every state and the U.S. territory of American Samoa, Guam, Puerto Rico, and the Virgin Islands. The FWS places high priority on the acquisition of lands and waters essential for the recovery of threatened and endangered species and the protection of habitats critical for the survival of rare species.

During high school, my goal entailed working with fish and wildlife in the outdoors; later, during college, it morphed into working with wildlife in the mountains. I first learned of national wildlife refuges and the FWS from my older brother Ernesto after he visited Aransas NWR with his wildlife biology class from Texas A&I University, now Texas A&M University - Kingsville. I first set foot on a refuge at the Santa Ana NWR in the Lower Rio Grande Valley during my second year at SFASU and hiked all of its foot trails in one day with binoculars and a bird field guide in hand. Although my work with the FWS in WY brought me closer to montane environments, I conducted most of my fieldwork at lower elevations in sagebrush and short-grass prairie communities and ultimately in oilfields retrieving bird carcasses from oil pits. Throughout my career with the FWS, I hearkened back to Maurice Hornocker and his approach to achieving success in wildlife conservation – interpersonal communication skills. It took me a few years to grasp how to communicate effectively with civil engineers, especially those in the U.S. Army Corps of Engineers (COE) and the U.S. Bureau of Reclamation. After several unsuccessful efforts to convince an engineer to modify the design of a leveed containment area within a critical habitat for the endangered whooping crane and use a former disposal area located adjacent to the Intracoastal waterway, I asked the engineer why the modification could not be done. The civil engineer pointed out that the sandy composition of the existing levees, which were severely eroded, would not support reconstructing them, risked continued erosion, and would likely fail over time, thus releasing the dredged material into the bay. I delved into COE technical manuals on the design and construction of dredged material containment areas as well as the behavior and fate of dredged material disposal in shallow bays. This allowed me to understand the engineering and hydrological constraints in the planning and locating of disposal areas. When assessing oil and gas development and the maintenance and operation of oil and gas production sites in Wyoming, I asked oil and gas regulatory agency staff as well as oil company employees to describe the equipment used to extract, store, and transport oil and gas from the field and eventually to a refinery for processing. I also read books on oil and gas production to help me learn the technical terms and processes. Showing an interest in their work and in them allowed the engineers and pumpers to gladly answer my questions and listen when I pointed out best management practices to avoid exposed oil and the entrapment and mortality of migratory birds. When first meeting them, I would try to find something in common by asking them the following questions. "Do you hunt or fish? I have a son in grade school. Do you have any kids? Where did you go to school?" Reading several 'how-to-books' such as: *"How to Talk So People Listen;" "How to Listen So People Talk,"* and *"Getting Past No"* helped me achieve conservation successes in the field. In addition to discussing best management practices with oil industry staff in the field at oil and gas production sites, I developed slide presentations covering the function of feathers, such as body temperature regulation, flight, defense, courtship display, species recognition, camouflage, and waterproofing. Emphasizing these details helped the audience understand the importance of preventing leaks, drips, and spills of oil and oilfield-produced water. My curiosity on how things worked extended to my inspections of other industrial sites that had wastewater treatment ponds, including oil refineries in Casper, Wyoming; a coal-fired power plant; in situ uranium mining facilities; open-pit coal mines; and a trip 800 feet or more down an elevator into an underground trona mine. My expertise with the environmental impacts of oil and gas exploration and production and my numerous presentations to state and federal agencies as well as industry led to my serving as a co-instructor in a short course on that topic for FWS refuge managers in 2001. Five years later, the NWRS recognized the need to develop a more intensive course focusing on existing NWRS regulations and federal and state laws applicable to oil and gas exploration and production in refuges. We taught the course twice a year in order to rapidly provide as many refuge managers and biologists, as well as biologists from the Ecological Services field offices, with information on oil and gas exploration and production and hands-on techniques on inspecting and identifying problems in oil and gas facilities located on NWRS lands. Instructors included refuge staff with experience in dealing with oil and gas exploration and or production on their refuge location, a DOI Solicitor (attorney), Pat O'Dell,

National Park Service (NPS) petroleum engineer, and Eddie Kassman, NPS regulatory specialist (attorney). We taught the course in Louisiana, Montana, North Dakota, and Texas, alternating the course location to reach as many refuge staff as possible that dealt with oil and gas exploration and production. Oil industry staff managing wells on NWRS lands also attended some of the courses we offered. A few years later, we offered the course once a year. Several years later, Pat O'Dell transferred to the FWS and was joined a year or two later by Ella Wagener after she completed her law degree from the Lewis and Clark Law School in Portland, Oregon.

Arriving home with my family from a Thanksgiving holiday trip to visit my friends Dan and Susan Kutvirt at their cabin near Chama, New Mexico, I was greeted with a brief voicemail message on our answering machine urging me to phone the Assistant Regional Director (ARD) of Ecological Services in Denver. I called the ARD and was asked if I would be interested in a job with the NWRS HQ office and work in Fort Collins at the NWRS National Resource Program Center (NRPC). NRPC consists of an interdisciplinary science team that provides technical assistance on planning and management to refuge managers. NRPC staff included wildlife biologists, air and water quality specialists, and human dimensions staff. Human dimensions staff assisted HQ NWRS staff as well as refuge field staff with issues involving landowners, industry, state and federal agencies, nongovernmental organizations, and the public. Needless to say, I was ecstatic and accepted the offer, as I would no longer have to commute 60 miles to work in Cheyenne.

I reported for work at NRPC on the last week of January 2013. Most, if not all, the staff and contractors had master's and PhDs with expertise in computer mapping (geographic information systems or GIS), statistics, human dimensions, and fish and wildlife management. After getting settled at NRPC, I gave the staff a slide presentation on the proposed work I would do for the HQ Branch of Wildlife Resources office and described oil and gas exploration and production and the impacts on refuges. My first task involved working with their GIS specialists to map oil and gas wells and pipelines located on refuges as well as wells within approximately one-half mile from the boundaries of NWRS lands owned or managed by the FWS. The following month, I joined staff from the Branch of

Wildlife Resources on a tour of oil and gas well sites in McFaddin, Anahuac, San Bernard, and Brazoria National Wildlife Refuges located along or near the Gulf Coast in southeast Texas. We noted impacts from following the tour. I commenced working with GIS Specialist Sheri Mosley, who converted spatial data on oil and gas wells and pipelines located on and adjacent to NWRS lands into spreadsheets so that I could sort the data by well types (oil, gas, water), well status (active, inactive, shut in, abandoned, orphan). Sheri and I published our results in a peer-reviewed scientific journal. I also worked with Branch of Wildlife staff Scott Covington, and Branch chief (supervisor) Kim Trust. Petroleum engineer Pat O'Dell transferred from the NPS to join our NWRS Branch of Wildlife oil and gas team in 2014. Ella Wagner joined our team in 2014 as a regulatory specialist, given her law degree. Most of the NWRS lands were located in areas with a minimal to non-existent potential for the exploration and development of oil and gas wells. However, when lands in oil and gas-producing states were obtained by the FWS for inclusion into the NWRS, the agency only acquired the surface and not the underlying mineral rights for two reasons: one, the FWS was only interested in the surface and not the minerals; and two, mineral estate owners rarely offer their mineral rights for sale, especially in oil-producing states.

Our team's task after the tour entailed updating regulations on oil and gas exploration and development on NWRS lands and preparing an environmental impact statement. The team contacted refuge managers from refuges that had oil and gas wells, informed them of our effort to update the regulations, and asked them if they or a member of their staff would participate in a meeting to obtain their input on the impact of oil and gas activities on their management of refuges.

On November 9, 2016, Republican Donald Trump was elected President, and Republicans gained a majority in the U.S. House of Representatives. The political climate was drastically changed, thus placing the enactment of regulations for oil and gas activities on refuges at risk of getting quashed by a Republican administration. The oil and gas team fast-tracked the drafting of proposed regulations for oil and gas exploration in NWRS. Fortunately, the proposed rule was approved by President Obama's administration and became effective on December 14, 2016. We developed a training course to provide technical assistance to refuges on oil and gas issues, instruct refuge staff on how the industry explores and produces oil and gas, and to prepare for and teach the NWRS Oil and Gas Course. The course provided attendees with information on minimizing the impacts of oil and gas exploration and development on NWRS lands, oil and gas laws and regulations, and key items to look for and document when visiting an oil and gas site on NWRS lands. During the last seven years of my career with FWS, I visited NWRS lands from the US-Mexico border in the Lower Rio Grande Valley in Texas to our country's border with Canada in North Dakota.

Chapter 22 – Passing The 'Baton' To My Successor

A year prior to my retirement, I drafted a document entitled *"Management of Oil & Gas Activities On National Wildlife Refuge System Lands"* to provide my successor(s) with information on the management of oil and gas activities on NWRS lands. The document described the purpose of the Energy Team "to improve an understanding of energy development impacts on Refuge lands and waters, and to develop effective strategies and tools to avoid or minimize impacts from energy development." The document listed several strategic goals: the protection of fish, wildlife, and habitat managed by the NWRS from the adverse impacts of oil and gas activities through the implementation of oil and gas regulations; ensuring access to accurate and relevant data on oil and gas facilities/activities occurring on NWRS lands by verifying the locations and number of oil and gas structures, including tank batteries, wells, and pipelines, in each refuge having oil and gas facilities; and, developing spatial databases to record compliance with the NWRS oil and gas rule. The

Energy Team would provide refuge managers and staff with technical assistance and the tools needed to manage oil and gas activities in their refuges effectively.

One month before my retirement, I joined Scott Covington and my supervisor, Debbie DeVore, on a field trip to Deep Fork NWR in Oklahoma and Hagerman NWR in north central Texas. Scott and I provided Debbie with "the good, the bad, and the ugly" of oil and gas exploration and production in the two refuges. Upon returning to our respective offices and homes, we faced the COVID-19 pandemic shutdown. I spent the last few weeks alternating between working at home and from the office. My colleagues, along with my wife, planned a collaborative retirement party at the Rio Grande restaurant in Old Town Fort Collins. The COVID shutdown threw a monkey wrench into those plans, so my send-off celebration became a virtual send-off on the Microsoft Teams application, which was not quite the end-of-career bash my colleagues and I had hoped for. After the virtual send-off, I stepped out of my home onto the backyard deck and tried to absorb the reality that my 41 years as a wildlife biologist with the U.S. Fish and Wildlife Service had come to an end. I recalled the advice given to me years before by Dennis Buechler, an FWS retiree who went on to work with the Colorado Wildlife Federation and served on the Colorado Wildlife Commission; "when you retire, have something to do, have a purpose." I took his advice and continued volunteering as an Assistant Scoutmaster on my son Erik's former scout troop, Troop 97. From 2010 to 2019, I participated in six wilderness treks with Troop 97 in the Weminuche, Mount Zirkel, and Flat Tops Wilderness areas in Colorado and the Bridger Wilderness area in the Wind River Range in Wyoming. I continue to participate in day hikes in the Colorado Rockies with my wife, Julie, our son Erik, and our daughter Rita. In 2015, Julie and I joined Poudre Wilderness Volunteers (PWV), a Fort Collins organization that assists the Canyon Lakes Ranger District of the United States Forest Service (USFS) in managing and protecting wilderness and backcountry areas within the Canyon Lakes Ranger District. Julie and I hike the trails with other PWV members and provide day hikers and backpackers using the trails within the ranger district with assistance if needed. We also record data for the ranger district on the number of hikers we encounter on the trail, and maintenance needs at backcountry campsites and trails. The data helps the USFS in determining the amount of use on the trails and in prioritizing the maintenance of the hundreds of miles of trails within the Canyon Lakes Ranger District. We also assist with outreach to inform the public about PWV and assist with the recruitment and training of new members.

ABOUT THE AUTHOR

Pedro Ramirez, Jr. has spent a lifetime embodying the principles of resilience, dedication, and the pursuit of knowledge. Born and raised in the close-knit ranching community of Encino, Texas, Pedro was deeply influenced by the values instilled in him by his parents. His father, a World War II veteran and county commissioner, and his mother, a hardworking homemaker, emphasized the importance of education and service to others.

Pedro's journey from the rural expanses of South Texas to a distinguished career in environmental conservation is a testament to his unyielding determination and passion for wildlife. After earning his degree from Stephen F. Austin State University, he continued his academic pursuits at the University of Idaho, where he conducted groundbreaking research on predator ecology under the mentorship of renowned conservationist Dr. Maurice G. Hornocker.

Over a remarkable 41-year career with the U.S. Fish and Wildlife Service, Pedro became a respected environmental contaminants specialist. His contributions to wildlife conservation have left an indelible mark on the field, particularly in the protection and preservation of endangered species and their habitats.

Pedro's life is also a powerful narrative of overcoming adversity and embracing cultural identity. As a Mexican American, he navigated the challenges of racial prejudice and societal expectations with grace and strength, drawing deeply from his heritage and the support of his family.

Beyond his professional achievements, Pedro is a devoted husband and father, whose love for his family is a central theme in his life story. His memoir, "Reaching for the Stars.. and Grabbing One," is a tribute to the power of education, the importance of family, and the beauty of pursuing one's dreams.

Pedro continues to inspire others through his writing and community involvement. His story is a beacon of hope, encouraging readers to reach for their own stars and grab hold of their dreams.